D1347754

INFORMATION AT YOUR FINGERTIPS

*Up-to-date and comprehensive, Pitman Dictionaries
are indispensable reference books, providing clear,
crisp explanation of specialist terminology
in an easy-to-use format*

A Concise Dictionary of Accounting and Finance
Accounting Terms Dictionary
A Dictionary of Economics and Commerce
A Dictionary of Management Terms
Dictionary of Business Studies
Dictionary of Banking
Dictionary of Banking and Finance
Dictionary of Law
Information Technology Dictionary
Office Practice Dictionary

DICTIONARY OF BUSINESS STUDIES

SECOND EDITION

M STEER

Pitman

Pitman Publishing
128 Long Acre, London WC2E 9AN

A Division of Longman Group UK Limited

First edition 1985
Second edition 1989
Reprinted 1990

© Longman Group UK Ltd 1985, 1989

British Library Cataloguing in Publication Data

Steer, M. (Margaret)
Dictionary of business studies.
1. Business enterprise. Encyclopaedias
I. Title II. Steer, M. (Margaret). Business
studies dictionary
338.6

ISBN 0 273 03077 9

Printed and bound in Singapore

PREFACE

Teaching within the vocabulary of the student is of the utmost importance if they are to fully understand what is being taught. Naturally, many students start their business studies with very little knowledge of the language of the business world; indeed, many everyday words take on a different meaning entirely in an office or factory environment. It was this problem that forced me into the practice of providing a precise definition of any new word before it was introduced into a lesson, and the collection of years became a dictionary.

Apart from the necessity of learning a new 'language' – always with an examination in view – I used to say that if, at the end of the course, students could read and understand the business pages of a daily newspaper it had all been worthwhile. I hope in this respect that the dictionary will be of assistance to others who find the dynamics of commerce and industry fascinating.

Finally, I would like to say that this dictionary is the result of a joint effort of my husband and myself. Without him it would have taken me twice as long to prepare, and for this I thank him.

There are others over the years who also deserve my thanks, not least the writers of business pages in our daily newspapers, and the very many authors whose books and articles I have enjoyed.

M Steer, January 1989

M Steer was formerly Head of the Commerce Department of Roundwood Park School, Harpenden and has taught widely in further education.

INTRODUCTION

The aim of this *Dictionary of Business Studies* is to provide a comprehensive reference companion for students of Business Studies at intermediate and advanced levels.

Full coverage is given to all terms likely to be met at GCSE, A level, B/TEC National and Higher, RSA, LCC and similar level examinations.

Topics covered include:

Abbreviations
Accounts
Advertising
Banking
British Constitution (functions of the Cabinet, legislature and judiciary)
Business organisation
Business organisations
City of London markets and institutions
Commercial services
Communications
Consumer protection
Economics
Employment and employer/ employee legislation
European Community (The Common Market)
Government organisations and services relating to commerce and industry
Industrial relations
Information technology
Insurance
International trade and its documentation
Law (in relation to British business)
Limited companies and company law
Marketing
Methods of payment
Physical distribution
Retailing
Stock Exchange
Transport
Warehousing
Wholesaling

Cross-references to terms included elsewhere in the dictionary are in small capitals to aid easy use.

ABBREVIATIONS

A1	first class, first-rate (at Lloyd's)
aar	against all risks
a/c	account
ACAS	Advisory, Conciliation and Arbitration Service
ACT	Advance Corporation Tax
ADP	automatic data processing
ADR	American Depository Rights
ad val	*ad valorem* (Latin); according to value
AFBD	Association of Futures Brokers and Dealers
AGM	Annual General Meeting
agt	agent
AI	Artificial Intelligence
AICES	Association of International Courier and Express Services
AMD	Aggregate Money Demand
AOB	any other business
APR	Annual Percentage Rate
ASA	Advertising Standards Authority
assn	association
av	average
a.v.	*ad valorem* (Latin); according to value
BAA	British Airports Authority
bal	balance
BBC	British Broadcasting Corporation
b/d	brought down
B/E	Bill of Exchange
BES	Business Expansion Scheme
b/f	brought forward
bkpt	bankrupt
B/L	Bill of Lading
BOTB	British Overseas Trade Board
bpd	barrels per day (of oil)
BR	British Rail

BRS	British Road Services
BSI	British Standards Institution
BTG	British Technology Group
C/A	Capital Account
CAB	Citizens' Advice Bureau
CACM	Central American Common Market
CADCAM	computer-aided design/computer-aided manufacture
CADMAT	computer-aided design, manufacture and test
c & f	cost and freight
cap	capital
CAP	Common Agricultural Policy (EC)
CARICOM	Caribbean Community and Common Market
CB	Cash Book
CBA	cost benefit analysis
CBI	Confederation of British Industry
CC	County Council
CCT	Common Customs Tariff (EC)
C/D	Certificate of Deposit
c/d	carried down
CDA	Cooperative Development Agency
CET	Common External Tariff (EC)
cf.	*confer* (Latin); compare
c/f	carried forward
CH	Clearing House
cif	cost, insurance and freight (sometimes cfi)
CIM	computer integrated manufacture
C/N	consignment note, cover note, credit note
co	company
COD	cash on delivery
COI	Central Office of Information
COM	computer output on microfilm
COMECOM	Communist Economic Community (Council for Mutual Economic Assistance)
comm	commission

Consols	Consolidated Annuities
COREPER	(French abbreviation) Committee of Permanent Representatives (EC)
CPA	critical path analysis
cpi	characters per inch
CPRE	Council for the Protection of Rural England
cps	characters per second
CPU	central processing unit
cr	credit, creditor
C/R	company's risk
CRE	Commission for Racial Equality
CRS	Cooperative Retail Society
CSO	Central Selling Organisation, Central Statistical Office
CT	Community Transit (EC), credit transfer
cum div	with dividend
cum pref	cumulative preference (shares)
CV	*curriculum vitae* (Latin) (see Dict)
CWO	cash with order
CWS	Cooperative Wholesale Society
D/A	documents against acceptance
DCE	Domestic Credit Expansion
DCF	discounted cash flow
DD	direct debit
deb	debenture
def	deferred
DES	Department of Education and Science
DESO	Defence Export Services Organisation
disc	discount
div	dividend, division
D/N	debit note, despatch note
DNS	Department of National Savings
do	ditto (repeat the same)
DOE	Department of the Environment
DOS	Disk Operating System
DP	data processing
D/P	documents against payment
dr	debtor, doctor

DTI	Department of Trade and Industry
DTP	desktop publishing
E & OE	errors and omissions excepted
EAEC	European Atomic Energy Community (*also* EURATOM)
EC	European Community
ECGD	Export Credit Guarantee Department
ECOWAS	Economic Community of West African States
ECS	*échantillons commerciaux* (commercial samples)
ECSC	European Coal and Steel Community
ECU	European Currency Unit
EDP	electronic data processing
EEC	European Economic Community
EFT	electronic funds transfer
EFTA	European Free Trade Association
EFTPOS	Electronic Funds Transfer at Point of Sale
e.g.	*exempli gratia* (Latin); for example
EGM	Extraordinary General Meeting
EIB	European Investment Bank
ELA	Equipment Leasing Association
EMS	European Monetary System
enc(s)	enclosure(s)
EOC	Equal Opportunities Commission
EOE	European Options Exchange
EPOS	electronic point of sale
eps	earnings per share
ERDF	European Regional Development Fund
ESOPS	Employee Share Ownership Plans
etc.	*et cetera* (Latin); and other things (especially of the same kind)
et seq	*et sequens* (Latin); and the following
EURATOM	European Atomic Energy Community (*also* EAEC)
EXBO	Export Buying Offices Association
ex div	ex dividend; without dividend

faa	free of all average (marine insurance)
fac	facsimile
FAO	(United Nations) Food and Agriculture Organisation
faq	fair average quality
fas	free alongside ship
FAX	facsimile transmission
Fed	(United States) Federal Reserve Board
FEOGA	(French initial letters) European Agricultural Guidance and Guarantee Fund
fga	free of general average (marine insurance)
FHA	Finance Houses Association
FIFO	first in, first out (of stock)
FIMBRA	Financial Intermediaries, Managers and Brokers Association
fis	free into store
fo, fol	folio
fob	free on board
for	free on rail
fpa	free of particular average (marine insurance)
FT	*Financial Times*
FTA	Freight Transport Association
fwd	forward
g/a	general average (marine insurance)
GAFTA	Grain and Feed Trade Association
GATT	General Agreement on Tariffs and Trade
GDP	Gross Domestic Product
GEMM	Gilt Edged Market-Maker
GNP	Gross National Product
HC	House of Commons
HL	House of Lords
HMC	Her Majesty's Customs
HMSO	Her Majesty's Stationery Office
HO	Home Office
HP	hire purchase

IATA	International Air Transport Association
IBELS	Interest-Bearing Eligible Liabilities
IBRD	International Bank for Reconstruction and Development
ICCH	International Commodities Clearing House
ICS	International Chamber of Shipping
IDB	Inter-Dealer Broker
IDD	International Direct Dialling
IDIS	Interbourse Data Information System
i.e.	*id est* (Latin); that is
IEA	Institute of Economic Affairs
I/F	insufficient funds
IFS	Institute for Fiscal Studies
III (3i)	Investors in Industry
ILO	International Labour Organisation
IMF	International Monetary Fund
IMRO	Investment Management Regulatory Organisation
inc	increase, incorporated
inf/info	information
int	interest, interim
inv	invoice
IOD	Institute of Directors
IPE	International Petroleum Exchange
IPR	Inward Processing Relief
IRR	internal rate of return
ISBN	International Standard Book Number
ISO	International Standardisation Organisation
IT	Information Technology
ital	italic
JET	Joint European Torus (EC)
JP	Justice of the Peace
K or Kb	kilobyte
LAFTA	Latin American Free Trade Association
LAN	Local Area Network

LAUTRO	Life Assurance and Unit Trusts Regulatory Organisation
lb	pound (in weight)
lc	lower case (small characters)
L/C	letter of credit
LDC	less developed country
LDMA	London Discount Market Association
LDT	Licensed Deposit-Taker
LGS	Loan Guarantee Scheme
LIBID	London Interbank Bid Rate
LIBOR	London Interbank Offered Rate
LIFFE	London International Financial Futures Exchange
LIFO	last in, first out (of stock)
LME	London Metal Exchange
LOCH	London Options Clearing House
LS	*locus sigilli* (Latin); the place of the seal
ltd	limited
LTOM	London Traded Options Market
LV	luncheon voucher
M or Mb	megabyte
MAFF	Ministry of Agriculture, Fisheries and Food
MBO	management by objectives
MD	Managing Director, market day
MEP	Member of the European Parliament
mfg	manufacturing
mfr	manufacturer
MICR	magnetic ink character recognition
misc	miscellaneous
MLR	Minimum Lending Rate
MMC	Monopolies and Mergers Commission
MOD	Ministry of Defence
MORI	Market and Opinion Research International
MPC	marginal propensity to consume
MPS	marginal propensity to save
MTFS	Medium-Term Financial Strategy
mtg	meeting

NATO	North Atlantic Treaty Organisation
nav	net asset value
NBFI	Non-Bank Financial Intermediaries
NCR	no carbon required
NEDC	National Economic Development Council
NEDO	National Economic Development Office
nem con	*nemine contradicente* (Latin); no-one contradicting
nem diss	*nemine dissentiente* (Latin); no-one dissenting
N/F	no funds
NHS	National Health Service
NI	National Insurance
NIC	newly industrialised country
NIFO	next in, first out (of stock)
nom	nominal
npv	no par value; net present value
NYMEX	New York Mercantile Exchange
o/a	on account
O & M	Organisation and Method
o/c	overcharge; out of charge (Customs)
OCR	Optical Character Recognition
o/d	on demand; overdraft; overdrawn
OECD	Organisation for European Cooperation and Development
OFGAS	Office of Gas Supply
OFT	Office of Fair Trading
OFTEL	Office of Telecommunications
OMR	optical mark recognition
OPEC	Organisation of Petroleum Exporting Countries
OPR	Outward Processing Relief
OR	Official Receiver; Operational Research; Owner's Risk
o/s	outstanding
OSI	open systems interconnection
OTC	Over-the-Counter (market in unlisted securites)

p, pp	page, pages
pa	per annum, personal assistant
PABX	Private Automatic Branch Exchange
P & L	Profit and Loss
p & p	postage and packing
PAR	programme analysis and review
para	paragraph
PAYE	pay as you earn
PBR	payment by results
PBX	Private Branch Exchange
PC	personal computer; Privy Councillor
P/E	price/earnings (ratio)
PEP	Personal Equity Plan; Projects and Export Policy (BOTB)
PERT	programme evaluation and review technique
PESC	Public Expenditure Survey Committee
pft	profit
PIN	personal identification number
PLC	public limited company
PO	post office, postal order
POP	post office preferred (envelope sizes)
pp	*per procurationem* (Latin); for and on behalf of (*per pro*)
PPI	printed postage impression
pqe	post qualification experience
PR	Public Relations
PRO	Public Records Office; Public Relations Officer
pro tem	*pro tempore* (Latin): for the time being
PSBR	Public Sector Borrowing Requirement
PSDR	Public Sector Debt Repayment
QB	Queen's Bench
QC	Queen's Counsel
qv.	*quod vide* (Latin); refer to
RAM	random access memory
R & D	Research and Development

R/D	refer to drawer
reqn	requisition
ROI	return on investment
ROM	read only memory
RO/RO	roll on, roll off (ferries)
RPB	Recognised Professional Body
RPI	Retail Price Index
SALT	Strategic Arms Limitation Talks
SAYE	save as you earn
SDR	Special Drawing Rights
SEAQ	Stock Exchange Automated Quotation System
SEMB	Stock Exchange Money Broker
SERPS	State Earnings-Related Pension Scheme
SIB	Securities and Investment Board
SITPRO	Simplification of International Trade Procedures
S/N	Shipping Note
SO	Standing Order
SRO	Self-Regulatory Organisation
SSAP	Statement of Standard Accounting Practice
STD	Subscriber Trunk Dialling
std	standard
stet	(Latin); let it stand
SWIFT	Society for Worldwide Interbank Financial Telecommunications
THE	Technical Help to Exporters
TIR	*Transport Internationale Routiers* International Road Transport
TSA	The Securities Association
TUC	Trades Union Congress
TWI	training within industry
UAE	United Arab Emirates
UK	United Kingdom
UKASS	United Kingdom Association of Suggestion Schemes

ULS	unsecured loan stock
UNCTAD	United Nations Commission for Trade and Development
UNEP	United Nations Environment Programme
UNFAO	United Nations Food and Agriculture Organisation
UNO	United Nations Organisation
USA	United States of America
USM	Unlisted Securities Market
USSR	Union of Soviet Socialist Republics
U/W	Underwriter
v	*versus* (Latin); against
VAT	Value Added Tax
VDU	visual display unit
viz	*videlicet* (Latin); namely
vlcc	very large crude carrier
vlsi	very large scale integration
WAN	Wide Area Network
WB	waybill
WEDA	Women's Enterprise Development Agency
WHO	World Health Organisation
wip	work-in-progress
WP	word processing
wpa	with particular average (marine insurance)
wpm	words per minute
xc, xcp	without coupon
xd	without dividend
xr	without rights

A

absenteeism. A persistent and deliberate absence from work or duty.

absorption costing. A costing system whereby all overhead costs – both fixed and variable – are apportioned first to cost centres and then to products. The costs are thus directly traceable and chargeable to such products and can act as a valuable guide to pricing policy.

accelerator. An economic concept that explains why investment demand fluctuates to a greater degree than demand for consumer goods. An increase in demand for a consumer good will raise the demand (the DERIVED DEMAND) for the factor of production, perhaps a machine, that makes it. But this derived demand will rise even faster than the demand for the product. This is because demand for investment (producer) goods is composed of a replacement and an expansion element.

acceptance credit. Amount for which a bank will undertake payment in settlement of an international trade debt.

acceptance of bills of exchange. A BILL OF EXCHANGE is said to be 'accepted' when it is signed by the debtor, who promises to pay the amount shown when the debt falls due.

accepting houses. The Accepting Houses Committee is an asociation of 17 MERCHANT BANKS, the accepting of BILLS OF EXCHANGE drawn on London being one of their main functions; bills so accepted are BANK BILLS.

access time (computers). The time taken to retrieve information from a storage location.

accident insurance. All insurance not covered by marine, fire or life assurance. This can be: *Insurance of liability.* This covers employers' liability for accidents at work; accidents which occur at public functions (the organiser will pay for insurance cover against such eventualities), and liability for accidental personal injury to or accidental damage to the property of third parties. *See* ACCIDENTS AT WORK. *Insurance of property* which covers a wide range of risks, including burglary and vandalism. *Motor vehicle owner's comprehensive policy* which may cover damage to the car as a result of an accident, theft, fire, injury to the insured, and third-party risks. (The first party is the insured, the second party is the insurer; third party may be other persons affected by the contract – passengers, pedestrians, cyclists, etc.). Car insurance is compulsory before taking a vehicle on the road. *Personal accident insurance* covering personal injury. Short-term policies may be purchased to cover rail or aircraft journeys for persons travelling on their own, or for parties or groups. A *fidelity guarantee* which can be taken out by firms to protect against dishonesty of employees, e.g. moneys embezzled from clients can be restored, but usually only after the employee has been charged in the courts. A professional firm may take out cover against the possibility that one of its members may have to answer for giving incorrect professional advice.

accidents at work. If an employee is injured at work and considers the injury to be due to the negligence of his employer, he may bring an action for damages against the employer under common law. An employer may also be held responsible for accidents caused by the action of his employees if these happen in the course of their employment. The Employers Liability (Compulsory Insurance) Act 1969 requires employers to insure against such claims. *See also* ACCIDENT INSURANCE.

accommodation bill. *See* BILL OF EXCHANGE.

account (Stock Exchange). The principal division of the International Stock Exchange calendar. Normally an Account runs for two weeks (10 working days). At the end of each Account, 'bargains' cease and a new dealing period commences at once. The first seven working days of every period are spent in clearing and settling the accounts. During the first week, speculators can make arrangements to carry bargains over to the new Account period, the following continuation facilities being available: *Contango* – a payment made by a buyer to a seller of shares to postpone delivery to a future day of settlement. *Backwardation* – a payment made by a seller to a buyer of shares to postpone delivery to a future day of settlement. Transfers are completed on Settlement

Day in the second week of the account, when payments are made and stock delivered.

account day (Stock Exchange). Day on which all bargains effected during the previous Account period are settled – normally the second Monday following the end of the Account. *Also called* SETTLEMENT DAY.

account rendered (a/c rendered). The opening entry on a Statement of Account which shows any balance which was outstanding at the beginning of the period covered. It is usually an amount which has appeared on a previous statement but which has not been paid.

account sales. This is easier to understand if it is regarded as an account of a sale – it is a detailed statement of a transaction and is sent by an agent to his principal giving details of the goods sold on his behalf. It includes charges for freight, dock dues, MARINE INSURANCE, and also the commission charged by the agent and expenses incurred by him in selling the goods. The final figure is the net proceeds of the sale. Sometimes there is an additional *del credere* commission shown; this is an extra charge by the agent for guaranteeing, and becoming responsible for, payment of the account on behalf of his principal.

accountability (in business). In general the principle of accountability is that those who conduct an enterprise should be accountable to those who provide the means which enabled the enterprise to be set up.

accounts. An account is a statement of moneys received and paid with calculation of the balance. The accounts of a firm show the exact cost of the goods and services offered, what overheads are involved, and the exact revenue of the business. A study of the accounts is essential to the formulation of a sound business policy for the future. All LIMITED COMPANIES are required by law to keep proper books of account, to record their transactions with regard to the purchase and sale of goods, the receipt and payment of moneys, and the assets and liabilities of the company. They must also prepare annually for the SHAREHOLDERS a PROFIT AND LOSS ACCOUNT, BALANCE SHEET, Source and Application of Funds Statement, and a Report of the Auditors.

accruals (accounting). Amount of payments owing for accrued expenses incurred during a period which remain unpaid at the end of the period. *Accrued revenue* is the amount of debt owing to a business which is payable at some date in the future.

acid test ratio. The critical test of a firm's ability to meet its immediate commitments. The formula for calculation is:

Liquid assets (less stock) : current liabilities

A ratio of at least 1 : 1 is generally required. If this is not met and the firm cannot cover current liabilities, then additional cash must be obtained. The term may also be referred to as the *quick* or *liquid ratio.*

acoustic coupler. When plugged into a telephone handset, converts pulses of sound from a telephone line into signals which can be received by a computer.

acronym. A word formed from the first letters, or first few letters, of several other words. ERNIE (Premium Bonds) is an acronym for Electronic Random Number Indicator Equipment.

activity sampling. A technique widely used within O & M. In order to establish the actual time taken to perform clerical tasks, periodic observations are made of the activities under investigation. Observation times are calculated using random number tables and the overall length of the exercise is designed to capture information throughout a complete job cycle. The information gained is used as an aid to planning improved clerical methods.

actuary. An expert in life assurance who estimates premiums from statistical analysis of probabilities in the mortality, sickness and retirement fields.

ad hoc. Beginning of a Latin phrase meaning 'for this particular purpose'. An *ad hoc meeting* is a meeting called for a particular purpose.

ad valorem **duty.** Duty charged according to value; one varying with the declared value of the goods, usually calculated as a percentage.

ad valorem **stamp duty.** Government duties on Stock Exchange contracts charged according to the value of the stocks and shares involved in the transaction.

added value. *See* VALUE ADDED.

adjudication order. An order of the BANKRUPTCY COURT, adjudging a debtor to be a bankrupt, and transferring his property to the OFFICIAL RECEIVER, or a trustee appointed for the purpose.

administration. The functions concerned with management of a business, or organising and conducting public affairs.

administrative law. Defined by Sir Ivor Jennings as 'the law relating to the Administration. It determines the organisation, power and duties of administrative authorities.' The activities of government departments, local authorities and public corporations require lawyers to be familiar with administrative processes likely to affect the rights and obligations of their clients. The ordinary courts are ill-equipped to deal with the conflicts which arise – problems mostly associated with the increase in social and welfare services now available. The use of administrative tribunals, regulated by the Tribunal and Inquiries Act 1971, to settle such socio-legal disputes, is becoming more common. Examples of such tribunals are the Land Tribunal and the Employment Appeal Tribunal; such tribunals are outside the ordinary court system, but have extensive powers of decision-making. *See* OMBUDSMAN.

advance corporation tax. *See* CORPORATION TAX.

advertising. The means by which firms or individuals make known to the market what they have to sell, or what they want to buy. There are many reasons for advertising but these fall broadly into two categories: *informative advertising* – announcing a new or modified product or service – and *persuasive advertising* to show the merits and claims of a particular product as superior to the competition. *Media advertising* – also known as above-the-line advertising – refers to the five traditional media of press, television, radio, cinema and outdoors (posters). This is mostly handled by advertising agencies who receive commission on the purchase of space, air time and sites. There is an increasing trend nowadays for firms to employ below-the-line advertising techniques, often handled by their own in-company advertising department. Six principal media come under this heading – direct mail, point-of-sale, sales promotion and merchandising, exhibitions and sales literature.

advertising agency. Besides undertaking market research and the planning of advertising campaigns for companies wishing to advertise, the agent will create, produce and distribute advertisements using whatever media are suitable.

advertising media. The main fields of advertising are the daily press, radio and television, the cinema, point of sale displays, hoardings, postal advertising, sample advertising, and telephone selling.

Advertising Standards Authority (ASA). Financed by the Advertising Association and established as a limited company, this has been set up to improve the quality of informative advertising, to maintain standards within the industry, and to control dishonest and undesirable advertisements. It supervises a code of advertising practice which is a detailed document setting out general principles to which advertisers and advertising agents should adhere; it is a voluntary code. There is provision for complaints made by the public about advertisements to be investigated, and for the authority to make recommendations where appropriate.

Advisory, Conciliation and Arbitration Service (ACAS). Established by the Employment Protection Act 1975, the duties of ACAS are: to offer conciliation and advisory services in an industrial dispute; to provide conciliation services in any complaint about the working of INDUSTRIAL TRIBUNALS; to refer matters which require arbitration, after advice and conciliation services have been offered, to the Central Arbitration Committee; to conduct enquiries into industrial relations in any particular industry or organisation; to publish advisory material, guidance on 'codes of practice', and generally promote good industrial relations.

affidavit. A written statement made on oath for use as judicial proof.

after-hours dealing (Stock Exchange). Dealing done after the end of the mandatory Quote Period, 9.00 am to 5.00 pm.

after-sales service. Maintenance and repair services which are made available by the retailer to the buyer of consumer durables (washing machines, television sets, etc.). These often carry a guarantee for a specified period, during which time the manufacturer is obliged to remedy the defects.

agenda. A list of items, drawn up by the chairman of a meeting and sent out by the secretary, which are to be discussed at a meeting in the order in which they are shown. The first three items are (normally): apologies for absence from those unable to attend; minutes of the last meeting; matters arising from the minutes. The item AOB (any other business) appears on an agenda after details of all known subjects for discussion have been listed. It allows an opportunity for urgent matters which have arisen and cannot wait until the next meeting to be brought forward. The agenda should be distributed before the meeting to all those due to attend, and extra copies made available at the meeting itself.

agent. One who is authorised by another to act for him and in his name, the person who authorises him being called the principal. The two most common types of mercantile agent are brokers and factors. A BROKER merely sells the goods for his principal and arranges delivery, but never actually has the goods in his possession; he charges brokerage for his services. The FACTOR actually has the goods in his possession, sells and delivers them to the buyer, and renders an account, less his commission, to his principal. Factors are particularly useful in the export trade. *See also* COMMISSION AGENT, FREIGHT FORWARDING AGENT, INSURANCE BROKER, OVERSEAS AGENT, AUCTIONEER, DEL CREDERE AGENT.

Aggregate Money Demand (AMD). Total demand by the public for entrepreneurial goods and services, i.e. those produced by business enterprises.

agricultural cooperatives. Formed by groups of farmers or growers who between them finance the purchase of processing plant and distribution centres; profits are shared by the owners.

aids to trade. *Commerce* is a comprehensive term covering all the operations involved directly or indirectly in the purchase or sale of merchandise or services. Trade is that section of commerce involved in buying and selling; the aids to trade are the commercial services necessary for trading to take place – banking and finance, communications (including advertising), insurance, transport and warehousing.

air charter party. A written agreement between the owner(s) of an aircraft and the merchant or other organisation wishing to transport goods or passengers by air; it gives details of the aircraft, the flight, and the price to be charged. The Baltair 1962 Air Charter Party originates from the AIR FREIGHT MARKET of the BALTIC EXCHANGE.

air consignment note/air waybill. Takes the place of the BILL OF LADING which is used in sea freight consignments and is a detailed list of the goods being conveyed. The consignee must present his copies of the air consignment note, insurance policy and the invoice, before the goods can be claimed when they are landed.

air couriers. The Association of International Courier and Express Services (AICES) undertake collection, international transportation and delivery of time-sensitive business documents and small packages from all parts of the UK to countries in every continent.

air freight market. The Baltic Air Freight Market of the BALTIC EXCHANGE operates very similarly to the FREIGHT MARKET where those in search of a vessel to carry cargo are put in touch with those who have shipping space available. The Baltic Air Freight Market finds aircraft for cargoes and cargoes for aircraft, and deals with 'tramp' aircraft who will fly anywhere with a cargo to make a profit. Though costly, air transport is ideal for small, expensive items (such as diamonds), light perishable goods where speed of delivery is important, and time-sensitive business documents.

ALGOL. A computer programming language useful for mathematical applications.

algorithm (computers). The procedural steps for the solution of a special problem. A simple example is a food recipe.

aligned documents. Export documentation has been made simpler by the introduction by SITPRO (Simplification of International Trade Procedures Board) of the 'aligned series' of export documents – a complete set of documents of the same standard size with the same information in the same position. A master sheet records all the information required; where certain details are not required on a document they are blanked off. Documents required for carriage by sea and air are: BILL OF LADING/SEA WAYBILL, AIR CONSIGNMENT NOTE/AIR WAYBILL, COMMERCIAL INVOICE, CERTIFICATE OF ORIGIN, CERTIFICATE OF INSURANCE, STANDARD SHIPPING NOTE.

allonge (bill of exchange). A slip of paper annexed to a bill of exchange to give room for further endorsements.

alpha shares. Shares of 70 very large companies in which a high proportion of Stock Exchange dealing takes place.

alphanumeric (word processors). A type of field within a record that can hold letters or numbers. Also describes a character that can be either a numeral or a letter of the alphabet.

amalgamation. The union of two or more firms into one concern in order to achieve an improved return on the firm's resources.

amortisation. The provision for the paying off of a debt, usually by means of a sinking fund.

analog computer. A computer which represents data by a measurable physical quantity, such as length or voltage.

Annual Abstract of Statistics (government publication). Covers hundreds of aspects of national activity. Among many entries of interest to the business world are statistics concerning production, energy, iron and steel, industrial materials, building and construction, and manufactured goods.

annual general meeting (AGM). The AGM of a LIMITED COMPANY is a statutory meeting which must be held once a year in addition to any other general meeting. Notice of the meeting must be sent to all SHAREHOLDERS. The Annual Report and Accounts, and the declaration of dividends are presented to shareholders at this meeting. Societies and clubs hold AGMs, to which all members are invited, and at which the election of a committee takes place.

annual inventory. This is the *annual stock count* which involves stocktaking of furniture, equipment, fixtures and fittings and is usually made in addition to the annual stocktaking of items in the stockrooms. It is needed for accounting purposes, and the information is also useful when it comes to assessing the amount of insurance cover needed by the firm against fire and theft.

annual percentage rate (APR). HIRE PURCHASE interest rates are often shown in such a way that they mislead consumers. It must be remembered that a flat rate quoted on the amount borrowed – either to purchase goods or on taking out a loan – means that the rate is applied to the full amount borrowed over the whole period of the repayment. In fact, every time a repayment is made, the amount owing is reduced and, strictly speaking, the interest payable on the remainder of the money owing should also be reduced. A true APR shows the amount of interest paid when this fact is not taken into consideration and is therefore a higher figure than the percentage rate quoted. Under the Consumer Credit Act 1974, any interest quoted by the seller must be the true annual percentage rate, calculated to an agreed formula.

annual report and accounts. The independently audited report which must be produced by all publicly quoted companies, and sent to their shareholders following the completion of each financial year; it records the year's trading results and the company's financial position at the year end. Statutory documents which must accompany the report include: the PROFIT AND LOSS ACCOUNT – a summary of the resources of a firm and how they have been allocated during the financial period; it must give a true and fair view of the financial position of the company; the BALANCE SHEET showing SHARE CAPITAL and the RESERVES, any liabilities and provisions such as loans and taxation, and the fixed and current assets; Source and Application of Funds Statement which shows the way in which funds have been generated and absorbed by the operations of the business; the Directors' Report. The Companies Acts cover certain exemptions – a small company with not more than 50 employees, a TURNOVER which does not exceed £2 million and a balance sheet of not more than £975,000 may file an abbreviated form of accounts and is not required to submit a Profit and Loss Account. These statements must comply with rigid formats; financial statements may be presented in either horizontal or vertical form. *See* NATIONALISED INDUSTRIES.

answering and answering/recording machines. *See* ELECTRONIC OFFICE (telephone systems).

any other business (meetings). *See* AGENDA.

application form. When a company offers shares to the public, the official application form must be used to apply for them. This form is printed in the PROSPECTUS and in a national newspaper.

application software. A complete, documented program for a computer application.

apportionment. The method of fairly dividing overheads between the cost centres of a business.

appraisal. *See* INVESTMENT APPRAISAL and STAFF APPRAISAL.

appropriation account. A part of the PROFIT AND LOSS ACCOUNT which shows how the net profit of a firm has been dealt with. Normally, appropriation covers: interest payable on loans, corporation tax payable on profits, dividend payable to shareholders. Any unappropriated balance is added to the shareholders' capital in the balance sheet.

arbitrage. Buying securities in one country and selling them in another, with the object of making a profit; also now used to describe the practice of taking strategic stakes in companies involved, or likely to be involved, in a takeover bid.

arbitration. The referring of a dispute to an independent body for hearing and decision, when the parties involved have failed to agree a settlement. *See* TRIBUNALS, and ADVISORY, CONCILIATION AND ARBITRATION SERVICE (ACAS).

arbitrator. A senior member of the BALTIC EXCHANGE who assists in the settlement of marine disputes. The London Maritime Arbitrators Association was set up in 1960 to encourage international arbitration in London.

arithmetic/logic unit (ALU). Part of the central processing unit of a computer where calculations and logical operations are carried out.

Articles of Association. An important document drawn up on the formation of a company. It regulates the internal administration; details the classes of shares to be issued; the rights of shareholders and the qualifications required of directors; sets out the rules relating to company meetings and accounting; details provision for winding up the company. *See* FLOATING A COMPANY.

assets. All the property and possessions owned by a business, including all debts due to it. *Fixed assets* are items acquired for use in a business over a prolonged period. Examples are plant and machinery, land and buildings, furniture and fittings, motor vehicles, trade marks, goodwill. *Current or circulating assets* are acquired by a business for disposal in the course of trade and will quickly be renewed again. These are stock, sundry debtors, cash in hand and cash at the bank. *Liquid assets* are those which are available in cash or near cash form – the total of cash, bank moneys and debtors together form the liquid capital of a business.

Association of Futures Brokers and Dealers (AFBD). Self-regulatory organisation covering those operating in the commodities futures markets and the financial futures markets.

assurance. *See* LIFE ASSURANCE.

attitude survey. A study designed to determine people's attitudes to or beliefs about specific factors. Because attitudes are relatively enduring in nature they have a particular interest for marketing strategists.

auction sales. Auction sales on the London commodity markets occur where the commodity cannot be standardised, and has to be sampled to decide its quality. One example is the London Tea Auctions at the Tea Trade Centre, where brokers representing growers from all over the world auction their lots to the highest bidders.

auctioneer. An agent for a seller; he is authorised by licence to sell goods by public auction.

audio-conferencing. Where two or more people are linked by telephone and can take part in the same telephone conversation. Drawbacks can be two people talking at the same time and difficulty in recognising who is speaking.

audit. A checking of accounts by reference to witnesses and VOUCHERS. *Internal check.* Applied to entries at the time they are being prepared; it is a BOOKKEEPING arrangement which minimises the possibility of errors and fraud. Whenever possible, no one person carries out all the jobs or prepares all the records connected with a particular activity. *Internal audit.* Additional to the internal check, it is performed by officials of the business; it is a physical check of the entries *after* they have been made. *External audit.* An examination of the accounts made by a person or persons outside the organisation, usually a professional auditor who acts for and is appointed by the owners or shareholders. In the case of PUBLIC LIMITED COMPANIES a company must appoint an auditor or auditors at its ANNUAL GENERAL MEETING to hold office until the next AGM. The auditors have access at all times to the company's books, accounts and vouchers. They must report to the members on the accounts examined by them.

auditor's report. *See* AUDIT.

autarchy (*also* autarky). National (economic) self-sufficiency and independence. The idea that a country should produce all it requires and cease to import foreign goods.

authorised (share) capital. The *nominal capital,* the maximum amount of money a company is allowed to raise by the issue of shares.

authority. In any organisation there is a delegation of authority from higher to lower levels; the *style* of authority has an important impact on the organisation concerned. *Legal* or *'line' authority* can be illustrated by an hierarchical organisation chart and is usually called *line management;* it is impersonal and formal, loyalty being owed to the office and not to the individual. The system tends to bureaucracy, but is efficient in larger organisations. *Charismatic authority* is earned rather than given; the informal relationships formed by such managers with other personnel ensure that their instructions will be implemented. Charismatic managers are usually seen as having superior knowledge and experience, deal wisely with problems, and generally relate well with others in the organisation. *Traditional authority* is usually found in small-scale organisations, usually family firms, which are run on paternalistic lines.

automatic teller. A computerised cash dispenser that offers bank customers instant cash withdrawal facilities;

information on balances and requests for statements and cheque books are also dealt with; some also take deposits.

autonomous corporation. A corporation with legal status conferred on it by Act of Parliament which is not subject to day-to-day parliamentary control by the House of Commons' question-time procedure.

average adjuster. Average adjusters and ships' valuers assist in preparing and settling marine insurance matters.

average clause. If a policy-holder is under-insured (i.e. has insured his interest for a sum less than its actual value), his compensation will be paid in the same relative proportion as his insurance bears to the true value of his interest.

average rate of return (ARR). The ratio of net PROFIT (after DEPRECIATION) to CAPITAL cost. Net profit is more commonly used than gross profit.

average stock. The average stock figure is obtained by adding the opening stock figure to the closing stock figure and dividing by two. To find the average stock held during a year the average should be taken of stock held at the end of each month (i.e. the annual total divided by 12). The value of stock can be taken at cost price or selling price, but consistency in the use of one or other value must be maintained.

B

back-up (computers). With all methods of storage it is essential to make extra back-up copies in case the originals are damaged or lost.

background (word processing). Part of a word processor that takes care of work not needing attention. For example, printing can be done in background leaving the operator free to enter or edit text.

backing store (computers). Data or programs currently stored in the memory can be transferred to disks or tapes separate from the computer.

backward vertical integration. *See* MERGERS.

backwardation. *See* ACCOUNT (STOCK EXCHANGE).

bad debts. When debtors cannot pay their debts, they are said to be irrecoverable. Bad debts must be written off the books by the end of the trading period as they represent actual losses, and must be charged against profits in the PROFIT AND LOSS ACCOUNT. DEBT FACTORING is one method of minimising the harmful effects of bad debts on a business.

balance. The sum required to make the two sides of an account equal, hence the surplus or the sum due on an account. A bank statement shows the customer whether he has a credit balance or is overdrawn.

balance of payments. The difference between payments into and out of a country in a given period. *See* CAPITAL ACCOUNT (BALANCE OF PAYMENTS) and CURRENT ACCOUNT (BALANCE OF PAYMENTS).

balance of trade. The excess of imports over exports, or exports over imports is called the balance of trade. This is the figure for 'visibles', i.e. trade in goods.

balance sheet. A summary of an organisation's ASSETS (what the business owns) and LIABILITIES (what the business owes), which sets out the financial position of an undertaking at a given point in time. There must be sufficient detail to enable a correct judgement to be formed, and brief enough to make rapid assessment possible. The Companies Act 1985 requires that a balance sheet be presented annually, showing SHARE CAPITAL and RESERVES, liabilities and provisions for loans and TAXATION, CURRENT LIABILITIES, FIXED ASSETS and CURRENT ASSETS.

balance sheet gearing/capital gearing. The ratio between a company's borrowings and shareholders' funds.

ballot. A method of voting used as an alternative to a show of hands, and which protects an individual member's right to secrecy.

Baltair 1962 Air Charter Party. *See* AIR CHARTER PARTY.

Baltic Exchange. Properly 'The Baltic Mercantile and Shipping Exchange', the basis of the operations there being the verbal contract. The three main activities of the Baltic Exchange are: the FREIGHT MARKET where cargoes are arranged for ships and ships for cargoes; the AIR FREIGHT MARKET, the GRAIN FUTURES MARKET and the OIL AND OILSEEDS MARKET. The Baltic Exchange also earns large sums by the sale and purchase of ships, and by acting as agents for dry-dock and ship repair specialists and for bunkering (the provision of fuel – nowadays oil) for ocean-going vessels. Senior members of the exchange act as arbitrators in international maritime disputes, and average adjusters and ships' valuers are available for assistance in marine insurance matters.

bank/banking. The main 'High Street' banks in the UK are CLEARING or joint stock banks. Bank customers may hold different types of account, *see* CURRENT ACCOUNT, DEPOSIT ACCOUNT, BUDGET ACCOUNT. Some banking services are offered to non-account holders; among these are the supply of foreign currency and traveller's cheques, banker's credit cards and safe-deposit facilities. The functions of banking are: collecting of money from the public; safeguarding such money; transferring money by means of cheques, credit transfers, direct debits and standing orders; discounting BILLS OF EXCHANGE; facilitating foreign trade; lending money to individuals or as institutional investors. Banks earn a living by lending the money deposited with them to gain interest, and also by charging customers for their services.

bank bill/banker's acceptance. *See* BILL OF EXCHANGE.

bank certificate. A certificate issued by a bank for AUDIT purposes, certifying the amount of a company's BALANCE in the bank's books at a certain date.

bank clearing. *See* CLEARING BANKS.

bank credit/bank lending. There are two requirements for a sound credit policy in banking: that depositors shall be content to leave funds on deposit without making sudden demands; that borrowers are credit-worthy. Bank credit can be given in the following ways: *Bank loans.* These can be made to any credit-worthy individual or organisation (who need not have bank accounts with the lending bank) for a specific reason and for an agreed length of time. Interest is paid on the loan, repayment of which may be made by instalments or by a lump sum. COLLATERAL SECURITY may be asked for by the bank for the duration of the loan. *Bank overdraft.* Permission for current account holders to over-draw on their accounts may be granted by the bank. This permits the drawing on an account of a sum in excess of one's credit at the bank, interest being charged on the day-to-day balance of the overdraft. COLLATERAL SECURITY may be asked for by the bank. *Bankers' credit cards.* (Access, Barclaycard, etc.) Holders of such cards (who need not have a bank account) are allowed credit at establishments showing the relevant sign. The card holder is given a personal credit limit.

bank draft/banker's draft. A method of payment through the banks. It is, in effect, a cheque drawn on the bank itself. It is used if businesses are uncertain of the credit-worthiness of persons or firms who owe them money. They may then insist on payment being by means of a banker's draft rather than by the normal cheque. This means that the firm which owes the money makes arrangements with its bank, and the bank will then make out a cheque drawn on itself (a banker's draft) and made payable to the creditor.

Bank for International Settlements (Basle). The BIS acts as a clearing house for the world's central banks.

bank loan. *See* BANK CREDIT.

Bank of England. The Bank of England was chartered by Act of Parliament in 1694 to enable William III to carry on the war with France; in 1844, The Bank Charter Act was passed which split the organisation into two departments – which continue today – the *Issue* and *Banking Departments*. The Bank was nationalised in 1946. The Bank of England issues a *weekly return* covering the liabilities and assets of the two departments. The *Issue Department* is concerned solely with the issue of Bank of England banknotes, which are issued to the public as required; it is largely a *fiduciary issue* – backed by British government securities. The return shows the amount of the weekly issue. The *Banking Department's return* covers the banking functions of the bank; the most fundamental service which it performs for the government is managing its major bank accounts.

MAIN FUNCTIONS OF THE BANK OF ENGLAND

The Bank as banker. The money paid into government accounts comes largely from taxes and purchases of government stock; the money flowing out ranges from salaries and social security benefits to payments to government contractors. *Money markets.* From day to day there may be a difference of several hundred million pounds between what is flowing in and flowing out of the national exchequer. To iron out these differences the Bank's money markets and gilts dealers sell TREASURY BILLS and government bonds to the market when the market is in funds, and will buy them in when the market is short. These transactions are made with the DISCOUNT HOUSES and other institutions which act as intermediaries between the Bank of England and the commercial banks; these operations ensure that the banks can all balance their books at the end of the day and also gives the Bank considerable influence over interest rates (*see* LENDER OF LAST RESORT). If the Bank feels interest rates should rise, it can make the most of a shortage of funds in the market to force the discount houses to borrow the money they need at a higher rate than the one currently prevailing in the market. *Fundraising.* Today the Bank raises money for government by selling gilt-edged stock ('gilts'). These are bonds which the government issues to financial institutions and private investors to make up the difference between what it receives in taxes and what it needs for spending on public services. These loans comprise the bulk of the National Debt.

The nation's reserves. The Bank manages the government's assets as well as its debts. Although gold no longer backs the currency, the Treasury keeps substantial gold reserves; it also looks after gold belonging to foreign governments and London bullion dealers. In addition, it manages the Treasury's reserves of foreign currency, which may be needed from time to time to counteract instability in the foreign exchange markets. *Economics.* The Bank's Economics Division closely monitors the national economy, looking at what is being spent, borrowed and invested by industry, the public and the government. Its forecasts play an important part in forming decisions about a wide range of economic policies as well as providing the background to much of the Bank's advice to government. Its International Divisions keep government departments informed about financial and economic developments around the world. *Supervising the financial institutions.* The Bank of England licenses all British and foreign banks operating in Britain; it ensures that they are prudently run by trustworthy managements and that they always have resources to meet any demands likely to be put on them. The Bank of England has legal powers to compel banks to disclose information and can, in extreme cases, revoke a bank's licence if it is not being properly managed. The Bank is also responsible for supervising institutions which act as buyers and sellers of gilt-edged stocks, foreign exchange and gold; it also appoints members of the Securities and Investments Board, the 'watchdog' organisation set up to protect investors in the various financial fields. *International banking.* As one of the world's major central banks, the Bank of England plays an important part in international financial strategy. The Bank offers its expertise and staff to developing countries, especially Commonwealth countries, to help them establish their own central banks to regulate their monetary and economic affairs. In collaboration with the INTERNATIONAL MONETARY FUND, the WORLD BANK, the *Bank of International Settlements* and other central banks, the Bank of England tries to work out strategies which will allow many developing countries with international debt problems to continue repaying the loans. The

Bank also plays an active part in drawing up international standards for banking practice and banking supervision. *Finance for industry.* Although the Bank of England does not lend its own money to industry, it can offer its services as adviser and honest broker if a company or institution is having difficulties in its relationship with its bankers, or needs reorganisation. *Stock registration.* The Bank is the registrar of government stocks.

bank overdraft. *See* BANK CREDIT.

bank rate. The official rate charged by the Bank of England for discounting first-class BILLS OF EXCHANGE; it influences the rates of interest charged by all banks for the loan of money, and the rate of interest allowed on deposits.

bank reconciliation statement. The bank balance shown in the cash book of a firm does not often agree with the figure shown on a bank statement of the same date. This is quite normal but it can conceal an error. It is therefore the practice in most firms to arrange to receive daily bank statements on which the individual items are checked each morning with the balance in the cash book. When completed, the bank reconciliation statement should show in detail the entries causing the discrepancy.

bank return (banking department's return). *See* BANK OF ENGLAND.

bank statements (current and deposit accounts). The bank statement of account is a copy of the account holder's personal computer account and is given or sent to a customer at regular intervals or when requested. It provides a record of all the transactions of the customer with the bank.

bankers' bank. Name given to the BANK OF ENGLAND as the depository for the working balances of commercial banks.

bankers' clearing house. *See* CLEARING BANKS.

bankers' credit card. *See* BANK CREDIT.

Banking Act 1979. Gave the Bank of England legal powers to supervise the activities of recognised banks and licensed deposit takers (LDTs) which accept deposits from members of the public. All banks are supervised by the BANK OF ENGLAND with the assistance of the Board of Banking Supervision.

Bank(ing) Department. *See* BANK OF ENGLAND.

banknotes. In England and Wales, the printing and distribution of banknotes is the monopoly of the Bank of England. The money the 'High Street' banks pay for banknotes is invested by the Bank of England and earns the Treasury around a billion pounds a year. Banknotes are, by law, a valid means of clearing debts; they are, like coin, LEGAL TENDER.

bankruptcy. If the losses of a sole trader or partnership are serious the business becomes insolvent and cannot pay its way – it becomes bankrupt. (Companies are said to go into liquidation, and are dealt with by a procedure known as 'winding up'.) An insolvent business is put into the hands of the OFFICIAL RECEIVER who instigates a public examination of the firm's finances and business affairs. If it seems that debts cannot be paid, the owner(s) will be declared bankrupt, the business and stock sold and creditors paid as much as possible. Sole traders and most partnerships have unlimited liability and the personal effects of the owner(s) of such businesses can be sold to help pay off the debts.

bar chart/bar graph. A method of illustrating numerical data. Individual vertical bars represent the quantity for each period, instead of a continuous line as in a line graph.

bar code (computers). Supermarkets commonly use bar code data for pricing and stock updating. The bars on the packet identify the manufacturer and product and are scanned by the cashier at the cash desk. The data is transmitted to a computer that records each item, sends back the price to the sales assistant, reduces the stock level and, if necessary, creates a requisition or order for further goods to be supplied. Bar codes are increasingly used for recording data on all kinds of stock movement.

bargain. Any STOCK EXCHANGE transaction; despite its name, no special price is implied.

barter. The exchange of goods for goods, goods for services, or services for services. In international trade, barter (known as COUNTERTRADING) is becoming more common; this is due to the uncertainty of unstable exchange rates.

base rate. A rate of interest set by an individual bank to which the interest rates on most of its loans are linked. This rate is always at or near the rate at which the Bank of England is currently willing to lend.

BASIC. A computer programming language most commonly used for microcomputers.

basic human needs. The three basic human needs are food, clothing and shelter.

basket of currencies. *See* EUROPEAN CURRENCY UNIT (ECU).

batch production. The manufacture of a product in large or small batches or lots. Each operation is carried out on the whole batch before the next operation is started. It is a production method extensively used in the engineering industry or whenever a limited quantity of one type of product is authorised for manufacture at one time.

baud rate (computers). The number of times per second that a data transmission channel changes state. (*Baud* is a unit of transmission speed.)

bear. One who has sold a security in the hope of buying it back at a lower price; a *bear market* is a falling market.

'bearer cheque'. A cheque payable to 'bearer' requires no endorsement, and entitles anyone in possession of the cheque to present it for payment at the bank branch shown on it.

'bearer' securities. Stocks and shares for which no register of ownership is kept by the company concerned.

bed and breakfast. Selling shares one day and buying them back the next for tax purposes at the end of the financial year.

beneficial owner. The ultimate owner of a security, regardless of the name in which it is legally registered.

beta shares. The second of four groupings of shares, classified according to how actively they are dealt on the Stock Exchange.

bid. 1. Indicates what a buyer is prepared to pay for shares. 2. An approach made by one company wishing to purchase the entire share capital of another company. 3. To offer a price at an auction.

bidirectional (printers). Describes a printer that prints both when the printing mechanism moves to the right and when it returns.

'big bang'. Term used to describe the changes which took place in October 1986 in the way member firms of the London STOCK EXCHANGE operated. Stock Exchange members are now divided between MARKET MAKERS and BROKER-DEALERS, and dealing in shares and bonds takes place by telephone between dealers' offices. Fixed commissions have been abolished. The SECURITIES AND INVESTMENT BOARD (SIB) regulates the activities of the institutions concerned with the buying and selling of securities.

bill of exchange. The legal definition of a bill of exchange is that it is 'an unconditional order in writing addressed by one person to another, signed by the person giving it, requiring the person to whom it is addressed to pay on demand, or at a fixed or determinable future time, a sum certain in money to, or to the order of, a specified person or to the bearer'. It is, in effect, a promise to pay a debt to a creditor on a set date (usually in 90 days' time). A bill of exchange is said to be accepted when it is signed by the debtor, who promises to pay the amount shown when the debt falls due. The signed bill is a legally binding document and banks will accept such bills and pay the holders for them, knowing that on a certain date the money can be collected. The bank's charge for this service is known as a discount, and the service is known as *discounting bills of exchange.* A bill of exchange is a negotiable instrument and can therefore be passed into the possession of another person – not necessarily a bank. When this is done, the bill should be endorsed (signed on the back) by the holder before it is passed on. If a bill is endorsed so often that there is no room for further names, a piece of paper – an 'allonge' – may be pasted on to it to allow for further signatures. A bill of exchange is not an alternative to a bank loan or overdraft. It is a method of payment whereby the seller receives early payment and the buyer enjoys 90 days' credit, during which time the transaction will normally have been completed. An *accommodation bill* is one that has been issued without value having been received; it is used to advance a sum of *money* to the payee. *Bank bills* have been signed or endorsed by a reputable bank. *Foreign bills* are either drawn in Great Britain and payable in some other country, or *vice versa*. *Inland bills* are both drawn and payable in Great Britain. *Trade bills* are used in commercial transactions. A *documentary bill of exchange* is used in international transactions; it is sent to an accepting bank with the shipping documents, without which the importer cannot claim the goods when they are landed. This bill contains a clause to the effect that documents are to be surrendered to the importer only against payment (D/P), or in some instances against acceptance (D/A) of the bill of exchange.

bill of lading. An official detailed receipt given by the master of a vessel to the consignor, by which he makes himself responsible for safe delivery of the goods. (*See also* SEA WAYBILL and COMMON SHORT FORM B/L.) A ship's manifest is the total of all the bills of lading for one particular voyage.

bill of materials. A detailed specification listing every component used in the manufacture and assembly of a product. It is important to the work of many of the production team: to the production planner in scheduling work through the factory; to the materials controller for requisitioning stocks to meet production needs; and to the accountants for calculating the materials' cost for a product.

bill rate. Discount rate applied by discount houses and banks for discounting bills of exchange.

bill-broking. A means of dealing in money – taking from those who have a surplus and distributing it to those who need it – mainly by using the bill of exchange. Members of the London Discount Market Association specialise in bill-broking. To keep the profit margin to a minimum, no expensive paper work is involved, and almost all deals are by word of mouth. Bill-brokers deal with the Bank of England, the commercial banks, large commercial and industrial firms, and institutional investors. They specialise in the provision of short-term money by discounting bills to borrowers who require funds; dealings are in TREASURY BILLS, BANK BILLS, COMMERCIAL BILLS, short-dated GILT-EDGED SECURITIES, local authority bills, and CERTIFICATES OF DEPOSIT.

bill-leak. Bankers' acceptance of bills of exchange held outside the banking system.

binary. A number system using a base of 2, having the 2 digits 0 and 1; these are used in computing where they can represent the presence or absence of a signal such as an electrical impulse.

bio-data. Research has been carried out on the suitability of candidates for specific jobs on the basis of biographical details – commonly known as bio-data.

bit (computers). A binary digit, either 0 or 1. The smallest piece of information which can be stored.

black economy. Covers illegal, undocumented (usually 'cash') transactions on which tax is not paid.

blacking. Sympathetic action by a group of trade union members to support another group who are on strike. It covers refusal to handle goods or equipment but stops short of strike action.

block (word processors). A group of words, lines or paragraphs which is treated as one unit.

block discounting. *See* FINANCE HOUSES.

Blue Book. Name for the United Kingdom National Accounts published annually in September by HMSO.

blue chip. Term for the most highly regarded industrial shares.

blue-collar worker. Worker in industrial factory work (cf. WHITE-COLLAR WORKER).

bold (word processors). A way of producing text in which each character is darker and thicker than normal.

bond. 1. 'An agreement or engagement binding on him who makes it.' The Stock Exchange motto 'my word is my bond' uses the word in this sense. 2. The owners of bonded warehouses give a *bond* to the authorities promising not to release goods from the warehouse until the duty has been paid and a customs officer is present at the payment. Goods in such warehouses are said to be 'in bond'. 3. A security issued by a government, nationalised corporation or a company which carries a fixed rate of interest to the holder. *Company bonds* are called DEBENTURES.

bonded warehouse. Warehouse owned by a company or private individual but under the control of the Customs and Excise officers of the UK, where goods which are subject

25

either to customs or excise duties may be stored pending payment of duty; such goods are said to be 'bonded' or 'in bond'. The owner or occupier of such a warehouse enters into a 'bond' with the CUSTOMS AND EXCISE authorities undertaking that no goods in them shall be removed for home consumption until the duty has been paid. When the whole or part of the goods in the warehouse are sold, duty is then paid on the quantity withdrawn from 'bond'. This service relieves the importer of the obligation of paying a large amount of duty at one time. Preparation for sale, but not manufacturing, can eventually be carried out in a bonded warehouse before duty is paid; among these activities are the bottling of wines and spirits, blending and packaging of tea and coffee, and the packing of tobacco.

bonus. 1. Annual profit credited to certain life assurance policies, or discretionary payment which may be made on a matured contract. 2. Extra company DIVIDEND sometimes paid on exceptional profits. 3. An extra payment, usually given as an incentive to improve profitability, made to a person earning money. A bonus may be given for a specific reason (e.g. at Christmas); it may be based on earnings and/or length of service. Sometimes a *group bonus* is earned by a team of workers; it may be shared equally among the members or paid out in proportion to basic pay.

bonus share/issue. *See* CAPITALISATION ISSUE.

bookkeeping. A systematic method of recording the transactions of a business in books of account.

books of prime entry (bookkeeping). Because of the rule that transactions must be passed through the subsidiary books before being entered in the ledger, the subsidiary books are known collectively as books of original, or first, entry; the term applies also to the cash book. These subsidiary books are: purchases day book, sales day book, sales returns and purchases returns books.

boot (computers). To start up a computer by loading information, e.g. from a systems disk.

bought deal (Stock Exchange). Instead of placing shares with a number of investors, a company can invite bids for all the shares from a number of security houses. The house with the highest bid is offered the shares, pays cash for them, and makes a profit by selling them to a range of investors.

bought ledger (purchases ledger). Contains the personal accounts of creditors.

bought note. A contract note sent by a buyer to a seller stating the terms and conditions of a purchase arranged orally, or a note sent by an agent to his principal giving full conditions of a purchase of goods on his behalf.

bourse. A stock exchange or money market.

boutique. Small financial operation specialising in providing a single financial service, such as fund management, broking or arbitrage.

branding. A 'branded' article is one where the trade name or brand has been registered in some official way, and where the manufacturer has created and preserved a 'brand' image by advertising. Many large retailers buy 'own brand' goods from manufacturers. The manufacturer will package the goods for the retailer who often sells them more cheaply than goods bearing the manufacturer's own TRADEMARK.

break-even analysis. Technique concerned with finding the point at which revenues and costs coincide, i.e. neither a profit nor a loss is made. *Break-even* point is reached when the total costs of a firm equal the total sales revenue.

breaking bulk. Buying in large quantities and breaking down into smaller quantities before resale.

bridging loan. Money borrowed (usually from a bank) pending the sale of an asset. Often necessary in housing transactions.

British Government Stock. This forms a part of the 'gilt-edged' market of the Stock Exchange, and is issued by the government with the primary object of providing long-term funds for government expenditure.

British Overseas Trade Board (BOTB). The Department of Trade and Industry's export arm. The Board consists of representatives of industry and commerce, including the Confederation of British Industry and the Trades Union Congress. The DTI works through the BOTB to provide EXPORT SERVICES.

British Standards Institution (BSI). Organisation which lays down minimum standards in the manufacture of consumer goods; the BSI Kitemark sign indicates that goods are of the quality required by the BSI specification.

British Technology Group. Public corporation ultimately reporting to the Department of Trade and Industry. BTG's objective is to promote the development of new technology in commercial products, particularly where the technology originates from public sector sources such as universities, polytechnics, research councils and government research establishments.

broker. The most commonly used term for dealers on the commodity markets. *See* IMPORT BROKERS, INSURANCE BROKERS.

brokerage. The commission paid to a broker on the business done by him.

broker-dealer. An International Stock Exchange member firm, which provides advice and dealing services to the public.

budget (government). Budget Day is held on a Tuesday in March/April each year when the Chancellor of the Exchequer presents to Parliament the government's plan for raising the money needed in the coming year – the fiscal programme. *See* ECONOMY, CONTROL OF.

budget (of organisations). A statement of the probable expenditure, and proposals for financing them, for a defined period of time, based on a prepared plan which fixes standards of materials, wages and expense costs to be incurred during the period. *Budgetary control* is the name given to a general scheme, involving the planning and control of operations, whereby every effort is made to ensure that the performance of a business conforms to the figures predicted in the budget.

budget account. 1. A budget account with a clearing bank or Girobank will enable a bank customer to spread his payments more evenly. For instance, all household expenses (mortgage payments, gas, electricity, telephone, holidays, etc.) may be totalled for the year, and the total divided by 12. Each month this figure is taken out of the current account of the householder and placed in a budget account which has a separate cheque book. The householder can draw on this account up to three times the monthly figure. 2. Budget accounts are also schemes operated by shops for the benefit of regular customers. By paying a stipulated amount each month, the customer is able to obtain credit up to a stated number of multiples of the amount paid. As the debt is reduced monthly the customer is always able to obtain credit on further goods up to the limit of his individual credit; it is a system of *revolving credit*.

buffer (word processors). Part of the word processor's memory which holds text.

building society. Organisation which offers facilities to savers who receive interest, and uses the money deposited to provide mortgages for the purchase of property. Mortgagors pay interest on the money they borrow. Building societies do not make a profit – the money received from savers and the interest they receive from investment as INSTITUTIONAL INVESTORS is balanced against the money they lend to house buyers. Many building societies now offer banking services to their members. The Building Societies Ombudsman will investigate complaints against individual building societies who are members of the scheme.

bulk cargoes. Bulk cargoes of one primary commodity only are usually handled by the COMMODITY MARKETS whose middlemen finance, transport and warehouse the goods.

bulk carriers. Large ocean-going vessels used for transporting iron ore, coal and oil in bulk. A system of charges known as WORLDSCALE is used when they are chartered.

bulk transactions. There are advantages in dealing in large quantities. First, most suppliers offer discounts on large orders; secondly, the transport of large movements are generally less, especially when very large crude carriers or container ships are used; thirdly, the documentation of large orders is very much the same as that for small orders.

bull. One who has bought a security in the hope of selling it at a higher price; a *bull market* is a rising market.

bulldog bond (Stock Exchange). A sterling bond issued in Britain by a foreigner.

bullion markets. The price of gold is dictated by supply and demand, which at any particular time varies from one world centre to another. In London the price is 'fixed' by the merchant bankers who form the *London Gold Bullion Market,* and who meet twice daily in the Rothschild offices for the ritual 'gold-fixing'. Buying and selling prices are normally expressed in US dollars per fine ounce. *The Silver Bullion Market* operates in much the same way as the Gold Market; there is only one 'fixing' a day, and quotations are made in both sterling and dollars.

bunkering. The fuelling of ships.

business documents (transactions). The following is a full list of documents used in a business transaction; obviously no transaction would entail using every one. Usually the top copy is sent to the addressee and a varying number of copies are kept by the issuing firm for different purposes – accounts and stock records, for example. The order of the list below is that in which the forms would be used.

1 Enquiry	7 Dispatch note	13 Pro forma invoice
2 Estimate	8 Advice note	14 Credit note
3 Quotation	9 Delivery note	15 Debit note
4 Tender	10 Packing note	16 Statement of Account
5 Firm offer	11 Consignment note	17 Remittance advice
6 Order	12 Invoice	18 Receipt

See TRANSACTIONS.

Business Expansion Scheme. Government scheme for allowing investors to put money into an unlisted company with the benefit of tax relief.

business letters. *See* CORRESPONDENCE.

business system. The complete system for running the activities of an organisation which can involve the use of computers, manual routines and documentation, all of which contribute to the running of the concern.

business units. Any organisation engaged in business is a business unit; the type of unit can be determined by identifying who provided the CAPITAL (the owner or owners), and who receives the profits. The UK has a 'mixed economy', which means that some organisations are privately owned, and some are publicly owned and run by the government and local authorities.

TYPES OF BUSINESS UNITS

Private sector. Sole trader; partnership; private limited company (with 'limited' or 'Ltd' after the name); public limited company (PLC); holding company. *Non-profit-making units* (in PRIVATE SECTOR). Cooperative societies; friendly societies; many different clubs and societies; agricultural and productive cooperatives. *Public sector.* Central government departments; public corporations; local government (county councils and district councils).

C

cabinet. The council of ministers responsible for the government of the United Kingdom; it is the focal point of the *executive* which formulates government policy. *Cabinet ministers* are the body of men chosen from the political party in power to fill the highest executive offices of the state. They direct the government and are collectively responsible to Parliament for every act of the Crown.

call. The amount due to be paid to a company by the purchaser of nil-paid or partly-paid shares.

call money. Bill-brokers are prepared to borrow money from any source and repay as required. Money which is borrowed and repayable on demand is 'call money'.

call option. An option (right) to buy SHARES at a future date at an agreed price, whatever happens to the market.

capital. Together with labour and land, capital is one of the three factors of production; it is wealth set aside to produce further wealth. *A firm's capital* represents its total financial resources.

SOURCES OF CAPITAL

The primary source of capital is savings – either voluntary savings or by way of taxation – which are invested in businesses. There are many private individuals who are investors, but the funds of the large institutional investors provide the greater part of the investment funds available. Investors' moneys may be made available to organisations through bank loans, bank overdrafts, issues of SHARES (or additional shares), or by the issue of DEBENTURES. Profits can be 'ploughed back' (re-invested) in a successful business.

TYPES OF CAPITAL

Authorised capital. The amount of share capital a LIMITED COMPANY is authorised to raise. *Called-up capital.* The amount the company actually receives from the shareholders, who may not be required to pay the full face value of their shares on allotment. *Capital employed.* The sum of the assets the firm is using, whether borrowed or not – the FIXED ASSETS *plus* working capital. *Capital owned.* This is calculated by deducting the firm's liabilities from its assets. The surplus represents the capital owned by the firm at the date calculated. *Circulating capital* (sometimes called floating capital). The flow of money through an organisation – ie the current assets – provides the resources to use the fixed assets to the best advantage. Circulating assets are used only once in production; they comprise stock, cash and amounts owed to the firm. *Fixed capital.* This consists of material goods used for the production of further goods – premises, plant, machinery; they are used many times to make a profit. *Issued capital.* The amount of share capital which the directors decide to issue to the public. The amount they do issue, and which is actually paid for, is the *issued* or *paid-up capital* . Also called *allotted capital. Liquid capital.* That part of the assets of a business which can be easily transferred into cash or near cash; the total of cash, bank moneys, and debtors. *Loan capital.* What a company has borrowed, either on MORTGAGE or by issue of DEBENTURES. *Minimum capital.* 1. By law, a public limited company must have an authorised capital of at least £50,000. 2. The minimum amount of capital which is declared by the directors of a new company to be necessary for it to commence business. If the minimum amount is not subscribed, the amount already collected must be returned to those who subscribed it. *Net capital employed.* Total assets less current liabilities, except bank overdraft. *Nominal capital.* The authorised or share capital. The amount of capital the company is authorised to raise by the sale of shares. *Paid-up capital.* The part of a company's issued share capital on which the nominal value of the shares has been received by the company. *Share capital.* The total amount of capital subscribed by the shareholders. *Social capital.* Taxes and rates are enforced 'savings' which finance the building of roads, bridges, hospitals, schools, etc; these collectively form the 'social capital' of a nation. *Trading capital.* The total of the fixed and circulating capital of a business. *Working capital.* Amount of capital needed to carry on a business from day to day. It is calculated by deducting current liabilities from current assets. Amounts owed to creditors are the current liabilities; stock, cash in hand, cash at the bank, and the amounts owed by the debtors form the current assets.

capital account (balance of payments). Government account made up of long-term transactions – private long-term investments, long-term government loans, and transactions with overseas monetary authorities such as the INTERNATIONAL MONETARY FUND (IMF). *See also* CURRENT ACCOUNT (BALANCE OF PAYMENTS).

capital assets. Most businesses own certain equipment – premises, machinery, furniture, etc. These are capital assets and are used to increase the production of goods and services.

capital consumption. *See* CAPITAL FORMATION.

capital expenditure. The acquisition of FIXED ASSETS such as plant and equipment which will be used over a long period of time.

capital formation. The national accounts (the 'Blue Book') record all the output of capital goods in one year – the gross capital formation for the country. *Capital consumption* represents the amount of capital depreciation in the same period.

capital gains tax. When individuals sell assets such as securities, works of art, or land, they are deemed to be trading and consequently pay capital gains tax on any profit or gain made.

capital gearing/balance sheet gearing/leverage. The ratio between a company's different sources of finance – ie between a company's EQUITY (ordinary shares and dividend capital) and its loan capital (DEBENTURES). When deciding which source of finance to use, the cost of the sources and the company's expected yield will influence the balance between the different sources. A firm with a high capital gearing has a high proportion of loan stock.

capital goods. Goods which are produced for other producers to use in a further stage of production. Also called *producer goods.*

capital market. When an individual saves money he places it for safe keeping with a bank, building society, insurance company, unit or investment trust, and all pension schemes collect vast amounts of savings from members. These 'collecting' organisations are institutional investors who invest the money in profitable ways, either in other industrial concerns which have a need for capital investment, or by lending it to other borrowers, such as the government, whose income is inadequate to meet the current requirements. The capital market exists to bring the two sides together. *See* DISCOUNT HOUSES, MONEY MARKET, NEW ISSUE MARKET, STOCK EXCHANGE.

capital owned. *See* CAPITAL (TYPES OF).

capital reserves. Reserves created by some extraordinary activity of a company, such as revaluation of property; not generally available for distribution as dividend.

capital transfer tax. Replaced by INHERITANCE TAX.

capitalisation issue. The process whereby money from a company's reserves is converted into issued capital, which is then distributed to shareholders as new shares in proportion to their original holdings. Also known as a *bonus* or *scrip issue.*

captain's protest. In the case of claims in marine insurance, this is a sworn statement by the captain of the vessel which gives particulars of the loss and the cause of it.

cargo insurance. In the import and export trade, the existence of an insurance policy in conjunction with a BILL OF LADING is vital. *Cargo policies* refer to the insurance of goods moving into or out of a country. *Floating policies* give cover for a specified sum, and eliminate the necessity of insuring each cargo separately. When the amount is spent, the floating policy is renewed. *Open-cover agreements* are at a pre-arranged rate for any consignment up to a certain limit notified to the UNDERWRITER for a particular vessel, on a particular voyage. The policies are issued after notification.

cargo liners. Vessels which carry mainly cargo but which have a few cabins for passengers. They usually keep to definite routes and schedules.

carriage forward. The cost of carriage is borne by the buyer.

carriage paid. The cost of carriage is borne by the seller.

carried unanimously (meetings). A motion 'carried unanimously' occurs when all members present at the meeting have voted in favour of it. (*See also NEM CON*).

carriers. *Local carriers* operate on a fixed route in a local area. *Universal carriers* accept goods for any destination. *See* COMMON CARRIER.

cartel. An independent combination of commercial enterprises designed to limit competition by regulating production and price.

cartridge disk. A large, high-capacity disk housed in a round plastic cartridge.

case law. Law established by previous judicial decisions (judicial precedents); it is based on the law that previous decisions of a higher court are followed by lower courts.

cash. cash is usually understood to mean 'ready money', or money in a bank, but has also come to denote cheques and other documents containing an order to pay on demand. New notes and coins are issued to the public by the commercial banks though they originate from the BANK OF ENGLAND and the Royal Mint. Banks also withdraw badly soiled or mutilated notes from circulation.

cash against documents. For goods imported into a country the terms are nearly always 'cash against documents'. The foreign exporter draws a BILL OF EXCHANGE against the importing firm; to this document he attaches the INVOICE, BILL OF LADING, and the CERTIFICATE OF INSURANCE. This documentary bill is then sent to the banker in the importing country who will receive payment in favour of the foreign exporter, before the goods are delivered to the importer.

cash and carry warehouse. Competes with the traditional wholesaler and is like a 'wholesale supermarket', dealing in bulk; it offers neither credit (though some accept bankers' credit cards) nor transport facilities, this saving on overheads enabling it to charge lower costs to retailers. The 'cut-price' policy is attractive to the small shopkeeper for whom the warehouse is also open at convenient hours.

cash card. Allows holders of current accounts at a bank or members of a building society to obtain money from *cash dispensers* outside normal working hours.

cash discount. A small concession given to customers for prompt payment of a bill.

cash flow. The money obtained from selling goods or services which is used to finance further production. Any major delay in receiving money will probably cause a firm to have cash flow problems and so run into financial difficulties. Businesses should aim to maintain a constant flow of cash into the firm so that WORKING CAPITAL is always available; if the inflow is inadequate there will not be enough cash available to pay creditors, purchase raw materials or pay wages; without raw materials, production will suffer. The price of a product also determines how much income an organisation will obtain from its capital outlay. It greatly influences the cash flow into an organisation and, consequently, affects its acquisition of additional resources. On the other hand, holding too much cash is expensive and inefficient; money should always be employed to generate profit.

cash flow forecast. A statement which analyses all cash receipts and payments over the periods during which transactions are anticipated. An assessment is made of potential shortfalls or surpluses so that remedial action can be taken before the flow of cash into the organisation is disrupted.

cash limits. Local authorities and government departments do not make profits and are given funds from public sources which they allocate to different (and competing) projects, according to political policy decisions. The Budget sets cash limits on the amounts government organisations can spend, though local government councillors have powers of discretion on expenditure within the cash limits set by central government.

cash markets. *See* SPOT DEALING.

cash ratio (banking). Early bankers observed that only about 8 per cent of their customers' funds were likely to be demanded in cash at any time – the *cash ratio*; this left them free to lend the remaining 92 per cent at interest. In fact the Bank of England requires that specific ratios must be retained by the banks in cash, and occasionally a further small percentage – a 'special deposit' – may be called in by the Bank to control credit policies.

cash sales/cash transactions. Immediate payment for goods and services received. The advantages to a business of the cash trade are: a smaller CAPITAL is required; there are no bad debts; there is less bookkeeping.

casting vote. If the ARTICLES OF ASSOCIATION expressly provide it, the chairman of a meeting has a second or casting vote in addition to his right to vote as a member, and he may use this in the event of an equality of votes.

casual worker. Person engaged to work on an occasional basis and employed for irregular periods.

caveat emptor. Means 'let the buyer beware', and is an early rule from contract law which still applies today. In placing an order, it is up to the buyer to examine carefully what he is about to buy.

caveat venditor. 'Let the seller beware.' With legislation increasingly protecting the buyer, the seller must also learn to be careful.

census. A counting of the population and gathering of related statistics (e.g. age, sex, social class). In the UK a census is taken every 10 years in the first year of the decade (1971, 1981, etc.).

central bank. The main banking institution of a country, primarily concerned with influencing affairs in its own country. *See* BANK OF ENGLAND.

central bank balances. The balances or deposits that commercial banks keep with the central bank.

central government. *See* GOVERNMENT (FUNCTIONS OF).

Central Office of Information (COI). An independent government organisation which issues many publications, including reports on particular industries and areas; it also runs an intelligence service which answers individual enquiries from commerce and industry. The COI offers a very comprehensive publicity service for British exporters, and advice on all aspects of international trade.

central processing unit (CPU) (computers). Made of microchips, this part of the computer contains the memory; the data in the memory is also processed in the CPU.

Central Selling Organisation (CSO). A London-based marketing organisation whose companies sort, value and sell rough diamonds to the world's major diamond-cutting centres and industries.

centralisation. The concentration, at one centre, of the government of a country or the administration of an organisation.

certificate of deposit. When an organisation, such as a bank, wishes to earn interest on funds lying idle, but does not wish to tie up its money in a term deposit (i.e. for a definite length of time), it will lodge the money with a DISCOUNT HOUSE and receive a certificate of deposit which is negotiable, and which can therefore be turned into cash. For the major banks these certificates are a simple way of buying funds in the market, and for the smaller banks they are a liquid asset which can be traded.

certificate of incorporation. Sent by the Registrar of Companies to a newly-registered company as its 'birth certificate', after initial documents (including the MEMORANDUM OF ASSOCIATION and the ARTICLES OF ASSOCIATION) have been lodged and approved by him. This gives the company a legal personality and allows its shares to be sold to secure the capital it needs.

certificate of insurance (international trade). Provides proof that goods have been insured against loss or damage during transit. It is one of the necessary documents which must accompany a documentary BILL OF EXCHANGE, others being the BILL OF LADING and the INVOICE.

certificate of origin. Certifies that goods have been manufactured in the country stated, and is used by customs to indicate the amount of duty payable on a particular item. The duty that an importing country imposes on goods varies according to the country from which they originate.

certificate of trading. When the SHARES of a PUBLIC LIMITED COMPANY have been sold and the minimum CAPITAL assured, the new company must apply to the Registrar of Companies for a certificate of trading, which will be granted if all the statutory documentation is in order. When this is received by the company, it can commence business.

certiorari. A writ by which cases are removed from inferior courts into the High Court of Justice.

chain of distribution, chain of production. Alternative titles for the route by which consumer goods reach the final consumer. *See* DISTRIBUTION.

chain store. A multiple store which sells a variety of goods; it is one of a large number of branch shops, each of which usually exhibits the same appearance, especially in the shop front and window design.

challenging. Method of dealing on the London Gold and Silver Bullion Markets. Brokers meet and challenge one another until a firm price is fixed.

chambers of (industry and) commerce. Many towns and cities have chambers of commerce. Membership is made up of the representatives of local firms engaged in industry and commerce. Their purpose is to promote trade and help members with problems connected with trade and manufacturing, both at home and abroad. The London Chamber of Commerce also conducts examinations in commercial subjects. Many chambers of commerce throughout the country are concerned with export promotion and will provide information for those wishing to export; in association with trade associations and export clubs, they undertake specific overseas research. There is an International Bureau of Chambers of Commerce.

chambers of trade. Many town and cities have a local chamber of trade. Membership is made up of representatives of large shops and smaller shopkeepers. They promote efficient trading and protect the interests of local retailers.

character (computers). A letter, number, space, mark or symbol.

charter party. In maritime law this is a contract between the owner or master of a ship and a person who hires the ship or part of the ship for the purpose of conveying goods from one port to another. The charter is a 'document of rights'. Vessels may be hired for a particular period of time (time charter) or a particular voyage (voyage charter).

chartering agents. Agents who represent merchants or organisations wishing to charter ships. *See* CHARTER PARTY.

charts. Bar charts, flowcharts and pie charts, line graphs, histograms and pictograms are all used in offices to display essential facts and figures in a way which can be quickly assimilated.

check trading. A type of credit for small purchases. Checks are available in various denominations from agents (tallymen) who make a regular round to collect payments. The checks may be used to buy goods at a large number of shops participating in the scheme. The checks are often known as 'Provident Checks' because the biggest issuer is the Provident Clothing and Supply Company Ltd.

cheque. A cheque is a written order to a bank to pay on demand a stated sum of money to the bearer or to the person named on it. A cheque is a bill of exchange drawn on a banker and payable on demand (Bills of Exchange Act 1882).

ESSENTIALS OF A CHEQUE

Cheques can be accepted for clearing (ie the money transferred from the drawer's (payer's) account either to the payee, or into his account), only if the following five items appear:

1. *the date*
2. *the payee's name* (unless it is made out to 'cash' by the owner of the account who intends to cash it at his own bank branch)
3. *the amount written in words*
4. *the amount written in figures*
5. *the drawer's signature*

PARTIES TO A CHEQUE

There are always three parties to a cheque:

1. *the drawer* (payer), who is the one who signs the cheque
2. *the drawee*, who is always the banker
3. *the payee*, who receives payment

RETURNED CHEQUES

Cheques returned to the payee by the bank may be marked:

R/D – refer to drawer
I/F – insufficient funds
N/F – no funds

In all cases the cheques should be referred back to the drawer of the cheque.

TYPES OF CHEQUE

Bearer cheque – made out to 'Pay Bearer', it is very unsafe. It does not require endorsement and can be cashed by any person presenting it at the counter of the bank branch shown on the cheque. *Blank cheque* – a cheque on which the amount of money to be drawn is not shown. It is advisable to write a monetary limit on such a cheque between the lines of the crossing. *Crossed cheque.* If two parallel lines are drawn across the face of a cheque, it must be paid into a bank account; this is a 'general crossing'. *'A/c payee only'* ('Account payee only') appearing between the parallel lines which cross a cheque, means that it can be paid only into the account of the payee. Occasionally the bank and branch of the payee's account are clearly stated – this is a 'special crossing'. *Eurocheque.* For use when travelling; can be written in most European currencies. *Open cheque.* Has no crossing and can be paid over the bank counter of the bank branch printed on it. *Post-dated cheque.* Cheque made payable on a later date than the present date. It will not be cleared until the date shown. *Stale cheque.* A cheque is stale if it is more than six months old, in which case it may not be accepted by the bank. *Traveller's cheques.* Obtainable from banks and travel agents in set denominations, they may be cashed at any bank and are frequently accepted by hotels and large stores at home and abroad. They may be purchased in a foreign currency.

Mistakes made in the writing of a cheque

If a mistake is made in the writing of a cheque, the drawer should sign his name as near as possible to the alteration, in addition to his usual signature.

To stop payment of a cheque

The drawer of a cheque may wish to stop payment if he learns that it has been lost or if, for some reason, he does not wish the particular payment to be made. To stop a cheque, a form is filled in and presented to the bank branch of issue.

cheque card. A guarantee by the issuing bank branch that it will pay cheques drawn in association with the card up to a specified limit for any one transaction.

Chinese wall. An imaginary barrier blocking inside information flowing from one part of a business to another which ought not to know about it – between corporate finance and investment management operations, or between share analysts and dealers. Physical segregation of staff is the most common form of Chinese wall.

chip (computers). A silicon chip is made from wafers of pure silicon crystal, treated so that a complete electrical circuit is formed within the solid material (solid-state). Chips may be made into data storage units (memories), microprocessors, or a combination of both.

circulars/circular letters. *See* CORRESPONDENCE.

circulating assets/circulating capital. *See* CAPITAL (TYPES OF).

Citizens Advice Bureau. A voluntary organisation formed to assist people with their shopping and other domestic problems, and which makes available a considerable network of advice throughout the country. CABs form an essential part of a nationwide consumer protection service.

civil law. The branches of civil law are contract law, the law of tort, the law of property, the law of succession, and the law of trust. An aggrieved person who seeks justice under any one of these branches must issue a summons against the wrongdoer so that the action can be heard. Civil law is concerned with the rights and duties of individual members of the community towards one another rather than towards the state itself, and is therefore sometimes referred to as private law. It is administered in the civil courts.

civil service. The administrative service of a government or international agency; it provides impartial advice to ministers and assists and advises any type of government regardless of politics.

claim (insurance). This must be made on the appropriate claim form, and details entered with 'utmost good faith'. If a fair valuation is agreed the insurance company will pay the agreed sum. If an insurable risk has been 'spread' over several insurers the insurance companies concerned will contribute to the loss proportionately, the exact division (known as *contribution*) depending upon the terms of the original policies.

clearing banks. The main 'High Street' banks are the most important members of the Bankers' Clearing House. The ·

prime purpose of the Clearing House is to make a daily settlement of the 'net indebtedness' of the clearing operations which exists between its members. This means that once a day all the transactions which make up the sum of this net indebtedness are recorded and totalled as they pass through the head offices of the various members. At the Clearing House these totals are balanced against each other and the debit or credit figures settled over their accounts at the Bank of England.

clerical function and the duties of office staff. The clerical function involves writing, copying, computing, checking, filing and indexing, sorting, and all forms of communication. Computers are used extensively in these areas. Employees engaged in the clerical function are known as *clerks*.

close company. A company which is controlled by five or fewer persons or groupings of connected persons.

closed shop. A workplace practice requiring compulsory unionisation of employees in certain jobs. The Employment Act 1982 extended protection for individuals from compulsion to join a union.

COBOL. A high-level computer language designed for business applications.

code of practice. Usually developed with the aid of a professional or trade association, it proposes its own code of conduct which members of that profession or grade will be expected to follow.

coins. Coins are now used only for petty transactions. *See* LEGAL TENDER.

cold calling. Any kind of selling where the salesman – not the buyer – makes the first approach.

collateral security. A person borrowing from a bank by means of a loan or overdraft may be asked to offer some sort of security; this is known as collateral – i.e. security lying alongside the debt. The deeds of a house, life assurance policy, or stocks and shares may be used.

collective bargaining. Term applied to those procedures by which the wages and conditions of employment are settled by a bargain in the form of an agreement between employers or associations of employers and workpeople's organisations such as a trade union.

COMECOM. The Council for Mutual Economic Assistance whose objectives are to combine and coordinate economic development of the member 'iron curtain' countries – Bulgaria, Czechoslovakia, the German Democratic Republic, Hungary, Mongolia, Poland, Rumania and the USSR. Yugoslavia is an associate member.

commerce. The term 'commerce' covers all commercial services which, together with direct (personal) services, form the third or tertiary branch of production. Commerce covers the distribution and exchange of all the surplus goods produced so that they reach the final consumer in the right place, in the right condition, at the right time, in the right quantity, and at the right price. This involves trade of all kinds – retail and wholesale, home and foreign – and the ancillary commercial services (the aids to trade): advertising, banking and finance, insurance, transport and warehousing. Producers (i.e. those who exchange their services for an income) who are engaged in trade or in the ancillary commercial services, are said to be employed in *commercial occupations*.

commercial banks. *See* CLEARING BANKS.

commercial bill. A bill of exchange created by commercial and industrial companies and guaranteed by an accepting bank.

commercial court (Queen's Bench Division). This court hears cases on commercial matters, such as banking and insurance.

commercial invoice. An important document in international trade, it must be sent with the documentary BILL OF EXCHANGE to the importer's bank or agent, together with the CERTIFICATE OF INSURANCE and the BILL OF LADING. The invoice is sent by the seller to the buyer, giving full details as to quantity, prices and descriptions of the goods, method of carriage, name of ship or air freight detail, shipping marks and details of precise terms of sale. Many overseas countries require that special prescribed invoice forms be used for all consignments to the countries concerned. If the appropriate form is not used there may be delays or a possible refusal to accept the goods at the port of entry. In international trade, a CONSULAR INVOICE is sometimes necessary.

commercial paper. A form of short-term promissory note issued to investors by a large, listed company or other acceptable borrower.

commission. 1. An agreed percentage paid to a company's agents or salesman on sales achieved. 2. A fee charged to clients (as on the Stock Exchange) for dealing on their behalf.

commission agent (international trade). It is essential that an exporting agent be appointed who is familiar with all aspects of the potential foreign market. There are several organisations – among them the DTI, chambers of commerce and trade associations – who will suggest the names of possible agents.

Commission for Racial Equality. The Race Relations Act 1976, established commissions to investigate discrimination in employment. The Commission for Racial Equality can institute legal proceedings against persistent offenders and must promote equal opportunity and elimination of discrimination on grounds of race, colour or nationality.

committee. The committee and officers of the committee are elected at the annual general meeting of a club, association or society, and to them the special business of running the organisation is committed. Members of the committee attend regular meetings at which the activities of the organisation are discussed and decisions taken. The *elected officers* of such committees are normally the chairman, treasurer and secretary.

Committee of Permanent Representatives (COREPER). *See* EUROPEAN COMMUNITY.

committee system. In a business organisation, the delegation of powers and responsibilities to committees. A *standing committee* usually covers the activities of a continuous function in an organisation. The members of such committees are drawn from all the departments involved. Standing committees meet regularly, and prepare reports and recommendations for management. The 'reporting back' process is vital, and an effective communication system must operate so that all concerned are supplied with up-to-date information. *Ad hoc committees* are called to deal with one particular eventuality which is unlikely to be repeated. They exist only until the matter in hand has been effectively dealt with. Often persons with some special knowledge or qualification are drafted (coopted) as additional members of such committees. *Executive committee.* A body with power to govern or administer. *Subcommittee.* A committee may appoint one or more of its members to a subcommittee formed to undertake a specific investigation, or to relieve the present committee of some of its routine work. *Joint committee.* Formed to coordinate the activities of two committees. It may be a permanent committee, or instigated for one particular purpose.

commodity markets. Raw material markets or exchanges mostly deal in natural products which are basic to the needs of industry. The LONDON COMMODITY EXCHANGE deals in more that 20 commodities, including coffee, sugar, spice and gums. Other exchanges concentrate on one particular type of product, such as the LONDON METAL EXCHANGE (LME) and the London Wool Terminal Market. All these markets are highly organised and only experts may deal on them in very large quantities. Primary commodities are usually brought into the country as bulk cargoes, and handled by middlemen whose function it is to finance, transport and warehouse the goods until required. Alongside the trade in actual goods are 'FUTURES' or 'terminal' markets, which can only be set up for goods which can be accurately described by grade or quality. In the futures markets the goods being sold are not available but will become so in the future; goods are therefore sold at an agreed price for delivery at a future date. The practice lends itself to speculation since a person may sell for delivery at a future date in the hope that by the time of delivery the price will have fallen, and he can repurchase on the market at a cheaper rate. The risk that concerns the buyer is that the price will rise; by buying on the futures market at an agreed price he can shield against this. *See* HEDGING.

Common Agricultural Policy (CAP). The variable nature of agricultural production has led the EUROPEAN COMMUNITY to develop a common agricultural policy to control the price and distribution of goods within the Community. To ensure that farmers are fairly rewarded, CAP imposes a minimum price. A farmer who cannot sell his product in the market can sell it to his state Intervention Board, the *intervention price* usually being about 90 per cent of the *target* or guide price. Since the price cannot fall to an equilibrium position, supply exceeds demand, with the result that there are butter mountains, wine lakes, etc.

common carrier. Common carriers include any person or firm that makes a business of carrying other people's goods from one place to another. A fixed rate of payments must be charged, and payment can be demanded in advance; delivery must be effected as soon as possible. Common carriers become responsible for the goods, their safety and prompt carriage, as soon as they are accepted.

Common External Tariff (CET). The members of the EUROPEAN COMMUNITY permit free circulation of goods manufactured or services provided by its member states. The CET operates to exclude foreign goods which could as easily be made by one of the member states; in practice, however, free trade agreements exist between members of the European Community and other countries who have a history of trade with them.

common law. In England this is the body of legal principles evolved by judges from custom and precedents of previous cases. It is complementary to the statute law contained in Acts of Parliament. The term is used to distinguish it from EQUITY – i.e. legal principles developed originally by the Lord Chancellor to mitigate hardship caused by the rigid application of common law. Common law matters are tried by the Queen's Bench, while equity cases are dealt with by the Chancery Division of the High Court.

Common Market. *See* EUROPEAN COMMUNITY.

common short form bill of lading. Introduced by SITPRO, this form retains all the legal protection of the 'long form' bill of lading, providing a receipt for taking over the goods by the carrier and their surrender by the carrier or his agent against presentation of an original bill of lading, and evidence of the contract of carriage for the goods as described. Like the 'long form', it is a document of title to the goods. Use of the 'short form' produces savings in documentation costs and increases efficiency.

communications. 1. This word covers all the ways used to transmit information, ideas, or feelings from one person to another, or others. *See* COMPUTERS, CORRESPONDENCE, ELECTRONIC OFFICE, INFORMATION TECHNOLOGY. 2. *See* TRANSPORT. 3. (Word processors) An additional unit of hardware which, when coupled with certain software, enables a word processor to exchange text or other information with other equipment, such as telexes or other word processors.

Communist Economic Community. *See* COMECOM.

community charge (Poll Tax). A tax of a fixed amount per person levied on adults which is to replace the present rates system in Scotland (1989) and England and Wales (1990).

community transit (CT). Goods moving between member nations of the EUROPEAN COMMUNITY are documented by a system of documents called the CT system, by which goods are enabled to move across frontiers without being inspected by customs. Goods are sealed into containers on departure and only opened in the country of destination.

company. A registered company – one which is registered under the Companies Acts with the Registrar of Companies – may be either a public or private company. Private limited companies may be identified by the abbreviation Ltd (limited) after the name; the abbreviation PLC after the name refers only to a public limited company. A limited company is distinct from the members composing it; it is an artificial 'person' created (incorporated) by law. It can sue and be sued in its own name in an action at law, and neither the death nor bankruptcy of its members, nor any change in the personnel of the membership affects its existence. Companies limited by share are of two kinds: a *private limited company* is one which, by its Articles of Association restricts its rights to transfer its shares and prohibits any invitation to the public to subscribe for any shares or debentures of the company; a *public limited company* is one which invites the public to subscribe to its shares and debentures. (A *holding* *company* is a PLC which has acquired control of another company by the purchase of at least 51 per cent of its voting shares.) Limited companies are owned by the SHAREHOLDERS and run by the directors who are accountable to the shareholders. Shareholders of companies *limited by share* are protected from losing their private possessions by LIMITED LIABILITY. *See also* COMPANY LAW.

company formation. *See* FLOATING A COMPANY.

company law. This is concerned with the formation, administration and working of limited companies which are not exempt from either civil or criminal liability. The 1985 Act consolidated the early Companies Acts of 1948, 1967, 1976, 1980 and 1981. These covered a vast amount of legislation which included a requirement that PLCs should publish annually a PROFIT AND LOSS ACCOUNT, BALANCE SHEET, and DIRECTORS' REPORT, and codified the appointment and resignation of external auditors. They also strengthened the external auditor's position in relation to the disclosure of information by company officials, and access to company records.

Points from the 1985 Act

Statutory books must be maintained containing, among other information, details of the company's membership, its directors, and mortgages and charges affecting the company's property; any alteration of the MEMORANDUM OF ASSOCIATION or ARTICLES OF ASSOCIATION must be in accordance with the 1985 Act; the Department of Trade may require a company to alter its name if it too closely resembles that of an existing company; a company's liquidation must be in accordance with the requirements of the Act; joint stock companies are accountable to the shareholders through the statutory AGM, at which they can, in theory, exercise control over the running of the company; firms must publish annual accounts in a specialised format.

company secretary. The chief administrative officer of a company with extensive duties and responsibilities.

Company Securities (Insider Dealing) Act 1985. Under this Act, insider dealing – the misuse of inside information which may affect the price of a company's shares – becomes a criminal offence.

company's risk. Goods carried by common carriers are carried at the carrying company's risk, that is, the carrier is responsible for the safe delivery of the goods.

compatibility (technological). Compatibility between all types of technological products manufactured by all companies (including microcomputers, printers and fax machines, etc.) is important if the benefits of the electronic office are to be realised quickly. The International Standards Organisation, backed by national standards bodies such as the British Standards Institution, is developing a standard for computer networking called Open Systems Interconnection (OSI) which when fully developed will greatly simplify the linking of computers from different manufacturers.

compensation fund. A fund maintained by the STOCK EXCHANGE to recompense investors should a member firm fail to meet its obligations and be 'hammered' (liquidated).

competition. In the business world, a desired form of conflict. *See* MONOPOLY and PERFECT COMPETITION/MARKET.

compiler. A computer program that translates instructions written in a high-level symbolic language (e.g. COBOL) into machine code.

composite offices. Proprietary offices (i.e. they have SHAREHOLDERS) usually set up as limited companies, which offer more than one type of insurance.

compound trading. Retailers now tend to extend the range of goods handled beyond their expected province. Grocers sell tights, butchers sell tinned fruit. Prepackaging of goods by the manufacturer or wholesaler has had a considerable influence in this area.

compulsory purchase order. Under the Acquisition of Land (Authorisation Procedure) Act 1946, a statutory procedure is laid down by which land may be acquired compulsorily for such uses as airfields, roads, cemeteries, reservoirs, hospitals, etc. Compensation is usually assessed by a Land Tribunal.

computer modelling. Includes everything from models of the economy to financial forecasts and computer simulations used in training.

computers. A programmable electronic device that can store, retrieve and process data. Computers need instructions from trained personnel. The instructions are *programs*, and are written by *computer programmers*, using *programming languages* (e.g. BASIC, COBOL, etc.).

TYPES OF COMPUTER

Mainframe computers. Large computer installations with considerable capacity found in computer centres catering for the needs of very large corporate systems. *Minicomputers.* Smaller than mainframes, these will support a limited number of users at the same time. *Microcomputers.* A general term describing personal computers which are mostly single-user. *Portable computers* can be folded into a carrying case and transported. With a modem and appropriate software it becomes a computer terminal to send information back to a firm's computer base.

COMPUTER HARDWARE

This is the computer equipment and has four main parts: *Input devices.* The most common method used in offices to input data is by way of a keyboard linked to the computer. Other methods include: OMR (optical marks recognition) as on multiple choice examination answers; OCR (optical character recognition) where specially shaped characters can be recognised by the computer; MICR (magnetic ink character recognition) as used on cheques; bar codes as at a supermarket point of sale; by using a mouse or lightpen. *Central processing unit (CPU).* Made of microchips, this part of the computer contains the memory. The data in the memory is also processed in the CPU. The greater the capacity of the processor and the higher the 'clock speed' (the rate at which data can be read to and from the internal memory), the faster will be the performance of the computer. *Output devices.* Processed data can be output from the computer in a number of forms, e.g. on paper using a *printer* which produces *hard copy*; on the screen of a *VDU (visual display unit)*; on *microfilm* – COM (computer output on microfilm). *Backing store.* Data or programs currently in the memory can be kept. Examples of backing store are floppy disks, hard (Winchester) disks, rigid disks, magnetic tapes and cassette tapes, optical (video and laser) disks.

COMPUTER SOFTWARE

The programs (sets of instructions) that the microprocessor can act on to control the operation of the hardware. *Systems software.* These form the *operating system* and act as an interface between the computer hardware and the *applications software*. (An interface is a place at which independent systems meet – in this case the hardware and the applications software). *Applications software.* These are the programs written to perform individual operations. They may be prepared packages for sale to anyone, programs written by in-house programmers, or specially tailored for a particular firm by a specialist software agency. *Integrated packages* are single packages which cover more than one area of application. Many *business programs* have been developed for mainframe, mini and microcomputers. Applications software is available in the following areas: accounting, word processing, financial modelling (spreadsheets), statistical, time management (electronic diaries), databases (for stock control, membership details, marketing data, etc), CAD (Computer-Aided Design) for draughting and engineering drawings.

FURTHER EXAMPLES OF COMPUTER USAGE

CIM – computer-integrated manufacturing, used in highly automated manufacturing industries; Desktop publishing – *see* ELECTRONIC OFFICE; EFTPOS – electronic funds transfer at point of sale; EPOS – Electronic point of sale at retail outlets; this is the computerised recording of stock and sales information for control purposes. *See* ELECTRONIC OFFICE, INFORMATION TECHNOLOGY.

conditional sale agreement. A type of hire purchase agreement.

conditions of sale. The general conditions of sale are concerned chiefly with quantity, quality, price, time of delivery and payment.

conditions of work. The factors of work including pay, hours, holidays, etc., that comprise an individual's total employment package. *See* CONTRACT OF EMPLOYMENT.

Confederation of British Industry (CBI). A body was formed in 1965 to promote British industry, safeguard its interests, promote its efficiency and maintain close contacts between industry and the government. Many trade associations are members of the Confederation which is the managers' counterpart of the TUC, and as such is one of the best known pressure groups in business affairs. Many CBI officials sit on government economic planning bodies.

conference lines. *See* LINER CONFERENCES.

confirmed credit. A method of financing overseas transactions by using a confirmed irrevocable letter of credit. Here the credit arranged by the customer's bank is confirmed by the London bank, so that it actually makes itself responsible for the payment to the exporter.

confirming houses. Specialist firms in the export field which take full responsibility for export orders, the exporter having no worries about payment. A transaction through a confirming house does not deprive the manufacturer of personal contact with the overseas customer, which is preserved because the customer, the confirming house and the exporter act as a team.

confravision. An inter-city conference service by British Telecom with vision plus sound communication between two groups in their respective cities.

conglomerate. An industrial group made up of companies which often have diverse and unrelated interests. *See* MERGERS.

consensus ad idem. *See* CONTRACT LAW.

consequential loss. *See* FIRE INSURANCE.

consideration. 1. *See* CONTRACT LAW. 2. The money value of a STOCK EXCHANGE transaction (number of shares multiplied by the price) before adding commission, stamp duty, VAT, time of deal, etc.

consignee. The named receiver of a consignment of goods.

consignment. All the goods delivered at any one time, whether all or part of an order.

consignor. The person responsible for transporting a consignment of goods.

consolidated fund (National Exchequer). An account in which are recorded all taxation moneys received and expenditure disbursed.

consols. Bonds, issued by the British government, which the owners can never ask to have repaid; an investor in consols simply buys a right to a perpetual annual payment of interest, though investors can generally recover their money by selling such bonds on the STOCK EXCHANGE.

consortium. A syndicate or association common to large-scale enterprise where because of the scale of the business or the amount of capital involved several firms agree to pool their resources.

constitution. 1. The system or body of fundamental principles according to which a nation, state, or body politic is constituted and governed. 2. Also called STANDING ORDERS, these are the rules compiled by an organisation to regulate the manner in which its business is to be conducted.

constitutional law. A system of law which has been established by the sovereign power of the state for its guidance. Its main object is to fix the limits and define the relations of the legislative, judicial and executive powers of the state.

consular invoice. This is a certified invoice which the consul or other representative of the importing country, residing in the country of origin, has certified as showing the correct price. This is necessary when the import duty on goods is to be paid according to the value of the goods, and prevents falsification of the records.

consultants. Individuals or groups of specialists who have gained expert knowledge in a particular field of business and offer professional advice for a fee. The increasing sophistication of business and the accelerating rate of change make it harder for firms to meet the challenge of competition from their own internal staff resources. In recent years the demand for specialist knowledge has led to consultancy becoming one of the major growth areas in the tertiary sector of business.

consultation. Joint consultation provides employees with the opportunity to discuss welfare matters with their employers, and enables employers to assess the impact of policy decisions on employees. Joint consultation committees consist of representatives from all levels of an organisation. The changing attitude towards consultation is supported by the European Commission; in line with this, the Employment Act 1982 requires company reports to contain a statement on the steps directors are taking to develop employee involvement.

consumer. The consumer is the final link in the chain of distribution; he buys the goods or services for his own use.

consumer councils. *See* NATIONALISED INDUSTRIES.

consumer credit. Credit is buying something and being given time to pay for it, or borrowing money and paying it back later. In addition to the cost of the goods or services, the credit has also to be paid for: this additional payment is called INTEREST. There are many different forms of credit: loans may be made by banks, finance houses, moneylenders, credit unions and others; a MORTGAGE, HIRE PURCHASE or credit sale, use of a banker's CREDIT CARD, budget account or monthly account, MAIL ORDER or the use of trading checks and vouchers are all forms of credit trading.

Consumer Credit Act 1974. This applies a comprehensive system to consumer credit and consumer hire agreements; it replaces the Moneylenders Acts and Hire Purchase Acts which previously applied, except for parts of the 1964 Act dealing with the purchase of motor cars by HP. There are two important provisions in the Act. The first concerns CREDIT BROKERS who now need a licence from the OFFICE OF FAIR TRADING before they can operate. The second concerns the rate the credit trader is charging (usually shown as a percentage rate). Now all traders must calculate their interest and credit charges in a standard way. The APR (annual percentage rate) is the true cost of credit, and includes in it all the costs which go to make up the credit charge and the total credit price. If it is thought that the amount of interest being charged is extortionate, application may be made to the courts. Under the Act a consumer has the right to know what information *credit reference agencies* divulge to credit traders about their customers. If a consumer is refused credit he has the right to obtain a copy of all the information a credit reference agency has on him in order to have any mistakes corrected. The local Trading Standards Department (sometimes called the

Consumer Protection Department), Citizens Advice Bureaux, Consumer Advice Centres, or neighbourhood law centres will all give advice on consumer-related matters. *Consumer Councils* deal with complaints about nationalised industries.

consumer credit agencies. *See* CONSUMER CREDIT ACT 1974.

consumer durables. Goods which are purchased and used by the general public but which do not need frequent replacement. Examples are washing machines, television sets and vacuum cleaners.

consumer goods. In addition to primary (basic) needs, people require a range of manufactured goods such as food, clothing, household goods, etc. These are consumer goods; PRODUCER GOODS are used by manufacturers to aid them in the production of other articles.

consumer protection. The Citizens Advice Bureaux, Consumer Advice Centres and local Trading Standards Departments (sometimes called the Consumer Protection Department) will all give advice to consumers on the best action to take if they, as consumers, have a grievance. The following Acts are the main legislative measures in force for the protection of consumers: *Consumer Credit Act 1974.* Applies a comprehensive system to consumer credit and consumer hire agreements. *Consumer Safety Act 1978* gives the Secretary of State for Trade the power to issue safety regulations in order to prevent or reduce the risk of death or injury from the use of goods and products. *Fair Trading Act 1973.* Set up the OFFICE OF FAIR TRADING (OFT) to act as 'watchdogs' on traders who break the law. The Director can bring actions in the Restrictive Practices Court against those who do not obey rules of trading. *Food and Drugs Act 1955* laid down that ingredients must be displayed on packaging; it became criminal to sell food or drugs unfit for human consumption. *Monopolies and Restrictive Practices Acts 1948 – 76* outlawed the enforcement of resale price maintenance. Practices considered to be against the public interest could be brought before the Restrictive Practices Court. *Sale of Goods Act 1979* lays down rules as to when ownership passes from seller to buyer and implies the condition that where goods are bought from a person who deals in those goods, and the buyer relies on the skill and judgement of the seller and makes known to him, expressly or impliedly, the purpose for which he requires the goods, then the goods shall be reasonably fit for that purpose and of marketable quality. Goods sold by sample must correspond with the sample. *Supply of Goods and Services Act 1982* protected persons from being deprived of their rights by unfair bargaining. *Trade Descriptions Act 1968* was designed to prevent misleading descriptions of goods in shops, labelling and advertising. *Trading Stamps Act 1968* stipulated that every trading stamp must have its cash value stated on it, and that holders should be able to choose to exchange them for either cash or goods. *Unfair Contract Terms Act 1977* restricted a trader's ability to limit his liability. Finally, the ADVERTISING STANDARDS AUTHORITY provides for complaints by the public about advertisements to be investigated, and for the authority to make recommendations where appropriate. The banking industry, building societies, insurance companies and the law are among those who have appointed 'ombudsmen' to investigate complaints made by consumers about their services.

consumer services. In some occupations the object is not to provide consumer goods but *personal* consumer services. These are part of tertiary production and are known as direct services (direct from the producer to the consumer); they exist in the social, commercial and professional fields. Doctors, teachers, firemen and entertainers provide such services; these producers 'service' the work force and ensure its efficiency.

consumerism. A movement that traces its origins to the campaigns of Ralph Nader in America in the early 1960s for more stringent safety standards in manufactured products. The movement encouraged consumers to be more sensitive to the quality of products on the market, and there are now a number of major institutions whose object is to protect consumers' interests. Their activities have resulted in improved safety standards and after-sales service, safer motor cars, better customer information and guarantees, control of environmental pollution, and open dating of perishable foods; in general, a much stricter regulation of market-place behaviour.

Consumers' Association. An independent, non-profit-making body set up in 1957, now strongly established as a watchdog for customers' complaints; it operates mainly by conducting comparative tests on goods and publishing reports on them in *Which?* magazine, for which annual subscriptions are paid by members of the Consumers' Association.

consumption. One of the four main elements of economic activity, the others being production, exchange and distribution. Consumption implies the satisfaction of our demands for goods and services over a period of time. Each individual has a propensity to consume, dependent on income and the utility derived from a particular consumption.

containerisation. Goods packed in standard-sized containers can be mechanically transferred from lorries on to purpose-built rail wagons, or on to ships, then back again to lorries for final delivery. Containerised goods are safer, protected both from weather and pilfering. Sealed with the authority of the customs, their use considerably reduces formalities at the port of arrival. Though containers are best when used with large consignments, small exporters can use the services of a freight forwarding agent, who treats the goods of several consignors as one load. Although train ferry services have been available for many years, the provision of container services has revolutionised deliveries to the continent of Europe, particularly at the container ports where roll-on roll-off (RORO) facilities are available for lorries. Specially-built vessels now provide the facility for a road vehicle to be packed at the exporter's factory and to make a door-to-door delivery to a customer in Europe.

contango. *See* ACCOUNT (STOCK EXCHANGE).

contango day. The first dealing day of a STOCK EXCHANGE ACCOUNT, on which contango is arranged.

continuous production. Manufacturing technique used in the production of liquids and semi-liquids.

continuous stocktaking. *See* PERPETUAL INVENTORY.

contract hire fleet. Where an independent haulier undertakes the entire transport requirements of an organisation.

The hiring organisation has complete control over drivers and vehicles, and vehicles are usually painted in the hirer's livery. There are no maintenance costs to the hirer who knows by agreement what the total cost will be. Contract hire fleets can be more expensive for a firm than running its own transport. Ideally, the hired fleet should be fully employed, but it is often difficult to organise return loads.

contract law. A contract is a legally enforceable agreement; it is a bargain between two or more persons, either orally or in writing. The essential element of a contract is that there must be an *offer* made by one person and an *acceptance* of that offer by another. Immediately the offer is accepted, a contract is concluded, but the parties to a contract must be clear as to what they are agreeing about otherwise there is no agreement. (*Consensus ad idem* – 'agreement to the same idea'.) *Consideration* is another important element of a contract, which is something in return for the promise made by the other party. The most common example is money exchanged for goods or services, i.e. the price in a contract of sale. The parties must have *the intention of creating a legally binding relationship*, and must be *persons with a legal capacity to contract* – this means that minors cannot enter into a contract with another person. Basically, the legal rule in contract law is that if an agreement is not carried out, or not performed correctly, the 'injured' party has the legal right to claim some form of redress.

contract note (Stock Exchange). On the day a bargain takes place, a member firm must send to a client a contract note detailing the transaction.

contract of employment. Under the Employment Protection (Consolidated) Act 1978, every employer is obliged to give every employee a written statement about his main terms of employment within thirteen weeks of starting work. This must show: the names of employer and employee; date of commencement of employment; title of job and description; rate of pay; whether weekly or monthly paid; hours of work; conditions relating to pay when absent through sickness; pension rights; length of notice to be given by either side to terminate the contract; holidays and payment for holidays;

the right to belong to a trade union; the right not to belong to a trade union; the procedures for registering a grievance; the steps for the subsequent grievance procedure.

contract of insurance. This is a CONTRACT under which one party undertakes for a consideration to indemnify another against certain forms of loss.

contract of sale. A properly constituted contract of sale is enforceable by law. To make an agreement legally valid, one party must make an offer to perform some function or to pay a particular price, and the other party to the agreement must unconditionally accept that offer. A feature of the sale of goods is that it is the purchaser who makes the offer to buy at a particular price. The price on an article is not an offer, but an *invitation* to offer. The seller can accept or reject the purchaser's offer, but usually accepts.

contribution. 1. (Insurance) *See* CLAIM (INSURANCE). 2. (costs) The difference between selling price and variable costs.

control accounts. These are memorandum accounts that are maintained as a self-balancing check on small sections of the ledger.

control unit (computers). Interprets the instructions and controls the input, output and storage operations.

controlled economy. *See* ECONOMY (TYPES OF).

cooperative societies. The Rochdale Pioneers, who opened their store in Toad Lane in 1844, harnessed the cooperative idea to the supply of consumer goods. Basic principles of the Rochdale Pioneers have become those of the whole cooperative movement. The main points were and are: open membership; democratic control – one person, one vote; payment of limited interest on capital; distribution of surplus funds in proportion to transactions. The cooperative societies were pioneers of adult education, and finance a range of educational, political and social activities at the present day. *Cooperative Retail Societies (CRS).* These are the traditional 'coop shops' – the 'stores'. They are organised by a committee elected by members who have one vote each; the committee directs the society's policy and the trading surplus is shared by members. In recent years the retail societies have lost a large share of the market, and in an effort to make the 'coop' movement more competitive a number of retail societies have merged to form regional societies, in the hope that a more efficient organisation will result. *Cooperative Wholesale Society (CWS).* This is the national trading and manufacturing organisation of the CRS in England and Wales, and is owned by the CRS whose directors elect the directors of the CWS. Any trading surplus is returned to the Retail Societies. The CWS administers the Coop Bank which offers a full banking service to its customers.

cooperatives. These organisations are the results of co-operation – working together – for the production and/or distribution of goods or services. The capital is subscribed by members, and all profits are shared among members according to an agreed plan. Control of the venture is in the hands of members, who are all involved in decision-making. Cooperatives include those in the marketing of farmers' produce, and supply of their requirements and services (agricultural cooperatives), workers' productive societies, fishermen's societies for marketing and supply, and housing societies for financing and building.

copyright. The exclusive right of an author or artist to reproduce his works over a fixed period of time.

corporate database. The assembled and complete set of factual information available to an organisation by means of a computerised data-processing system.

corporate planning. Decisions on major capital investments, sources of finance for such investments, product and market choices, made by top-level management.

corporation (business unit). A corporation is an association of individuals which by a legal fiction is regarded as a single person. The distinguishing characteristic of a corporation is that it can never die, and consequently the death or change of the persons who administer the corporate property has no effect upon the ownership, which lies in the 'artificial person' or legal entity of the corporation. Corporate status enables a business to own its own property and enter contracts in its own right.

corporation tax. A tax levied on the profits and capital gains of public limited companies; companies can deduct allowances from their gross profits, and the remaining net profit is then taxed at a standard rate; this is *mainstream* tax. *Advance Corporation Tax (ACT)*. A company's payment of dividend to shareholders is paid after personal income tax at the full rate has been deducted. This deducted tax (ACT) must be paid to the tax authorities within two weeks of the end of the quarter in which the dividend was paid, but is then deducted from the *next* payment of *mainstream* corporation tax liability.

correlation. The reciprocal relationship that exists between sets of figures or variables. Positive correlation is said to occur when an increase in one variable is associated to a greater or lesser extent with an increase in another (e.g. advertising and sales). Negative correlation occurs when an increase in one variable is associated with a decrease in another (e.g. the use of electric light and gas lamp sales).

correspondence. 1. The complete set of letters on one particular subject, usually collected together in one file (a correspondence file). 2. All communications by letter and documentation. *Business letters* are a means of communication between firms, and between firms and individuals. *Circular letters/circulars* are duplicated letters sent to several addresses for information or to gain custom. *Form letters.* Standard letters used by businesses for correspondence of a similar or repetitive nature – acknowledgments of orders, reminder letters, etc. *Postcards* may be used for brief messages – confirming appointments, acknowledging orders, etc. *Official letters* are letters from government departments. Correspondence may be sent by post, Telex, Teletex, fax, or messenger. *See also* INTERNAL METHODS OF COMMUNICATION.

corruption (computers). The inadvertent destruction of text on a disk by exposure to stray magnetic rays.

cost. 1. (economics) Cost – the use of resources – is measured by the sacrifice of alternatives foregone or opportunities lost. This is because economists are interested in the efficient utilisation of real (as opposed to monetary) resources. 2. (accounts) To the accountant, cost represents the expenditure incurred on the goods and services which are consumed in producing an output of other goods and services.

cost accounting. Describes the procedures for classifying, collecting and analysing costs in respect of a business unit, process, product or service. A good costing system is a necessary prerequisite to management planning and control. *See also* MARGINAL COSTING, UNIT COSTS, JOB and PROCESS COSTING.

cost and freight (c & f). *See* DELIVERY COSTS.

cost centre. An identifiable section of a business – a department, a group of people or machines – in respect of which costs are accumulated and over which cost control can be exercised. *See* ABSORPTION COSTING.

cost, insurance and freight (cif). *See* DELIVERY COSTS.

cost of living. From the time of World War I, wages have been fixed for very large sections of the community on a cost of living basis, determined since 1947 by the RETAIL PRICE INDEX NUMBER, issued by the Department of Employment.

cost-benefit analysis (CBA). Technique where the costs of a project are listed and compared with the benefits, which has helped to improve the analysis and understanding of public expenditure. CBA takes into account all the socially hidden costs as well as the actual costs which society will have to pay and balances them against the benefits to society, whether there are actual payments or receipts to be taken into account or not.

cost-plus pricing. The most common form of pricing; the unit cost is calculated and then a profit margin added.

costs. The production costs of a firm may be divided into those which are fixed in the short term (i.e. those which do not vary as output or sales expand) and those which are variable or *direct* costs. *Fixed costs* are those which cover rent, rates, interest on loans, and depreciation, which an organisation has to pay, even when production is not taking place. *Variable costs* are those which vary with output, such as expenditure on raw materials, fuel, lighting, heating, and the wages of those directly engaged in production. Also known as *direct costs*. The *total costs* of production are made up of fixed and variable costs. The *unit (average) cost* is the total cost divided by the number of units produced. *Marginal cost* is the increase in total costs resulting from the production of one more unit of output. An important theory is that any profit-maximising firm will expand output to the point where marginal cost is equal to marginal revenue.

countertrade. *See* BARTER.

coupon (Stock Exchange). On bearer securities, a detachable part of the certificate exchangeable for dividends. Also used generally to denote the rate of interest on a fixed-interest gilt-edged SECURITY.

cover (Stock Exchange). The amount of money a company has available for distribution as DIVIDEND, divided by the amount actually paid. If this results in a figure of 1 or more, the dividend is that number of *times covered*. If the result is less than 1, the dividend is uncovered.

cover note. Issued when insurers agree to insure item(s) detailed on a proposal form. A cover note gives immediate cover on acceptance of risk, pending preparation of a policy.

craft union. *See* TRADE UNIONS.

credit. Time given for payment for goods or services provided, but not immediately paid for. Credit is *given* by the lender, *received* by the borrower.

credit brokers. Licensed under the Consumer Credit Act 1974, credit brokers are those who introduce people to sources of credit or hire, or to other credit brokers. Examples of such brokers are: a *shopkeeper* who asks a finance company to finance a purchase for a customer; a *mortgage broker* who helps a house-purchaser to obtain a loan from a building society; an *electrical dealer* who arranges the hire of a TV set from a rental company. All credit brokers must obtain a licence from the Office of Fair Trading.

credit cards. Cards issued by financial organisations, such as a bank, which enable the holder to buy goods or services at any shop, restaurant, garage, etc. which has joined the scheme, without paying by cash or cheque at the time of purchase. Each card holder is given an overall limit which cannot be exceeded. The card holder is presented with a statement at the end of each month showing all the transactions he has made during the month. He settles this account by one monthly payment, but may, if he wishes, pay back by instalments each month, at which stage interest will be charged. *A banker's credit card* also enables the holder to obtain cash up to a given limit at any of the branches within the issuing bank's system.

credit control. The purpose of credit control is to avoid bad debts. A new customer will be required to establish his 'credit-worthiness' before being granted credit and will be given a credit rating, showing the amount of credit he will be allowed. If he proves to be a reliable customer his rating may be increased. Every organisation should have a firm policy regarding bad debts and the amount of latitude which customers may be allowed.

credit creation. Bankers know from experience that it is rare for depositors to demand more than about 8 per cent of deposits at any one time, and are enabled, therefore, in practice, to lend 92 per cent of the money entrusted to them. The government, through the Bank of England, controls the creation of credit by exercising its regulatory powers and by controlling the interest rate.

credit period. *See* DEBT COLLECTION PERIOD.

credit rating. A certificate issued by a bank stating that a firm is financially sound.

credit reference agency. *See* CONSUMER CREDIT ACT 1974.

credit sale agreement. An agreement to sell goods by instalments, the property passing to the new owner at once. It is usually for the sale of clothing or similar articles where goods are not worth reselling. (This is also known as the deferred payments system.) It is widely used by mail order companies.

credit scoring. This measures the statistical probability that money lent will be repaid. Among the claimed advantages of credit scoring are savings in costs resulting from the increased use of automated techniques and the ability to devolve credit-granting authority. By reducing the administrative costs of granting credit, as well as the incidence of bad debts, credit grantors are also better able to contain the cost of credit tó their customers.

credit transactions. These are usual between firms who deal regularly with one another, payment being made at the end of a month or other agreed period. HP (hire purchase) credit transactions may be spread over longer periods.

credit transfer. The Bank Giro Credit Transfer System is a method of making multiple payments through the clearing banks. By issuing one cheque a customer is able to have any number of amounts transferred. A good example of this is of a company paying salaries to its employees. All the payments are listed on a schedule showing the employees' bank branch code numbers, and a slip is made out for each one. The customer draws one cheque for the total amount. Slips, schedule and cheque are taken or posted to the company's own bank which sends the credits through the clearing system to the banks to which they are addressed. These salary credits are then credited to the payees' accounts on the second or third working day after being paid in.

creditor. A person to whom a debt is owed.

credit-worthiness. When buyers wish to purchase on credit, the seller has to be satisfied that the customer will be able to pay. It is, therefore, usual for a prospective purchaser to supply references from his banker or other business concerns confirming his ability to pay. *See* CREDIT RATING, CREDIT SCORING.

criminal law. Crime – an act punishable by law as being forbidden by statute or injurious to the public welfare – affects the whole community. As such, criminal offences are considered to be against the state, and are punished by a system laid down and administered by the state. Individuals may suffer from the effect of criminal offences and, in addition to the punishment laid down by the state, may obtain compensation for personal loss.

critical path analysis (CPA) (operational research). Method whereby the policy to be adopted in carrying through a project is represented by a graphical model (network) in which the times necessary for all the different operations are shown. The model is analysed, time required for the total project calculated, and the times available for the different constituent operations worked out. CPA is a prediction technique which can shorten the time of projects, especially construction projects such as bridges, roads, buildings and ships. The technique can be refined to indicate the best time to allocate resources.

Crown agents. A non-profit-making organisation which provides financial, commercial and professional services to the public sector overseas.

cum. Latin for 'with', used in abbreviations. Cum cap, cum div, cum rights, etc. indicate that the buyer is entitled to participate in the forthcoming capitalisation issue, dividend or rights issue. *See also* EX.

cumulative preference shares. *See* SHARES.

Currency and Bank Notes Act 1954. Governs the note issue. The government reserves the right to issue notes and coins which reach the public via the BANK OF ENGLAND.

currency basket. *See* EUROPEAN CURRENCY UNIT (ECU).

current account (balance of payments). In international trade, the balance between British imports and exports (visible and invisible). *See also* BALANCE OF TRADE, CAPITAL ACCOUNT (BALANCE OF PAYMENTS).

current account deposits (banking). Deposits that can be freely transferred by writing a cheque.

current assets. *See* ASSETS.

current cost accounting. Method of accounting designed to reflect the effects of inflation, and so provide more useful information than figures based on historic (actual) cost.

current liabilities. *See* LIABILITIES, CURRENT.

current ratio. A test of LIQUIDITY; it is the ratio between CURRENT ASSETS and CURRENT LIABILITIES. The current ratio is a quick way of assessing the nature of the working capital. If the ratio is less than 2 : 1 then the firm could run into liquidity problems and might find it difficult to pay its way.

curriculum vitae. Summary of career and qualifications. It is a useful document to prepare for sending with applications for employment. At all times it should be kept completely up-to-date.

cursor (computers). Movable mark on the screen that indicates where the next character will appear.

Customs and Excise. Department responsible for collection of the following: Betting Duty – Gaming and Licensing

Duties; payments relating to the Common Agricultural Policy (CAP) of the EC; Import Duties; Revenue Duties – the excise on tobacco, alcohol and petrol; Value Added Tax (VAT). *See* INWARD and OUTWARD PROCESSING RELIEF.

Customs duties. Indirect taxes raised on goods being imported into the country; they are used to control imports. Customs duties may be SPECIFIC DUTIES which are based on fixed quantities, i.e. the rate is per unit of weight, volume, measure or number; or it may be an AD VALOREM DUTY which varies with the declared value of the goods. The amount of duty to be paid can be determined by reference to the Customs and Excise tariffs. (A tariff is a list or set of Customs duties.) Customs allow goods to be stored in BONDED WAREHOUSES and duty is then paid on any amounts as they are released. *See* INWARD AND OUTWARD PROCESSING RELIEF.

cut-and-paste (word processors). General name given to the task of moving pieces of text from one position to another.

cycle of production. Production, exchange, distribution and consumption are the four main elements of economic activity. Consumption destroys production, producing a cycle. After consumption, production must recommence.

D

daily list. A list issued officially by the STOCK EXCHANGE showing quotations for stocks and other securities dealt with on the Exchange.

daily settlement. The daily settling up of net-indebtedness between the CLEARING BANKS.

daisy wheel (printers). A single printing element which contains all the usual characters, each 'petal' of the daisy wheel holding a character of type.

data. Ideas and facts about people and entities represented in a formal way suitable for communication, interpretation or processing by human or computerised means.

data processing. The operation of collecting data, recording and processing it, and presenting results in a planned format; particularly, now, it means the conversion by computer of crude information into usable or storable form. Electronic data processing has many advantages over manual and mechanical systems of writing, copying, computing, checking, filing and indexing. It is quick, accurate and reliable; more complicated analyses can be effected easily, as can updating of information. Good quality finished copy (hard copy) is available when printers are used.

Data Protection Act 1984. Regulates all organisations in their use of personal information which is recorded and processed electronically; all such organisations must register with the Data Protection Registrar. *Personal data* is defined as information held on a computer about living, identifiable individuals, including expressions of opinion about them. Individuals may claim compensation from data users for any damage or distress they suffer as a result of misuse of the data held. A TRIBUNAL exists to hear appeals by data users against the Data Protection Registrar.

database. A centralised collection of data files logically arranged to serve the needs of users for a variety of applications. Although usually associated with computer systems (an organised file of information held in the computer's memory, or on tape or disk), a database can comprise manual storage media such as ledger and paper files, as well as magnetic media. *See* INFORMATION TECHNOLOGY.

daybooks. Chronological records of bookkeeping transactions. Original documents such as invoices and credit notes are recorded in these books of original entry prior to posting to the ledger.

dealer. One who deals on his own account and not as an AGENT.

debentures. Fixed-interest loans made to a company, they differ from other loans to a company in that they can be bought and sold on the STOCK EXCHANGE. They are issued with specific terms regarding interest, capital repayment and security, and are usually redeemable on a set date. They are not part of the share capital of a company, and the interest on them must be paid whether there are profits or not. *Fixed debentures* are secured against certain FIXED ASSETS, which cannot be disposed of in any way by the directors without the permission of the debenture trustees. *Floating debentures* 'float' over the assets of a company, particularly the current assets. *Mortgage debentures* are 'covered' by a particular part of the firm's property, which will be sold in order to repay debenture holders in the event of difficulty. *Simple* or *naked debentures* carry no charge on the assets. Trustees are appointed to look after the interest of debenture holders; if their interest is not received on time, the trustees can take over all or some of the company's assets and sell them off to repay the loan (known as *prior charges*, i.e. charges having *priority*).

debit note. A document made out by the seller whenever the buyer has been undercharged on an INVOICE, or when he needs to make an additional charge which increases the buyer's indebtedness.

debt collection period. The length of time it takes, on average, to convert money owed by debtors into cash. The average collection period can be expressed in the ratio – debtors : annual sales. A ratio of 1 : 3 indicates an average period of 4 months; a ratio of 1 : 2 indicates an average period of 6 months.

debt factoring. Factoring is a system of arranging payments which frees a businessman from the complications that can arise with debtors, particularly overseas debtors. The factor takes over the invoices of a firm, to whom a percentage payment, less charges, is made immediately. Factoring is especially effective for overseas debts, as the factors specialise in specific countries where they have knowledge of the language, customs, legal system, etc. By using the services of a debt factor a firm does not have to wait to obtain the cash for goods sold, which thereby increases the cash flow in the organisation. Services offered by factors include help with credit control, bookkeeping, and the collection of debts; they can also provide protection against bad debts. The London Finance Houses were among the first to undertake debt factoring.

debt ratio. *See* GEARING.

debtor. A person or firm who owes money to another.

decentralisation. The distribution of functions and powers from a central authority to regional or departmental centres. *Centralisation* can lead to ineffective communication and poor control in an organisation, and large concerns can decentralise in an attempt to overcome these deficiencies. Authority is then delegated by dividing the organisation into several autonomous units, each unit being responsible for its own performance. Performance is judged in regard to relationships between units and with other organisations. Central government, because of its size, has problems in internal and external communication; decentralisation helps to improve administration and to allow for better communication between the providers of services and the public.

decimal tab (word processors). Key used for entering numbers to ensure the alignment of the decimal point.

decision tables/decision trees. A mathematical technique for improving management decision-making when the outcome is uncertain. It is done by quantifying income and costs for all known alternatives to a situation. The purpose is to handle risk in a more certain and objective manner.

deductions from salaries and wages. Before salaries and wages are paid to employees, certain deductions are made. There are two types: *Statutory deductions.* Compulsory by law, they are income tax (PAYE) and National Insurance. *Voluntary deductions.* These include private medical insurance (e.g. BUPA), SAYE (save as you earn), social clubs and welfare schemes, superannuation and union dues.

default (word processors). Name given to a value, such as a margin setting, which the word processor automatically assumes in the absence of any other entry.

Defence Export Services Organisation (DESO). Part of the Ministry of Defence, this exists to help British firms market and sell their defence products and services overseas.

deferred payments. *See* CREDIT SALE AGREEMENT.

deferred shares. Also called *founder's shares. See* SHARES.

deflation. A deliberate contraction in the supply of money available to buy goods and services with the result that demand, production and prices fall, and unemployment tends to rise.

deindustrialisation. The decline of secondary industries (manufacturing) and the rise of tertiary industries (commercial and personal services).

del credere **agent.** Agent who believes he has found a buyer who will pay in due course, and agrees to assume the risk of any debts. If the buyer fails to pay, the agent bears the loss; he charges his principal an extra *del credere* commission for this service.

delegated legislation. *See* STATUTORY INSTRUMENTS.

delegation. Describes the management process of releasing to subordinates the authority and responsibility for undertaking particular tasks. Theoretically it should provide each employee with an even workload, allow for individual growth and prevent overloading at senior levels.

delivery costs. There are several ways in which export delivery prices may be quoted: *Cost and freight* (c & f). Covers the cost of goods and freight, the buyer being committed to making his own insurance arrangements. *Cost, insurance and freight (cif, sometimes cfi).* The exporter supplies the goods, meets all expenses involved in placing them on board ship or on the aircraft, pays the freight charges and insurance premiums, and renders the bills of lading, invoices and insurance certificates to the overseas buyer whose responsibilities commence when the goods arrive at the point of delivery in the buyer's country. *Duty paid.* The seller pays all costs including taxes and duties up to the buyer's point of delivery. *Ex ship.* Means that the importer must pay for the unloading of the goods from the ship once they have reached the port of destination, and must make arrangements for their transport therefrom. All charges up to this point are met by the exporter. *Ex works.* Covers the cost of goods at the factory, all additional charges being the responsibility of the customer. '*Franco*' or '*franco domicile*'. This must include in the price all prices up to and including delivery to the premises of the customer overseas. Such a quotation is made easier if an overseas branch or agent has been organised. *Free alongside ship* (fas). The risks and expenses are the responsibility of the exporter until the goods are delivered to the wharf alongside the ship which will carry them. *Free on board* (fob). The risks and expenses are the responsibility of the exporter until the goods are loaded on the vessel. *Free on rail* (for). The risks and expenses are the responsibility of the exporter until the goods are loaded onto the railway vehicle.

delta shares. Inactive shares whose prices are not shown on the SEAQ screen system.

demand. Demand for goods and services is the basis of all business operations, and the changing nature of demand is a permanent feature of business activity. Demand, as used in economics, is the effective demand by prospective buyers who are prepared to pay the market price in a given period of time. The ever-changing nature of markets and needs is the main external risk which an organisation faces. Shifts in demand may be due to a rise or fall in income, or changing tastes, possibly through advertising. The increased demand for some goods is complementary – an increase in cars on the road leads to a demand for more petrol. On the other hand, substitutes can cause a rise in demand of one product at the expense of a fall in another – compare plastic bags with paper bags, which once had no substitute. When the price of a good or service changes and the change in demand is small, demand is said to be *inelastic*; when demand does respond easily to changes in price then demand is said to be *elastic*.

demand and supply, law of. Under perfect competition, price is decided by the interaction of demand and supply; the market price is that price which equates demand and supply – the goods supplied by producers equals the quantity bought by consumers. Basically, an increased demand or decreased supply leads to a rise in price; in the same way a decreased demand or increased supply leads to a fall in price.

demarcation dispute. A dispute between trade unions when each claims that a particular area of work belongs exclusively to members of its own union.

demographics. The social study of people in their communities. Demography draws on data relating to births, deaths, marriage, health, etc. to draw conclusions about community behaviour.

demurrage. Charge made by a carrier to cover any delay in loading or unloading.

denationalisation. The ownership of a public organisation transferred to the private sector. Denationalised (privatised) industries acquire the status of a public limited company.

department store. Large shops in town and city centres, characterised by having 'many shops under one roof', with restaurants and other amenities. They offer credit facilities to their regular customers, such as budget accounts or account cards – which enable customers to charge purchases to their accounts; the store will send them monthly statements which should be paid, or partially paid, before the end of the following month.

dependency ratio. *See* POPULATION (STRUCTURE OF).

deposit account. A form of bank account that entitles the saver to earn interest on money deposited.

deposit, certificate of. *See* CERTIFICATE OF DEPOSIT.

deposit-taking institutions. *See* LICENSED DEPOSIT TAKERS .

depreciation. Depreciation of CAPITAL GOODS – the loss in their initial value over a period of time – eventually calls for replacement of or repair to premises, plant and fittings, and always leads to a fall in the monetary value of an ASSET. In accounts, depreciation is a way of measuring the cost of using a fixed asset. A set portion of the asset's cost is treated as an expense each period of its working life. The amount of money used to reduce the cost is deducted from the initial capital outlay in the BALANCE SHEET, and is also treated as a legitimate expense in the PROFIT AND LOSS ACCOUNT. The purpose of depreciation is to reduce the cost of a fixed asset to a scrap or realisable value to provide for future purchases. Under the *straight-line method* of charging depreciation the total wastage is estimated and the loss in value spread in equal instalments over the working life of the asset. In the *diminishing/reducing balance method* the value of the asset is reduced annually by the same *fixed rate per cent.*

derived demand. The demand for industrial (producer) products is dependent on (derived from) the demand for consumer products. *See* ACCELERATOR.

descender (word processors). The part of a letter that appears below a baseline, e.g. the 'tails' of g, j, p, q, y.

desk research. *See* MARKETING.

deskilling. The replacement of human skills by machinery.

desktop publishing. *See* ELECTRONIC OFFICE.

devaluation. Reduction in the value of a currency in relation to the value of another currency or currencies. A country with a devalued currency finds imported goods are more expensive, while overseas its exports are cheaper.

development areas. Defined areas in the United Kingdom where grants and inducements are offered to commerce and industry to locate, or relocate, in order to relieve the high rates of unemployment prevalent. Both the British government and the European Regional Development Fund are party to the scheme.

diamond market. *See* CENTRAL SELLING ORGANISATION.

dictionary (word processors). A collection of short pieces of text, stored on disk, which is reserved for special application, e.g. a disk-based spelling dictionary. Also called *library.*

differential cost analysis. Concerns the physical distribution of goods and is an analysis of the differences of cost involved when various ranges of goods are distributed in different ways.

differentials. Relative pay levels; the amounts by which the remuneration of different classes of workers differ.

digital computer. Computer which stores and processes data in the form of digits.

diminishing returns, law of. The law of diminishing returns states that as more and more resources are allocated to a fixed asset, then eventually output will diminish. In all systems there is an optimum mix of resources which will maximise output, and this mix can often be assessed by OPERATIONAL RESEARCH (OR) techniques.

diplomatic service. The commercial services offered by British diplomatic agencies overseas promote exports and assist in liaison between British and overseas companies and trade organisations.

direct controls (Bank of England). Controls on individual banks designed to regulate growth of money and credit. They work through direct instructions rather than through changes in interest rates. Although the Bank of England does have legal powers, its supervisory system still depends heavily on the voluntary cooperation of banks.

direct costs. *See* COSTS.

direct debit. A method of arranging for a bank to make periodic payments on behalf of its customer; it can be used for fixed amounts at fixed dates or for varying amounts at irregular intervals. A direct debit for an unspecified amount is called a variable amount direct debit. With the direct debit system, the company requesting payment draws on the debtor's bank account; it claims the amount due for a period, e.g. month, week, etc. from the bank. The company requesting payment will need its debtor's written authority before direct debiting can commence.

direct expenses (costing). Factory lighting, heating, fuel, etc.; these are added to the direct cost of raw materials and direct labour costs to reach the *prime cost* of manufactured goods.

direct importation. When a manufacturer needs regular supplies of raw materials, or where a firm has built up a strong link with a supplier overseas, direct importation – importation without the services of a middleman – is customary. Such commodities do not pass through the commodity markets.

direct mail/direct sales. Selling direct from the manufacturer to the consumer, cutting out both the wholesaler and retailer. Contact with the customer is made by post, advertisement in newspapers, etc, or by the manufacturer employing door-to-door salesmen.

direct production. The satisfying of a person's wants without help from any other person (cf. INDIRECT PRODUCTION).

direct services. *See* CONSUMER SERVICES.

direct taxation. Direct taxation is paid directly by a person or 'legal entity' to the government. The following are examples: INCOME TAX, CORPORATION TAX, SCHEDULE D TAX (paid on profits made by businesses operating as sole traders or partnerships), CAPITAL GAINS TAX.

directors, board of. The most important part of any limited company, and the chairman of the board is the true head of the firm; other members of the board are called directors. The board is elected by members in general meeting; the chairman of the company is elected by the board who also elect the managing director. The managing director actually runs the firm and puts the decisions of the board into effect. Other directors may be heads of departments and are thus executive directors and full-time employees of the organisation. Part-time directors have experience which will be of service to the company and make a valuable contribution to the organisation. Everything that happens in a firm takes place through the authority of the board of directors. The main functions of the board are, first, to determine and clarify company policy, and to formulate plans to put it into effect and, secondly, to ensure that the company complies with the requirements of the Companies Acts.

directors' report. Published annually with the registered accounts this statutory document now has to contain 'a fair review of the development of the business of the company and its subsidiaries'. In addition, since the Employment Act 1982, firms with more than 250 employees must state what action, if any, has been taken during the year to encourage employee participation in the management of the company.

discount. 1. A discount is a reduction in a bill, given as a favour. There are three kinds: *Cash discount.* Given to debtors who pay promptly for their goods when the time for payment arrives. Also known as *settlement discount. Quantity discount.* Given for large orders; the greater the quantity ordered the lower the unit cost. *Trade discount.* Often given by one trader to another. It is also the reduction in the catalogue price of an article, given by the wholesaler or manufacturer to the retailer to enable him to make a profit. 2. (Stock Exchange) The amount by which a newly-issued share is traded below its original price (*see* PREMIUM). 3. *See* BILL OF EXCHANGE.

discount houses/discount market. The discount houses are specialist financial institutions who are members of the London Discount Houses Association, and act as providers of sterling liquidity to the commercial banks. Until October 1988 the Bank of England's MONEY MARKET dealings were conducted with eight discount houses only, but since that time the Bank has opened the market to other financial institutions who have been prepared to accept certain stringent financial commitments. These institutions are now included in the weekly TENDER FOR TREASURY BILLS, and also deal in other money market instruments – local authority bills, bank bills, 'short' gilt-edged securities and Certificates of Deposit. *See* LENDER OF THE LAST RESORT.

discount rate. Rate of interest employed in discounting operations on the money market. *See* BILL OF EXCHANGE.

discounted. Used to indicate that some expected future event has already been allowed for in the current price.

discounted cash flow (DCF). A technique used in investment appraisal for examining the forecast 'inflow' and 'outflow' of money over the expected life of a project to provide a basis for calculating its profitability. Prepared *discount tables* are available for reference. *See also* INTERNAL RATE OF RETURN.

discrimination in employment. The three Acts of Parliament which relate to this are: Equal Pay Act 1970; Race Relations Act 1976; Sex Discrimination Act 1975. Discrimination occurs under these Acts when an employee, or an applicant, is treated less favourably than others because of his or her sex, colour or race.

diseconomies of scale. Though many advantages arise when large organisations employ effective mass-production methods, there are also disadvantages. Among these are difficulties in communication (both internal and external), poor coordination and control, slow reaction to change, and a failure to keep equipment up-to-date.

dishonoured cheque. Cheque on which a bank has refused payment. The cheque should be referred back to the drawer.

disk (computers). A storage device consisting of a flat circular plate, made of plastic or aluminium, coated with a magnetisable material. The disk may be exchangeable or fixed, hard or floppy (diskette).

disk drive (computers). Device consisting of a motor and an electromagnet which enables text to be stored on disks.

dismissal. An employee is dismissed when an employer terminates the contract of employment. This may be done with or without notice, but if the employer fails to establish a fair reason for the dismissal he may be liable in an action for UNFAIR DISMISSAL.

disposable income. The residue of a person's income after taxes and the basic needs for food and shelter have been met.

distribution (economics). The distribution of income between the factors of production: *rent* for land, *earnings* for producers, and *interest/dividends* for the suppliers of capital.

distribution, chain/channel of. When studying production and the vast quantities of manufactured goods produced by it, the chain of distribution is seen to be of vital importance; sometimes called the *chain of commerce* or the *chain of production*, it is the route taken by goods from their place of manufacture to the place where they are finally purchased by the consumer. Without it there would be little consumption and no point in producing anything that could not be 'consumed' at the point of manufacture. The distribution of the raw materials and components from which manufactured goods are made is not covered by the term 'physical distribution'; this is concerned solely with goods between their manufacture and the point at which they are sold to the consumer. The whole activity is part of tertiary production and is a commercial service; there are two aspects which have to be considered: 1. *the commercial aids to trade which assist distribution,* and 2. *the actual channel of physical distribution* by which goods travel from the manufacturer to the consumer.

COMMERCIAL AIDS

Commerce is that part of production which ensures that goods and services reach the final consumer at the right place, in the right condition, at the right time, in the right quantity, and at the right price. Below is shown the fundamental contribution which commerce makes in achieving this. *At the right place.* Wherever the goods are to be sold they have to be taken to the place of sale. This involves transport, finance, insurance and sometimes warehousing – all commercial services. *In the right condition.* Transport uses specially constructed vehicles if these are necessary: refrigerated vans; vans for carrying large panes of plate glass; road and rail tankers of many types; ships for different cargoes. *At the right time.* 'Movement through time' belongs particularly to the distributive trades. Consider the uses of warehousing in retaining ice-cream in cold storage which enables the trade to cope with a high demand during a heat wave; the warehousing of seasonal goods which are manufactured throughout the year but which the average retailer has no room to stock far in advance of requirements; the daily and unfailing delivery of food stocks which, though primary products, have been processed in some way. *In the right quantity.* Breaking bulk is a function of both wholesaling and retailing, providing the right quantity for the buyer in both cases. *At the right price.* The costs of commercial services always add to the price of an article; the greater their efficiency, the greater the savings in price and time.

PHYSICAL DISTRIBUTION

The traditional route for consumer goods from the manufacturer to the consumer – the physical distribution – involves particularly the commercial services provided by transport and warehousing, and is usually shown as:

Manufacturer *to* Wholesaler *to* Retailer *to* Consumer. Sometimes, however, the wholesaler and/or retailer are eliminated, though it must be remembered that the services they offer cannot also be dispensed with – they have to be performed by someone, somewhere. For instance, breaking bulk is regarded as a function of the wholesaler; large retailers who buy direct from the manufacturer must do this for themselves. Below are some variations in the traditional route taken by goods to their selling points: *Direct selling from manufacturer to consumer.* This involves a direct response by consumers to manufacturers' advertisements, eliminating the services of the wholesaler and retailer. *Wholesalers selling to consumers.* Having bought from manufacturers, wholesalers sell by means of a catalogue, eliminating the retailer's services. *Retailers who manufacture their own goods.* Some large organisations manufacture the goods themselves with their own brand names, so that the whole operation needs only a retail outlet to sell to the consumer. *Retailers who buy in bulk from manufacturers.* With the increased size of many retail shops, often part of a large chain, retail organisations often buy in bulk from manufacturers and eliminate the wholesaler altogether, providing their own warehousing and warehouse services. *Perishable goods.* These cannot always be sent by way of the 'traditional' routes. Sometimes farmers sell their produce direct to consumers (e.g. the 'pick-your-own' fruit and vegetable crops); and there is a strong link between farmers and local markets and shops. Agricultural cooperatives have their own warehouses from which large retailers obtain supplies, and the large produce markets, both regional and national, receive much of their perishable produce. These markets receive produce from both home and foreign sources, and both wholesalers and retailers buy from them. Finally, there may be a law compelling farmers to sell certain produce through a marketing board, which really becomes the wholesaler of that particular product. The Milk Marketing Board is an example of such an organisation. *See* TRANSPORT.

distribution mix. The different methods of distribution in one organisation for differing products.

district auditor. Government officials who exert financial control by checking the financial records of local authorities and government organisations.

diversification. The risks encountered by an organisation can be spread by diversification – that is, by an extension of its range of products and/or activities.

dividend. Payment from a company's post-tax profits to its shareholders. It is usually expressed as pence per share. (A dividend is also paid to members of the Retail Cooperative Societies who own shares.)

dividend cover. *See* COVER (STOCK EXCHANGE).

division of labour. Each industry specialises in one particular type of production, and within each industry there is further specialisation into different organisations, each having its own subdivisions of departments or branches. Even within one department or branch, *specialisation* is apparent. These examples illustrate how work is divided between producers, each producer or group of producers concentrating on one particular part of the productive process. The main characteristic of the division of labour is that the whole cannot function if one of the parts is ineffective; a breakdown of one section of production can lead to serious holdups.

dock dues. Harbour dues payable when goods pass through a dock either as exports or imports.

document of title. Documentary evidence that the holder of goods has legal ownership.

documentation (export trade). *See* EXPORT DOCUMENTATION.

documentation (home trade). *See* TRANSACTIONS.

documents against acceptance (D/A); documents against payment (D/P). *See* DOCUMENTARY BILL OF EXCHANGE (under BILL OF EXCHANGE).

domestic credit expansion (DCE). The chief means by which the BANK OF ENGLAND controls domestic credit (the money supply) are: open market operations (issue of Treasury Bills and gilt-edged securities); alteration of the bank rate; calling for *special deposits* from the banks.

domiciled bill. A BILL OF EXCHANGE that requires the holder to present it to a named bank for payment.

dot matrix (printers). Type of printer used with computers that prints characters as a set of fine dots within a grid of rows and columns called a matrix.

double-entry bookkeeping. The feature from which this type of bookkeeping derives its name is that every transaction is entered twice in the ledger, as a debit to one account and a credit to another.

double liability. Wrongful acts can be both criminal and civil, and can be regulated at the same time by criminal and civil actions (known as double liability).

double time (salaries and wages). Time worked which is paid for at twice the basic rate, for instance Sunday or Bank Holiday work.

Dow Jones industrial average. USA share index similar to the FT Index in the United Kingdom.

drawee. The bank charged with payment of a cheque.

drawer. The person who writes and signs a cheque.

duopoly. A special case of imperfect competition that exists where only two firms compete in the same market.

duties. *See* CUSTOMS AND EXCISE.

E

earnings. Money earned in return for goods or services supplied by the self-employed, or salaries or wages paid to employees for specific services.

earnings per share. The division of the net profit of a company by the number of shares in issue.

earnings rate. A company's net profits divided by its paid-up capital.

easement. A right to use the land of another, such as the use of a right of way.

economic rent. The surplus earned by a FACTOR OF PRODUCTION above the income necessary to keep the factor at work.

economics. A social science concerned chiefly with the production, distribution, and consumption of goods and services.

economies of scale. There are many advantages attached to large-scale organisation, both within the organisation itself and in its relationships with other organisations which provide it with goods and services external to its own activities. Among these are: a greater facility to obtain finance for expansion; greater opportunities for specialisation; better training facilities, either in-house or through local colleges; increased output leading to lower unit costs; better purchasing power; bulk buying.

economy, control of. Every government tries to control the economy in order to achieve prosperity for the nation; the Chancellor of the Exchequer's yearly Budget is an instrument for achieving control of the economy for the coming year, not just designed to raise revenue. *Financial measures* influence the credit policy of the government. An easy credit policy and a low rate of interest on borrowings encourages investment in new projects; a 'credit squeeze' makes it difficult for businesses to find the capital they require. *Fiscal measures/policy.* The fiscal policy of the government covers taxation policy in general, and is set out each year in the Budget. On Budget Day, the Chancellor of the Exchequer presents to Parliament the government's plans for raising money in the coming year – the fiscal programme. In Britain the aim of fiscal and other measures has been to influence the level of activity in the economy. Money can be 'taken out' of the economy by high taxation; conversely, money can be 'put back' into the economy by tax cuts and other measures. The government has to decide the balance between revenue from taxation and public borrowing, as well as between direct and indirect taxation. *See also* BANK OF ENGLAND (ECONOMICS).

economy, types of. The economy of a country is made up of two sectors – the private sector and the public sector. Private enterprises are privately owned and operated; public enterprise is socially owned and operated, and is run by the public for the benefit of the community. *Controlled (planned) economies* are those where a high degree of centralised control exists and almost all enterprise is in the public sector. Such economies are found in communist countries. *Free enterprise economies* are those where most of the wealth is in the hands of private enterprise. The United States has this type of economy, though public sector activity there is increasing. *Mixed economies* – such as that of the United Kingdom – have a mixture of public and private enterprise.

edit (computers). To rearrange text; to prepare data for a later operation.

editor. A program which allows a user to inspect and alter his program or data.

elasticity. An economic concept that describes the degree of responsiveness to a change in price. Demand is said to be elastic when a relatively small variation in price causes a marked change in the amount demanded. The same concept applies to supply when a small change in price causes a marked change in the amount supplied. The concept has important implications for government policy, e.g. on taxation and tariff setting, as well as for the businessman who must monitor closely the effects of price changes on demand for goods and supply of the factors of production.

electronic funds transfer (EFT). A system of automatic transfer of money transactions supported by advanced computer and telecommunications systems. Credit transfer between banks is carried out on a large scale using the Society for Worldwide Interbank Financial Telecommunications (SWIFT) network. At a more personal level, the opportunity of 'cashless' transactions is being offered to an increasing number of shoppers today as retailers increase their use of point of sale terminals for automatic payment (EFTPOS – electronic funds transfer at point of sale).

electronic office. Term used to describe an office setting that is highly computerised and employs the latest techniques and developments in office technology. In such an office the typing, filing, communications and retrieval of information are supported by electronic equipment. INFORMATION TECHNOLOGY is dealt with under its separate heading, but the following (in alphabetical order) are the more common components of an electronic office:

CONFERENCES

Audioconferencing/teleconferencing. Communication by two or more groups of people at different locations. If required, it may be supplemented by video aids, such as slow-scan TV or facsimile. Graphics pads can be used to add visual information in addition to the voice. *Confravision.* An inter-city conference service available from studios in London and other cities. It provides vision plus sound communication between two groups in their respective cities.

DESKTOP PUBLISHING

A microcomputer using a hard disk allows the combination of inputting text, insertion of photographs/diagrams, and final printing. A laser printer is necessary; also an electronic scanner for photographs or diagrams if these are required. Documents produced can be stored on disk, recalled to the screen and modified. Desktop publishing provides a fast method of producing good quality business forms, price lists, or any material which is required quickly where presentation is of importance.

DICTATING MACHINES

These enable executives to record letters and messages at any time convenient for them. The tapes are then transcribed by audio-typists using either earphones or a speaker. Some organisations install a centralised recording unit which records dictation from executives who are some distance away. The work received is shared out by a supervisor among the audio-typists.

ELECTRONIC MAIL (Email)

Mail – text, data and graphics – can be transmitted over telephone lines to one or more destinations without the need to print out hard copy. Methods used are: *Computers, electronic typewriters and word processors* (used in conjunction with a MODEM/ACOUSTIC COUPLER) can be connected for direct transmission of text, data and graphics between two different locations, using the public telephone network, *providing the machines are compatible.* Material can be prepared at one terminal and sent to another to be received almost instantaneously. With the addition of a TELETEX adapter and the appropriate software, microcomputers and word processors can be converted to transmit and receive material from other international Teletex terminals. (Do not confuse with Teletext.) *Telex.* The British Telecom 24-hour teleprinter service. Subscribers rent a teleprinter (in appearance this resembles a typewriter with a telephone dial attachment) and a line to the nearest Telex exchange. Calls are made by direct subscriber dialling to all UK subscribers and to most European countries and the United States; when the connection has been made, the caller types his message, which is printed simultaneously on *both* machines. New electronic Telex terminals store messages in the memory until accessed by the operator. If the machine is left switched on but unattended, it will receive any messages sent. Telex machines have editing facilities, and the same message may be sent to several locations (multi-addresses). *FAX (facsimile telegraphy).* Facsimile transceivers can transmit and receive any form of printed, typed or handwritten matter, drawings, diagrams and photographs from one location to another, at home or abroad, within a few minutes. Material can be transmitted over national and international telephone networks by the direct dial system. If the machine is left switched on but unattended, it will receive any messages sent.

It is important that sender and receiver have compatible facsimile equipment.

MAILBOX SYSTEMS

The storage unit of a 'host' computer is divided into separate *mailboxes*. Each mailbox is hired out to a separate subscriber with a compatible terminal, the terminal then being connected to the main computer via a telephone line. Messages may be sent or received through the 'host' mailbox. Mailboxes may be *external* – available for use between different organisations, or *internal* (in-house) where each executive is allocated the use of his own mailbox.

MAIL-HANDLING EQUIPMENT

Incoming mail. A *letter-opening machine* is used to cut a narrow slip off the tops of envelopes. *Outgoing mail. Electronic addressing machines* deal with large quantities of circulars, accounts, etc. For effectively speeding the sealing and wrapping of outgoing mail, there are envelope-sealing machines, inserting and folding, package-sealing, rolling and wrapping, tucking and folding machines. Postage is usually prepaid by means of a *franking machine* which prints on the label or envelope any denomination of postage. An electronic franking machine can also be linked to electronic scales which automatically combine the weighing, postage calculations and franking operations. Payment in respect of postage must be made in advance; electronic machines have a remote meter-resetting system using a special telephone data pad which enables additional units to be purchased, and the franking machine reset by telephone, without having to visit a post office.

MICROGRAPHICS (ELECTRONIC FILING SYSTEMS)

A camera and processor are used to store information on microfilm in place of storing the actual documents in filing cabinets. VDU terminals are used to communicate directly with a computer which is able to locate a specific document and then display the image on the screen; a reader/printer will provide a photostat copy of any document. CAR – computer-assisted-retrieval – indexes a document as it is filmed and aids rapid retrieval.

PHOTOCOPIERS

There are many varieties of photocopier; they all produce copies of an original and there is no need to prepare a master. Masters required for use with ink (stencil), spirit and offset-litho duplicating machines can be produced on certain photocopiers. The rapid collating and stapling of copies for long reports and for booklets may be effected in one operation by more sophisticated machines.

PRINTERS

Dot matrix, daisy wheel, ink jet and laser printers are all widely used with computers and word processors for printing 'hard copy'. All have a range of fonts and print styles, and use single sheet or continuous stationery.

SATELLITE COMMUNICATIONS See SATSTREAM.

TELEPHONE SYSTEMS

These are used for internal communications and also for contacting other firms and organisations. Computers 'talk' to each other over telephone lines using a MODEM or ACOUSTIC COUPLER, providing there is compatibility between the two computers. This is true of other equipment which also use telephone lines for communication: Telex, Teletex and fax. Telephones also connect with dictating machines if a centralised system is being used; the message is recorded on tape and stored for future transcription. If the office is unattended, an ANSWERING MACHINE can be switched on which will accept messages from a caller for future action; the machines can be used by businesses to take orders.

TYPEWRITERS

Electronic typewriters. These offer a varied range of facilities; the simplest machine has an electronic keyboard, daisy wheel, choice of pitch and an automatic error correction from a small buffer memory. Basic ELTs have no internal/permanent memories and few facilities. More sophisticated machines have 2 – 3 line correction memories and internal/permanent memories, sometimes larger than 4,000 characters; not all have visual displays. The most expensive machines offer more varied features, including unlimited external memories (e.g. removable disks). These can be interfaced with VDUs and upgraded to provide word processing facilities.

WORD PROCESSORS

A dedicated word processor is a microcomputer which does only word processing. Most word processing is effected on microcomputers by the use of word processing software. Typing, editing, storage, printing and communication of written information can be produced; merely by the operation of keys, text can be inserted, deleted or moved to another position. Layout adjustments are easily performed and corrections can be made by overtyping. Documents are printed out only when they are completely correct, and can be stored for future use.

electronic point of sale (EPOS). At retail outlets, this is the computerised recording of stock and sales information for control purposes.

electronic publishing. *See* INFORMATION TECHNOLOGY *(public on-line database systems).*

eligible banks. Banks whose bill 'acceptances' the BANK OF ENGLAND is prepared to rediscount.

eligible liabilities. A bank's STERLING deposit liabilities, excluding deposits having an original maturity of over two years, and any sterling resources obtained by switching foreign currencies into sterling.

elite type. A size of type which gives 12 characters to the inch (25 mm).

embargo. Embargoes, quotas and TARIFFS are methods of protecting home industries. Embargoes prohibit the import of particular commodities, or goods, from certain countries.

emboldening (word processors). A procedure whereby the word processor prints text in 'bold' face – in characters darker and thicker than normal.

employee participation. After the Bullock Report on industrial democracy, organisations were encouraged to allow workers to participate in decision-making. The European Community has also recommended that there should be 'worker directors' on company boards.

employers' associations/organisations/federations. These provide a wide range of services for members within the same industry. Besides negotiating and dealing with organised labour (trade unions), they help with technical problems, liaise with official and professional bodies, work to improve customer relations and encourage research. *See* CONFEDERATION OF BRITISH INDUSTRY.

employer's liability insurance. *See* ACCIDENT INSURANCE.

employment, contract of. *See* CONTRACT OF EMPLOYMENT.

employment legislation. Under the Contracts of Employment Act 1972, every employer must supply a new employee with a CONTRACT OF EMPLOYMENT. The Employment Protection Act 1975 added further requirements which are now incorporated in the contract of employment; the Employment Act 1984 makes detailed changes to employee/trade union relationships within employment. The three Acts which relate to discrimination in employment are: Equal Pay Act 1970 (amended by the Employment Act 1982); Race Relations Act 1976 (which set up the Commission for Racial Equality); Sex Discrimination Act 1975. Health and safety for employees are covered by: *The Factories Act 1961*, which consolidated all factory law passed between 1937 and 1959 concerning health, safety, welfare and the employment of women and young persons. *Offices, Shops and Railways Premises Act 1963* covers regulations dealing with the provision of suitable sanitary accommodation, satisfactory standards of cleanliness, ventilation, lighting and heating, the avoidance of overcrowding, fire prevention precautions and the safety of office machinery. *Health and Safety at Work Act 1974* covers everyone at work and also increases the protection of the general public from industrial hazards. The Act sets out certain minimum standards of safety, health and welfare, and employers' and employees' duties in relation to these aspects of the working environment.

endorsement. The act of endorsing is the writing of one's name on the back of a BILL OF EXCHANGE, cheque, note, etc.

endowment assurance. The most popular method of combining life cover with long-term saving, this provides a sum of money which is payable by the insurance company either at the end of an agreed period (the maturity period) or at death, whichever occurs first.

Enterprise Allowance Scheme. Allows payments of weekly amounts (from DTI) to persons starting up new businesses.

enterprise grants. Introduced by the DTI for investment and innovation projects by small firms in development areas.

entrepôt trade. The handling of goods in transit between two other countries. An *entrepôt* is a seaport, warehouse or other intermediary centre of trade and transhipment.

entrepreneur. One who is responsible for the initiation and organisation of enterprise in capitalist or free market economies out of a desire to maximise profits. *The entrepreneurial function* is to control a business, and its success largely depends on organising ability, foresight and general business capacity. The function may be performed by sole traders or partners who own the business, or by professional managers who are employees of an organisation. Some economists regard the entrepreneur as a factor of production.

'entry' form. Goods arriving in the United Kingdom must be entered for Customs clearance on an 'entry' form. *Non-dutiable goods and dutiable goods* are required to be entered for statistical purposes; in addition, dutiable goods are inspected by Customs and the duties collected.

envelope sizes. *POP (Post Office Preferred range).* Post Office sorting machines are designed to take envelopes within a certain range of sizes. Envelopes (and cards) should be at least 90 x 140 mm, and not larger than 120 x 235 mm.

International envelope sizes are as follows:

	mm		mm
C3	324 × 458	B4	250 × 353
C4	229 × 324	B5	176 × 250
C5	162 × 229	B6/C4	125 × 324
C6	114 × 162	B6	125 × 176
C5/6 (DL)	110 × 220		
C7/6	81 × 162		
C7	81 × 114		

environment. Organisations have to exist in an environment which limits their activities in the following areas: *economics* – by the variable demand and supply of goods and services; *legal* – by laws which control their formation, administration and working arrangements; *political* – which controls their financial operations, enforces the law, and determines the type of economy; *social* – they must exercise constraint in consideration of pollution and the preservation of the natural environment.

Equal Opportunities Commission (EOC). Set up under the Sex Discrimination Act 1975, it can institute legal proceedings against employers who do not allow women equal opportunities of employment.

Equal Pay Act 1970. Prevents discrimination against women in the terms and conditions of employment.

equilibrium. An economic term to describe the point at which the amount of a commodity demanded equals the amount offered for sale, at a price which is satisfactory to buyer and seller.

equity. 1. This popularly means natural justice or fair play. Lawyers use the term in a more technical sense as that system of law which has been evolved in the Chancery Court to provide relief for wrongs for which the common law offers no remedy. Equity follows the common law but if the common law should suffer a wrong to be without a remedy, it will 'see fair play' is administered in the Chancery Court. 2. Equity share capital is the true risk capital of a company, i.e. the 'ordinary shares'. Equity shares have a nominal value, but there is no guarantee that an investor in equity shares will get either a dividend or his money back; but he does get the chance of an income and possibly capital growth. Also, being a part owner of the company he has the right to vote proportionately to the number of shares he holds. There are more equity shares than any other type, but the owner receives a dividend only after other classes of shareholder have been paid the amounts due to them. If a firm is not prospering, there is sometimes no dividend and ordinary shares carry the greatest risk.

ergonomics. The scientific study of the way a human body works, and its physical dimensions. The results are applied to the design of equipment and machines for the workplace with a view to reducing fatigue, discomfort and strain.

error correction (word processors). A feature built into communications to ensure that any text sent to, or received from, another device has not been distorted during its transmission.

estoppel. The fact of being precluded from a certain action as a result of a previous action or statement.

Eurobonds. London has established itself firmly in the Eurobond market; outside the UK gilt market, this is one of the largest capital markets in the world. Eurobonds sprang from the interest equalisation tax introduced in the United States in 1963, which made it cheaper for US companies with overseas operations to raise capital outside the US; consequently, EURODOLLARS and Eurobonds were introduced. Now International Eurobonds are also issued in French and Swiss francs, Deutschmarks and yen. Although most issues are listed on the London Stock Exchange or on a continental bourse, dealing is mostly by international dealers and largely takes place over the telephone.

Eurocurrency. Eurocurrency is paper money on the books of a bank belonging to an overseas customer and can be used to settle debts in other currencies. It originated in Eurodollars which were simply dollar deposits in European centres. The international banking community in London is active not only in the financing of foreign trade, but in Eurocurrency lending, interbank and Eurobond operations, international PORTFOLIO management, corporate finance and consumer credit, all of which involve Eurocurrency, though this activity is no longer confined to Europe. FOREIGN EXCHANGE and Eurocurrency are two separate parts of the foreign exchange market. Eurocurrency concerns borrowing and lending – not the buying and selling of one currency against another.

Eurodollars. A US dollar held (e.g. by a bank) outside the USA, especially in Europe.

European Assembly/Parliament. *See* EUROPEAN COMMUNITY.

European Commission. *See* EUROPEAN COMMUNITY.

European Community (EC). The Common Market (the European Economic Community) was founded by the Treaty of Rome in 1957 with six signatories – France, Germany, Italy, the Netherlands, Belgium and Luxembourg – with the intention of setting up a free trade area and eventually a political and monetary union. Britain joined in 1973, together with Denmark and Eire; Greece joined in 1981, and Spain and Portugal in 1986. A 'Single Act', signed in February 1986 and submitted to national parliaments for ratification, spells out certain objectives of the Community: completion of the European internal market and the creation by 1992 of a great area without frontiers; technological development; progress towards economic and monetary union; strengthening of economic and social cohesion; improvement of the environment and the working environment. *See* SINGLE EUROPEAN ACT.

MAJOR INSTITUTIONS OF THE EUROPEAN COMMUNITY

The European Commission consists of two commissioners from each major member and one from smaller powers. They act to ensure that Community rules and the principles of the Common Market are respected; they propose to the Community Council of Ministers measures likely to advance the development of Community policies, they implement Community policies whether based on Council decisions or directly on Treaty provisions. The Commission manages the funds and common policies which account for most of the Community budget and provides the day-to-day administration services. *The Council of Ministers* consists of ministers from member state governments, each government acting as President of the Council for six months; the Council makes the major policy decisions of the Community. Meetings take place two or three times a year and deal with Community questions and with political cooperation. The Council is assisted by the *Committee of Permanent Representatives* (COREPER) which coordinates the groundwork for Community decisions. *The Community Court of Justice* is composed of learned judges from member nations and has sole authority to interpret Community law. Through its judgments and interpretations the Court of Justice is helping to create a body of Community law which will apply to all Community institutions, member states, national courts and private citizens. Judgments of the Court, in the field of Community law, overrule those of national courts. Also, in cases of non-application of Community law by the Council or member states, the Court has heard complaints brought by individuals and upheld the direct applicability of Treaty-imposed principles, such as equal pay for men and women and the right of the liberal professions to practise throughout the Community. *The European Parliament* has 518 members elected every five years by universal suffrage; they form political rather than national groups. The European Parliament does not have legislative powers like those of national parliaments – the Commission has the sole power of initiative and the Council plays the major role in taking decisions. The function of the European Parliament is to debate all matters of Community policy, to question both the Commission and the Council of Ministers and to supervise the Community Budget. It has the power to dismiss the Commission by a two-thirds majority. *The Economic and Social Committee and the Advisory Committee.*

Before a Commission proposal can be adopted by the Council, an opinion must be sought, not only from the European Parliament but from the Economic and Social Committee. This is a consultative body which represents employers, trade unions and other interested groups such as farmers and consumers. Many specialised advisory bodies help to further associate professional and trade union interests with the development of the Community. *The Community Budget* is no longer financed by national contributions but by the Community's own resources – customs duties and agricultural levies on imports from the rest of the world, and a proportion, on a uniform assessment basis, of VAT collected in the member states. The management of the budget is supervised by a *Court of Auditors. The European Regional Development Fund* (ERDF) is used to give direct assistance to investment projects and Community-based programmes which deal with unemployment and environmental decay. *The European Economic Community Agricultural Guidance and Guarantee Fund* supports farm prices and encourages the implementation of agreed agricultural arrangements. (FEOGA is the French abbreviation.) *The European Investment Bank* (EIB) borrows money on the world's capital markets and lends it out on a number of Community projects. *See*

COMMON EXTERNAL TARIFF (CET), COMMON AGRICULTURAL POLICY (CAP), and COMMUNITY TRANSIT (CT) SYSTEM, SINGLE EUROPEAN ACT.

European Council of Ministers. *See* EUROPEAN COMMUNITY.

European Court of Justice. *See* EUROPEAN COMMUNITY.

European currency unit (ECU). A currency 'basket', it is made up of the currencies of Germany, Great Britain, France, Italy, Holland, Belgium, Luxembourg, Denmark and Ireland, the proportion of each currency being directly linked to the value of international trade carried on by the participating nations. The value of the units is recalculated every day and officially announced, but if the rises and falls within one unit 'balance out' (e.g. should the mark rise and the franc fall) the fluctuation in the ECU will be less than that exhibited in a single currency. This currency unit is used as the unit of measure for all accounts of the member states, and as the medium for presenting financial statements.

European Economic Communities. The Treaty of Paris 1951 created the European Coal and Steel Community (ECSC); in 1957 two Treaties of Rome set up the European Economic Community (EEC); and the European Atomic Energy Community (EAEC or EURATOM). The three European Communities are managed by common institutions and as a consequence they are increasingly referred to, in the singular, as the EUROPEAN COMMUNITY to which reference should be made above. *See* SINGLE EUROPEAN ACT.

European Free Trade Association (EFTA). Since 1973 the European Community has formed a free trade area with the countries of EFTA: Switzerland, Austria, Sweden, Norway, Iceland and Finland. Customs duties and restrictions on trade in manufactured goods were abolished, and some reciprocal concessions were made for agricultural produce. In Luxembourg in 1984 the two groups decided to create a big European economic area by extending their cooperation beyond free trade agreements, in economic, monetary, and industrial policy, in research and technology and in regard to the environment, fisheries, the steel industry and transport.

European Monetary Fund (EMF). In 1979 the EEC (except for the UK, which though not an EMF member has a certain involvement with it) converted to the European Monetary System, by which members' currencies are tied to one another through a grid of currency parities; they are also all tied to the EUROPEAN CURRENCY UNIT (ECU) – a new international currency. When individual currencies rise or fall, the overall value of the ECU changes little, though a country with an obviously weakening currency should take remedial action.

European Parliament/Assembly. *See* EUROPEAN COMMUNITY.

ex. Without (Stock Exchange). The opposite of CUM, and used to indicate that the buyer is not entitled to participate in whatever forthcoming event is specified: ex cap, ex dividend, ex rights, etc.

ex officio. A Latin phrase meaning 'by virtue of his office'. An *ex officio* member of a committee is appointed to it because of some office he holds.

ex ship. *See* DELIVERY COSTS.

ex works. *See* DELIVERY COSTS.

exchange. 1. The term applied to the transfer from one person or institution of goods or services to another person or institution in return for another good or service, or for money. 2. Exchange, in commerce, is used in various senses of the giving or receiving of one currency in return for an equivalent sum in another currency. 3. Exchange is applied to the assemblage of merchants, bankers and brokers for the transaction of business in commodities, stocks, bonds, bills, etc., and also to the place in which they meet for such purposes, e.g. the Stock Exchange, Baltic Mercantile and Shipping Exchange, and the Royal Exchange. *See* MARKETS.

exchange controls. The official control of the movement of a country's currency between national frontiers. These were abandoned by the UK in 1979; nevertheless the Bank of England can influence the exchange rate by selling sterling when the government wants the rate to go down, and by using foreign currency reserves to buy sterling when the government wants the exchange rate to increase.

exchange disk (computers). A disk that can be removed from the disk drive. Using interchangeable disks means that more than one can be used to store text. Floppy disks are exchangeable. *See also* FIXED DISKS.

exchange equalisation account. This contains Britain's gold and foreign currency reserves; it is from this account that the foreign currency ultimately comes when it is needed by an importer to buy goods or by a traveller to spend abroad. It is also used as a defence against currency speculators, and to buy unwanted sterling. The main object of the account is to intervene in the international money market in such a way as to stabilise the value of sterling.

exchange rate. The rate at which one currency exchanges for another in the world currency markets. The price of STERLING (its exchange rate with other currencies) affects the price of imports and exports. If the exchange rate is low (i.e. there are fewer £s for one unit of foreign currency) then imports are more expensive and exports become cheaper; if it is high, the reverse happens. Movements in the exchange rate affect importers and exporters and, ultimately, the whole economy. When the exchange rate gets too much out of line and stability is required, the government may step in by raising interest rates, which attracts foreign money to correct the balance. It also restricts imports by imposing a low rate of exchange by devaluation. Since 1972 the price of the pound has been determined by the supply and demand for sterling. The BANK OF ENGLAND can influence the exchange rate by selling sterling when the government wants the rate to go down and by using foreign currency reserves to buy sterling when the government wants the exchange rate to rise. The INTERNATIONAL MONETARY FUND seeks to promote harmony in international monetary relations by discouraging erratic movements in exchange rates. *See* FOREIGN EXCHANGE MARKET.

exchequer account (Bank of England). Central account at the Bank of England to which all government receipts are eventually credited and from which all government payments are debited.

excise duty. Indirect tax, imposed on tobacco, petroleum products and alcohol. Excise duties are specific taxes (per unit) imposed at the point of production and which must be paid by the manufacturer before parting with the goods; the tax is later included in the price paid by the final consumer.

export agents. *See* EXPORT HOUSES, FREIGHT FORWARDING AGENTS.

Export Buying Offices Association (EXBO). An association of the London buying offices of leading overseas department stores and importers. The majority of consumer goods sold to department stores overseas are channelled through EXBO members who can advise manufacturers on the suitability of their goods for foreign markets.

export clubs. The idea of the export club is that members (industrialists) should pool their information and knowledge for the benefit of other members. *See* INWARD MISSIONS and OUTWARD MISSIONS.

Export Credit Guarantee Department (ECGD). A separate government department of the Department of Trade and Industry which provides credit insurance for UK exporters against non-payment risks, guarantees to banks for export finance, and insurance against political risks on new overseas investments. The usual principles of insurance apply to ECGD policies, which are accepted as collateral security by banks financing overseas trade.

export documentation. Details of the following documents used in international trade will be found under their own headings: bill of exchange: bill of lading or air waybill (*also* sea waybill); certificate of origin; commercial invoice; consular invoice; certificate of insurance; letter of credit; standard shipping note. *See also* SIMPLIFICATION OF INTERNATIONAL TRADE PROCEDURES (SITPRO).

export finance. Can be of three kinds: short- and medium-term, long-term, or forward trading.

SHORT- AND MEDIUM-TERM TRANSACTIONS

1. *Bank overdrafts and loans* can be used by exporters who cannot afford to finance their own sales. Collateral security in the form of an ECGD policy may be asked for. 2. *Export houses and export merchants* can be used by UK-based manufacturers as this is often a trouble-free method of selling. CONFIRMING HOUSES and EXPORT HOUSES undertake the sale, distribution and delivery to the overseas customer, and assume the financial risk involved in obtaining payment. 3. *Open accounts.* If a British exporter has a long-standing arrangement with an overseas buyer, the buyer will make payments directly into the overseas branch of the exporter's

commercial bank who will often credit the exporter in advance of receiving payment – especially if the transaction has been backed by an ECGD policy.

LONG-TERM PROJECTS

Projects such as the building of dams, oil refineries, etc. may be financed by international organisations such as the INTERNATIONAL BANK FOR RECONSTRUCTION AND DEVELOPMENT (IBRD), which pays the exporter and assumes responsibility for collecting payments from the countries concerned. High-value or project-related exports can benefit from an *ECGD Project Group Guarantee.*

FORWARD TRADING

An exporter can suffer serious losses if his export earnings are affected by a falling exchange rate. To prevent this happening, the exporter can sell *currency* 'forward'. 'Forward trading' is buying or selling currency forward at an agreed exchange rate for delivery in the future – in 3, 6, or 12 months' time. When the exporter receives payment, the exchange rate will be at the 'forward rate', whatever has happened to the £ in the meantime. This is a necessary function to equalise demand and stabilise rates.

export house/merchant. Type of intermediary who functions in one or more capacities as manufacturers' agent, export manager, buying or confirming house, export finance house and so on. Many are members of the British Export Houses Association and they generally specialise in particular markets or goods. Export houses cover the shipping, packing, insurance and finance of export orders. As CONFIRMING HOUSES they take full responsibility for export orders and remove from the exporter all worries about payment. These firms may receive their orders in the form of an 'indent' from abroad. An indent requires the export house to find a supplier for the goods required.

export insurance. *See* EXPORT CREDIT GUARANTEE DEPARTMENT.

Export Intelligence Service (BOTB). The Export Intelligence Service receives a non-stop supply of general market information and specific export opportunities from all over the world. Each item is given a computer coding and when that matches the type of information which has been requested by a British exporter an immediate printout is posted to him. The Export Intelligence Service is supported by a range of regional offices throughout Great Britain.

export invoice. *See* COMMERCIAL INVOICE and CONSULAR INVOICE.

export licences. The United Kingdom stipulates that a licence must be obtained before certain goods can *leave* this country. This restriction applies mainly to works of art, articles of historical value and 'strategic' commodities (arms and ammunition), where the restriction may apply only to specified countries. Export controls are administered by the BOTB, with certain exceptions: the Home Office is responsible for dangerous drugs, HM Customs and Excise for spirits (beverages), and the Ministry of Agriculture, Fisheries and Food for live animals.

Export Marketing Research Scheme (BOTB). Offers free professional advice to exporters on how to set about market research to the best advantage. When a market research project for an overseas market has been decided upon, the BOTB may make a grant of up to 50 per cent towards the costs.

export merchant. *See* EXPORT HOUSE.

Export Representative Service (BOTB). Helps exporters to find representatives to handle their trade in an overseas market. Once requirements are known, the BOTB will contact the Commercial Department of the British Embassy (or similar diplomatic post) in the country with which trade is expected to take place. The Department will send back a report listing local businessmen who have been sounded out and will be interested in selling the product or service for the British exporter.

export restrictions and controls. *See* EXPORT LICENCES.

export risks. The nature of a consignment determines the type of risk to which it will be subject. Physical journeys by sea or air can present a risk in themselves; rough weather and/or sea water can affect cargoes. Theft at the docks is a very real risk (modified now by containerisation), but the most serious risk is that of non-payment. These risks must be covered by adequate insurance. *See* MARINE INSURANCE, EXPORT CREDIT GUARANTEE DEPT.

export services provided by the British Overseas Trade Board.
The BOTB is the export arm of the Department of Trade and
Industry. The following is a list of services; details of each will
be found under its own heading: air couriers; Export Buying
Offices Association; export houses; Export Intelligence
Service; Export Licensing Branch; Export Marketing
Research Scheme; Export Representative Service; freight
forwarders; in-store promotions; inward missions; outward
missions; Overseas Projects Fund; overseas seminars;
Overseas Status Report Service; Project and Export Policy
Division; SITPRO (Simplification of International Trade
Procedures Board); Statistics and Market Intelligence
Library; Technical Help to Exporters (THE); trade fairs
abroad; trade missions; Trade Promotions Guide; World Aid
Section. BOTB publications include 'Hints to Exporters', a
series of booklets each about exporting to a different
country; export guides for small firms; *Overseas Trade*, a free
magazine for exporters; and *Countertrade* which gives advice
to exporters encountering COUNTERTRADE for the first time. *See
also* EXPORT CREDIT GUARANTEE DEPARTMENT.

export trade. Exporting is the selling of British goods
overseas. Britain is an important trading nation, but since
becoming a member of the European Community her
trading patterns have changed and her overseas markets are
now more concentrated on Europe and North America. The
stimulation of exports figures largely in government
economic policies, its aim being to balance exports against
imports. Imports are vital to a country which cannot produce
all its own food or the goods it requires – nor the raw materials
needed by industry. Goods can be sold on the export market
in any of the following ways: *By direct selling from the UK. See*
EXPORT SERVICES PROVIDED BY THE BOTB. *Selling by overseas agents.*
These are 'home nationals' who are able to understand the
complexities of trade in their own countries. *By setting up an
overseas base.* This is a typical activity of many international
companies who have resources not available to the small
exporter. In the 'invisible' export field, overseas manufacturers can be licensed to produce and market British
products, 'royalties' being paid to the British firm. The use

of licensing enables the British manufacturer to sell goods which otherwise could not be sold overseas by direct exportation. Local import restrictions, prohibitive tariffs, and even a lack of the right currency sometimes make such sales impossible. The competitiveness of Britain's exports are affected by movements in the exchange rate. *See also* INVISIBLE TRADE.

extractive industry (economics). The first stage of production – primary production – including the work of all producers engaged in making available raw materials and natural products (food, fishing, agriculture, mining, timber felling). Most primary production is in the form of raw materials which have to be manufactured into other goods at the secondary stage of production.

extraordinary general meeting (EGM). In addition to the statutory ANNUAL GENERAL MEETING, an EGM may be called at any time to discuss special business which cannot conveniently be held over till the next AGM.

F

face value. the value as stated on the face of a coin, note, share certificate, etc. The nominal worth.

facsimile transmission (fax). *See* ELECTRONIC OFFICE (electronic mail).

factor (trade). An agent representing the seller, who actually has the goods in his possession, sells and delivers them to the buyer, and renders an account, less his commission, to his principal. Factors are particularly useful in the export trade.

Factories Acts. *See* EMPLOYMENT LEGISLATION.

factoring of debts. *See* DEBT FACTORING.

factors of production. The factors of production are: *Land* – the term is used to cover all natural resources available to man, including land for factories, warehouses, etc. *Capital* is the stock of money and producer goods available to entrepreneurs for use in production. *Labour* – human resources – covers not only physical labour, but skilful use of human attributes. (*The entrepreneur* is not regarded by all economists as a factor of production.)

fair average quality (faq). Refers to the condition of goods for sale. This type of quotation often refers to goods which are already classified and graded by the trade.

Fair Trading Act 1973. *See* OFFICE OF FAIR TRADING.

family law. The family division of the law covers all matters concerning marriage and divorce, and maintenance claims for wives and children.

family protection policy. In this type of policy, if death occurs during the period stated in the contract the benefit will be paid, not in one lump sum, but by a series of regular payments, terminating with a final sum at the end of a period; it provides useful cover for a widow and young dependents. The period of the contract is usually arranged to cover the time before the children are able to support themselves.

fax (facsimile transmission). *See* ELECTRONIC OFFICE (electronic mail).

feasibility study. A study carried out prior to development of a new product or service; it should cover production, marketing, financial costs, and timing, and provide a sound basis for decision-making.

fee simple. In English law, one of the two legal estates in land. 'Fee simple', broadly speaking, covers the term 'freehold'; the other, 'the term of years absolute', can be described as 'leasehold'.

feedback. The return, to a source of information, about the results of an action or process. By this means the transmitter of a message can assess whether it has been understood.

FEOGA. The initials of the French title of the AGRICULTURAL GUIDANCE AND GUARANTEE FUND which supports farm prices and encourages the implementation of agricultural agreement arrangements.

fidelity bond/guarantee. *See* ACCIDENT INSURANCE.

fiduciary issue. That part of the Bank of England's note issue which is not backed by gold but by government and other securities ('fiduciary' means 'founded on faith or trust').

field (computers). A subdivision of a record which contains only a specific type of information, e.g. in a 'name and address' record, the post code and town are both fields.

field research. *See* MARKETING.

FIFO. *See* FIRST IN, FIRST OUT.

file. 1. An organised collection of related records.

2. (computers). An identifiable quantity of data, such as a set of names and addresses.

filing. The arrangement of documents in order for preservation and reference. A good filing system is essential to the smooth running of any firm or organisation. The five main systems are: alphabetical, chronological, geographical, numerical and subject filing. Two or more systems may be combined to aid efficiency. *See also* ELECTRONIC OFFICE (micrographics).

final dividend. The dividend paid by a company at the end of its financial year, recommended by the directors, but authorised by the shareholders at the company's ANNUAL GENERAL MEETING.

finance. The main financial functions are financial management (budgeting and budgetary control); accounting; providing information for management decision-making; the raising and provision of money. Finance plays a vital part in both government organisations and private industry. The funding, subsequent working within cash limits and provision of an adequate cash flow present perennial problems, more especially when businesses are faced with inflation and recession, and figures become distorted. Financial information in an organisation is essential to enable managers to formulate a sound business policy when they budget for the future. Only from the recorded accounts can an analysis be made of the actual cost of goods and services offered, the amount spent on overheads and the exact revenue of the business. Control over expenditure is made possible when figures can be examined and regulated.

PUBLIC SECTOR

Commercial organisations in the public sector face the same problems as those in the private sector – they should pay their way. Often, they do not and run on a perpetual deficit. *Non-commercial organisations* in the public sector are given money – and strict cash limits – by the government, which funds such services from direct and indirect taxes, rates, National Insurance contributions and motor vehicle duty. The government raises money in other ways: through the 'open market' operations on the STOCK EXCHANGE (the issue of 'gilt-edged securities' which are central or local government stock), through the issue of Treasury Bills and from overseas investment in sterling.

PRIVATE SECTOR – SHORT-TERM

Bank loans and *bank overdrafts* may be obtained. *Hire purchase* may sometimes enable small businesses to acquire equipment, but the system is expensive and mostly used when other forms of credit are not available. *Leasing* is increasingly popular – it is a combination of hiring, instalment credit and property leasing. No large sums of money are required to obtain capital equipment, and usually the payment of a fixed cost is made in advance, which facilitates budgeting. *See also* DEBT FACTORING.

PRIVATE SECTOR – LONG-TERM

Public and private limited companies obtain their initial capital from the sale of SHARES. Further shares may be issued to raise more capital, but only those of public limited companies may be offered to the public for sale. DEBENTURES may also be issued, though only those of public limited companies are sold on the Stock Exchange; they are not shares but *loans* to a company which will ultimately be paid back. *Mortgages* enable businesses to purchase premises. *Government assistance* is available for new businesses and in development areas. Established companies may use retained profits for expansion; unwanted assets can be sold to raise capital.

Finance Bill/Act. The legislation which implements the Budget proposals each year in the UK.

finance for export. *See* EXPORT FINANCE.

Finance Houses Association (FHA). These companies include all the large HP firms; between them they provide money for a continually enlarging market, and without them industrial growth and innovation would stagnate. Cars and consumer durables are generally financed for the consumer by a finance house. Industrial and commercial finance is the main area of activity of the larger finance houses, though all the houses concentrate on particular areas. The finance houses were pioneers in the field of LEASING and DEBT FACTORING. The credit industry itself is financed by deposits from the public, and industrial and commercial companies; it also borrows from the banks. It is because of high borrowing costs that HP charges are relatively high. The FHA has its own rate which is determined by an agreed formula. *Block discounting* is another activity of the finance houses. This involves the buying from retailers of blocks of instalment credit agreements, an immediate cash sum being paid to the retailer.

financial accounting. Covers the recording of all financial activities as they occur – the record of all transactions (buying and selling), the payment of wages – and payments to other organisations which result from this: to pension funds, Inland Revenue, National Insurance, etc.

financial control (of businesses). *Public sector.* Local authorities and government departments are accountable to district and internal auditors, and the Public Expenditure Survey Committee (PESC); they should observe 'cash limits' when such restrictions are set. *Private sector.* Financial control is exercised by budgeting. Implementation is in the hands of managers and accountants, the accounts being finally passed by external auditors.

financial control (of the economy). *See* ECONOMY, CONTROL OF.

financial futures market. *See* LONDON INTERNATIONAL FINANCIAL FUTURES EXCHANGE (LIFFE).

financial instruments. Certificates of deposit, bills, shares, bonds, etc. which can be traded in the money or stock markets.

Financial Intermediaries, Managers and Brokers Regulatory Association (FIMBRA). Self-regulatory organisation which checks on the solvency and competence of insurance brokers and investment advisers.

financial intermediary. Person or institution acting between others in a financial transaction.

financial markets. *See* CAPITAL MARKET, DISCOUNT HOUSES, FOREIGN EXCHANGE MARKET, ISSUING HOUSES, MONEY MARKET, STOCK EXCHANGE.

Financial Services Act 1986. Introduced competitive dealing between the City of London's financial institutions, such as banks, stockbroking firms, insurance companies and unit trusts. Its aim was to provide a uniform level of protection for customers across all the markets in the financial services industry. The Securities and Investment Board (SIB) is the chief City 'watchdog', and is the umbrella organisation for the other self-regulatory organisations (SROs). These are: AFBD – Association of Futures Brokers and Dealers; FIMBRA – Financial Intermediaries, Managers and Brokers Association; LAUTRO – Life Assurance and Unit Trust Regulatory Organisation; IMRO – Investment Management Regulatory Organisation; TSA – The Securities Association.

Financial Times (FT) /**Stock Exchange (SE) 100 share index.** ('Footsie Index.') An index of 100 leading UK shares listed on the International Stock Exchange to provide a minute-by-minute picture of how share prices are moving. It started in January 1984 with the base number of 1,000. Also forms the basis of a contract in the Exchange's *Traded Options Market*. The *FT Index* refers to the *Financial Times* Industrial Ordinary Share Index, also known as the '30 Share Index'. This started in 1935 at 100, and is based on the prices of 30 leading industrial and commercial shares, representative of British industry rather than of the Exchange. Government stocks, banks and insurance companies are not included.

fine rate. This is an agreed minimum rate below which the discount houses will not buy first-class bank bills. (Bank bills are BILLS OF EXCHANGE which have been accepted or endorsed by a reputable bank and are very reliable – hence the competitive minimum rate at which they may be discounted.)

fire insurance. This is a contract of indemnity in respect of loss or damage to material property by fire.

TYPES OF POLICY

Straightforward fire insurance on domestic and business premises and their contents; household policies which cover fire and a very wide range of risks, including burglary; *consequential loss or loss of profits insurance* which indemnifies an insured party for loss caused by the interruption to business activities resulting from fire. The normal fire policy covers only the value of damaged property, but other losses consequent upon a fire may prove to be even costlier to the business; *insurance of 'special risks'*, such as flooding.

first entry, books of. *See* BOOKS OF PRIME ENTRY.

first in, first out (FIFO). A method for controlling stock that assumes the goods received first will be the first issued.

fiscal measures/fiscal policy (of government). Directing the economy through government expenditure and taxes. *See* ECONOMY, CONTROL OF.

fiscal year. Year adopted for accounting and tax purposes; in the UK the government's fiscal year runs to 5 April.

fixed assets. *See* ASSETS.

fixed capital. *See* CAPITAL.

fixed costs. *See* COSTS.

fixed disk (computers). A built-in disk which cannot be removed from the disk drive. One disk stores all the text (cf. EXCHANGE DISK).

fixed-interest stock. Loans issued by a company (debentures), the government or local authority, where the amount of interest to be paid each year is set on issue. Usually the date of repayment is also included in the title.

fixings. The name given to the twice-daily meetings of members of the London Gold Market to establish the day's official gold price.

flat yield. The income received on *fixed-interest stock*.

flexitime. A workplace practice that allows staff some discretion in the time they start and finish work. It is the usual practice for employers to prescribe a core time (say 10.00 am till 4.00 pm) when all staff must be present, but outside those hours staff can choose arrival and departure times that best accommodate their personal needs, within a normal working week.

float. Money put into an account at its commencement. *See* IMPREST.

floating a company. After obtaining clearance from the Registrar of Companies that the proposed name for the company is acceptable, the PROMOTER joins with one other person in signing: the MEMORANDUM OF ASSOCIATION, governing the relationship of the company with the outside world; its 'objects clause' sets out the purposes for which the company was formed; the ARTICLES OF ASSOCIATION which control the internal affairs of the company; the PROSPECTUS; a statement of nominal capital; a list of DIRECTORS with their written consent and promise to take up shares; a statutory declaration that the Companies Acts have been complied with. These documents are then sent to the REGISTRAR OF COMPANIES who may grant a CERTIFICATE OF INCORPORATION. When this certificate is received, shares can be issued by: *a private limited company*, the shares being usually bought by the founders; at this point the private limited company can commence trading; *a public limited company* (PLC): these are bought by the public or by large institutional investors. Often financiers will underwrite public companies to ensure that the minimum capital is subscribed. When the required amount is received, documents of confirmation are sent to the Registrar of Companies who, if satisfied, will issue a

Certificate of Trading to the new company which enables it to commence business. *See* COMPANY.

floating capital. *See* CAPITAL (circulating capital).

floating currencies (foreign exchange). Currencies which do not have a fixed value – the market forces of supply and demand decide their value, which fluctuates from day to day and sometimes several times a day.

floating debentures. *See* DEBENTURES.

floating policy. *See* CARGO INSURANCE.

floppy disk (computers). A small magnetic disk designed for use with microcomputer systems.

flotation (Stock Exchange). The occasion on which a company's shares are offered on the market for the first time.

flowchart. A diagram that uses special symbols and interconnecting lines to represent the steps in a procedure.

folio. A numbered page in an account book.

font (computers). A set of characters of a particular style and type, e.g. Pica Cubic.

Food and Drugs Act 1955. *See* CONSUMER PROTECTION.

footer/footing (word processors). A short piece of text or other information that appears at the bottom of every page in a document.

footnote (word processors). A piece of text which appears at the bottom of a page. It is referenced by a number, and elaborates on material contained within the main text. Do not confuse with FOOTER.

forecasting. A technique used by governments and business planners to predict future behaviour in the economy or market place. A model is set up, taking account of known variables, and a number of statistical techniques employed to project past relationships into the future.

foreground (word processors). A part of the word processor that handles text entry and editing, and any other activities which need the operator's direct involvement (cf. BACKGROUND).

foreign bill. *See* BILL OF EXCHANGE.

foreign exchange market. The City of London provides the world's leading market for the exchange of currencies, though it is not based in one building of its own. Foreign exchange dealing is carried on in many separate city locations, but dealers keep in close touch by electronic communication systems. Members of the Foreign Exchange Brokers Association accept business only from banks actively dealing in the foreign exchange markets. Exchange dealing is a vital link in the chain of international trade. Exporters buying raw materials from abroad may have to pay in a foreign currency, but may require payment for finished goods in sterling. An exporter's local bank will arrange the necessary transactions through the foreign exchange market. The BANK OF ENGLAND supervises the exchange rate for the £, and is ready to take action if it moves too far one way or the other; further internal regulation is exercised by the British Bankers' Association. All member countries of the IMF (International Monetary Fund) must keep their exchange rates within limits. Foreign exchange and EUROCURRENCY are two separate parts of the foreign exchange market. The former is the buying and selling of one currency against another; the latter concerns borrowing and lending. *See* EXCHANGE EQUALISATION ACCOUNT, EXPORT FINANCE.

foreign trade. *See* EXPORT TRADE *and* IMPORT TRADE.

forfeiture. The procedure by which a company expropriates the shares of a member who has defaulted in paying part of the moneys due from him in respect of shares declared forfeit.

form letters. *See* CORRESPONDENCE (2).

format (word processors). The layout, presentation or arrangement of text on a screen or on paper.

formatting (word processors). The process of defining areas on a disk where text is to be stored. With some word processors the manufacturer's own brand of specially formatted disks must be used.

forms of address (correspondence). It is important that the correct form of address is used in correspondence with persons of rank or title, both in the letter and on the envelope. Among the reference books containing this information are Black's *Titles and Forms of Address* and *Debrett's Peerage and Titles of Courtesy.*

FORTRAN. A high-level computer language, primarily for mathematical and scientific applications.

forward dealing/trading. *See* EXPORT FINANCE.

forward vertical integration. *See* MERGERS.

founder's shares. *See* SHARES (deferred shares).

franchising. A franchise agreement is made between two parties when an individual or firm sells another individual or firm the right to market something in its possession according to an agreed format. The 'something' can be a process (like the 'secret formula' in a franchise food), a brand good, or a patented device. Almost always the agreement will be for a specific area, and other subsidiary agreements (dealing with supplies, equipment, servicing) will be involved with the package. The franchise is not buying just the rights to a name, but the blueprint for an entire, successful operation. There is a vast difference between a chain of restaurants and a franchise operation. With the former, a company may start one restaurant, make a profit, and then go on to own other restaurants using the same name. With a franchise operation, the 'parent' company may own one or two of the first restaurants opened – to create a 'name' – but the main part of the operation is to allow others to use its name and product by special agreement.

franco quotations/franco domicile. *See* DELIVERY COSTS.

franked income. Dividends received by one company from another company, whose profits have already borne CORPORATION TAX, and which are not subject to further corporation tax. *Unfranked income* has not borne tax, and is subject to corporation tax.

franking machine. *See* ELECTRONIC OFFICE (mail-handling equipment).

free alongside ship (fas). *See* DELIVERY COSTS.

free enterprise economy. *See* ECONOMY, TYPES OF.

free of particular average (marine insurance). An FPA policy covers only against total loss.

free on board. *See* DELIVERY COSTS.

free on rail. *See* DELIVERY COSTS.

free trade. Trade between nations which is free of all restrictions such as tariffs (customs duties), quotas, and the protection of home industries by subsidisation. Though universal free trade could be advantageous, from a national point of view the protection of some home industries is necessary. Free trade areas (customs unions) are groups of nations which offer each other reciprocal trading arrangements. The major groups are the European Community, EFTA, the British Commonwealth, and COMECOM (the communist economic community).

freehold. A buyer can become the *owner* of land by purchasing the freehold.

freeports. *See* PORTS.

freight forwarding agents. These agents carry out the handling, through-transport arrangements, and payment collection for the greater part of exports from the UK.

freight insurance. *Freight* is the *charge* for carrying cargo. The carriage charges are the income of the carrier, and freight insurance covers the *loss of freight*, i.e, the loss of this income.

freight market (Baltic Exchange). A highly-organised market where cargoes are arranged for ships and ships for cargoes. Cargoes are shipped by: *liners* operating on regular routes with international calls; *tramps* prepared to go anywhere with a cargo for profit. *Ships are chartered (hired) by chartering agents* who represent merchants and others who want to charter ships. *Shipbrokers (owners' brokers)* represent the shipowners. *Independent brokers* arrange both cargoes for ships, and ships for cargoes. A *charter* may be: *a voyage charter* which covers a particular cargo for a particular voyage, or *a time charter* which gives 'rights' over the vessel for a specified period of time. *See also* CHARTER PARTY and AIR FREIGHT MARKET.

friction. Friction is any market force which reduces the efficient fixing of prices. Examples are duties imposed on goods and transport costs.

frictional unemployment. *See* UNEMPLOYMENT.

friendly societies. Non-profit-making organisations maintained from members' subscriptions which are used for sickness, death, endowment and retirement benefits for the members.

fringe benefits. An addition to wages or salaries which form part of the regular non-cash remuneration from employment. Examples are pension schemes, subsidised meals, company cars, and private health insurance.

fully paid (Stock Exchange). Applied to *new issues* of shares when the total amount payable in relation to the new shares has been paid to the company.

function keys (word processors). Extra keys found only on a word processor keyboard. They are used to control editing, printing, storage and other processing of text.

functional organisation. A form of business organisation where specialists are appointed to undertake and advise on a certain type of work throughout the organisation. These specialists act in an advisory capacity only and do not exercise any authority over line management. The O & M team would be regarded as one such specialist function in most organisations.

funding. Literally, this is the conversion of a floating debt into a permanent one. It may be defined in national terms as persuading citizens and institutions to lend money on a long-term basis (creating a fund) to the government.

funds. 1. A resource, especially a sum of money, set apart for a specific purpose. 2. An available sum of money, such as working capital.

funds flow statement. The source and application of funds statement. *See* ANNUAL REPORT AND ACCOUNTS.

futures. Futures (or terminal markets) are markets where the goods being bought and sold are not yet available but will be available later. Goods are ordered at a specified price and delivered later at the price agreed, even if market prices have fallen or risen. A futures contract is essentially a transaction between two parties who require to cover themselves against opposite risks; one fears a rise in price, the other a fall. Speculators are also active in the futures markets and help to stabilise market prices. *See also* HEDGING, INTERNATIONAL COMMODITY CLEARING HOUSE (ICCH), and LONDON INTERNATIONAL FINANCIAL FUTURES EXCHANGE (LIFFE).

G

gamma shares. The third tier of Stock Exchange share groups, smaller and less active than beta shares.

garnishee order. An order on a bank, made by a judgment creditor, for an attachment of funds in respect of a customer's account. The bank stops the account and returns any cheques not yet presented.

gateway facilities (computers). A 'host' organisation's computer is linked to other users' terminal(s), which enables the distant terminals to communicate with each other through the central computer.

gearing. The proportional relationship between a company's debt capital (DEBENTURES) on the one hand and EQUITY capital on the other. The greater the proportion of borrowing, the higher the gearing.

General Agreement on Tariffs and Trade (GATT). Brought into existence at the Geneva Conference in 1947, GATT reflected a belief among the members in free international trade for the whole world. It has been very successful in its efforts to simplify and standardise international trade statistics, customs procedures and valuations, and has made valuable contributions to the understanding of international economic relations. A series of very long tariff-bargaining rounds has lowered the overall level of tariffs considerably. Trade agreements now normally follow the pattern of bilateral arrangements between pairs of countries product by product. Since its creation, GATT has been the only accepted international instrument which lays down rules of conduct for trade on a world-wide basis, and which has been accepted by a high proportion of the leading trading nations. During the last few years GATT has begun to devote more of its efforts to the task of expanding and stabilising exports of the less developed countries.

general ledger. The accounts book required for a proper record of the transactions of a business is called the ledger. In a large firm there may be several ledgers – the sales ledger contains the debtors' accounts, and the purchase (or bought) ledger contains the creditors' accounts. A third – the general or nominal ledger – contains the real and nominal accounts relating to the assets and liabilities and the gains and expenses of the business.

general meeting. A meeting which can be attended by all the members of an organisation (e.g. all the shareholders of a company).

general partners. *See* PARTNERS.

general union. After World War I many unions amalgamated and the large general unions were formed. *See* TRADE UNIONS.

geographical location. Some sites are more suitable than others for the location of a business; primarily the type of business is the most important factor which influences the choice of site. Following this it is necessary to consider: the availability of communications for physical distribution (facilities provided for electronic information technology are available everywhere); availability of raw materials, components and labour for industrial undertakings; availability of housing and other essential services for personnel. The government has declared certain areas of high unemployment to be enterprise zones, where employment is encouraged through tax and rate relief. This may provide a strong inducement for a business to choose a particular location.

Giffen goods. A term which refers to those essential and relatively cheap goods for which demand is likely to increase following a rise in price. The Giffen Paradox is named after a nineteenth century economist who noticed that when the price of bread increased, consumers bought more of it, being unable to afford more luxurious foods such as meat and fruit.

gilt-edged market (Stock Exchange). Government expenditure is not met entirely by taxation so there is a constant need for the government to borrow the money required. This is the primary function of the GILT-EDGED MARKET-MAKERS (GEMMs) and is achieved by the buying and selling of marketable government and local authority securities. These pay a fixed rate of interest throughout their lives, repayment being guaranteed. Most new stocks are announced in the financial press and anyone can apply for them, but buyers are mainly institutions – long-term stock is obviously particularly suitable for life assurance companies and pension funds. (Any member of the public can buy gilt-edged stocks which are on the register at a post office.) The banks and DISCOUNT HOUSES trade in short-dated government and local authority stock. These 'open market' operations help to implement the government's monetary policy; by selling such stock the government siphons money out of the system; to put money back it can buy back in the same markets. Government stocks form the core of the fixed-interest investments. They can be 'Longs': those *without* a redemption date within 15 years; 'Mediums': those *with* a redemption date between 7-15 years; 'Shorts': those *with* a redemption date within 7 years.

gilts. Popular name for government securities. *See* GILT-EDGED MARKET.

giro systems (banking). *See* CREDIT TRANSFER.

glossary (word processors). A term used by some manufacturers to describe a collection of standard paragraphs.

go slow. Industrial action which involves working at a very slow rate.

Gold Bullion Market. *See* BULLION MARKETS.

gold reserves. Today there is a shortage of gold. British gold reserves represent only part of the face value of the country's issued currency; another part is reflected in the amount of foreign currencies it holds. If the Bank of England intervenes in the foreign exchange market to stabilise the value of sterling against the currencies of other main trading countries, it does this through the Exchange Equalisation Account which includes Britain's gold and foreign currency reserves. The funds can be used by the Bank of England to buy unwanted sterling and stabilise the exchange rate.

golden share (Bank of England). A term applied to a share which has particular voting rights which can be used to exercise a vote in certain circumstances. The term is most frequently applied in privatisation issues to a share in a company, retained by the British government, which can be used to prevent the privatised company being acquired by another company contrary to the government's wishes.

goods. All the wants of mankind can be classified as either goods or services. Goods are tangible things such as clothes, motor vehicles, furniture, etc. Services are intangible things such as the services offered by a doctor, solicitor or entertainer. *Capital goods* (producer goods) are produced for other producers to use in a further stage of production. *Consumer goods* (consumption goods) are those goods required in addition to primary (basic) needs, e.g. clothing, household goods, etc.

goodwill (of businesses). The benefit acquired by an establishment or business beyond the mere value of the capital, stock-in-trade, and funds employed in it; it is the possession of a ready-formed connection of customers, and is considered as a separate element in the saleable value of a business. If demand for the type of business in question is high, then the price paid for the goodwill is high. Advertising helps to build up an important asset in the form of goodwill.

government aid for exporters. The BRITISH OVERSEAS TRADE BOARD is the export arm of the Department of Trade and Industry; its members are mainly businessmen with practical knowledge of exporting. It directs the government's export promotion programme and offers a large range of market and specialist advice on the rules and regulations which apply to exporting. A booklet is available from the BOTB called *Hints for Exporters. See* EXPORT SERVICES PROVIDED BY BOTB.

government aid for industry. The Department of Trade and Industry, through its network of regional offices, offers a comprehensive advisory service on all the types of aid available for industrial development. Besides covering the broader aspects of government policy in relation to areas of high unemployment, there is a special Small Firms Service, and the department allocates funds for research and development in many different industrial fields.

government bonds. Documents issued by the government or public authorities in return for loans to finance expenditure which is not met by taxation. *See* GILT-EDGED MARKET.

government borrowing. The main sources of government borrowing are: by open-market operations in bills and bonds (*see* TREASURY BILLS, GILT-EDGED MARKET), and by investment from overseas in British government stock.

government broker. An official of the Bank of England who is an *ex officio* member of the Stock Exchange Council; he keeps the Bank of England in close touch with the stock market.

government departments. The aims of government departments are laid down by statute; each organisation in the public sector has legal obligations to provide certain services in such areas as trade, employment, health, education, social services, defence and foreign affairs.

government expenditure. Government expenditure falls into two main categories: *expenditure on goods and services* (defence, education, hospitals, etc.): this is, for the most part, composed of salaries and wages, but vast quantities of goods are also required if these services are to function; *expenditure in creating 'transfer incomes'* such as social security and unemployment benefits, and retirement pensions. This provides personal incomes to the unemployed and retired, who are not supplying any productive services at the time.

government, functions of. The central government of a state carries out three functions: *the executive function* – performed by the Cabinet with the assistance of the Civil Service; *the legislative function* (the making of laws) – performed by the Queen in Parliament; *the judicial function* – performed by the judiciary led by the Lord Chancellor.

government income. Derived mainly from taxes (direct and indirect), rates and National Insurance contributions.

government monetary policy. To a considerable extent, the BANK OF ENGLAND – acting as the government's agent – can control the money supply in the following ways: by open-market operations in bills and bonds (*see* GILT-EDGED MARKET and TREASURY BILLS); by requiring 'special deposits' from the commercial banks; by alteration of the bank rate; by intervention on the foreign exchange market to stabilise the value of sterling against other main foreign currencies.

government policy objectives. The main objectives of every government, irrespective of political party, are: control of unemployment and inflation, a favourable balance of payments and economic growth.

grain futures market. A grain futures market operated by GAFTA (Grain and Feed Trade Association) is held in the Baltic Exchange.

graphics pad (computers). Information, such as technical drawings and graphs, can be put into a computer by drawing on a magnetically sensitive surface (a graphics pad) with a special pen.

Green Paper. Before a government Bill is introduced into Parliament, a pamphlet – called a Green Paper – may be issued to explain the proposals being put forward in order to promote public discussion.

greenmail. A form of corporate blackmail.

grey market. Trading in the shares of a company before the official date.

grievance procedure (industrial relations). Established rules to be followed should a dispute arise between employer and employee(s).

gross (investment). Income from an investment before deduction of tax. *Grossing up* is calculating the amount that would be required, in the case of an investment subject to tax, to equal the income from an investment not subject to tax.

Gross Domestic Product (GDP). Total value of output produced within the country's physical borders in a specified period.

Gross National Product (GNP). Equals GDP (Gross Domestic Product) plus net property income from abroad accruing to residents of the United Kingdom.

gross pay. The full amount of salary or wages before any deductions have been made.

gross profit. The difference between cost price and selling price. To calculate the gross profit made by a business, the cost of the goods sold during a particular period is deducted from the total value of sales made during the same period.

gross profit percentage. Gross profit is the difference between the cost price and the selling price of the goods sold.

$$\text{Gross profit percentage} = \frac{\text{Gross profit}}{\text{Turnover}} \times \frac{100}{1}$$

group bonus. *See* BONUS (3).

group life insurance. Small employers may take out insurance to cover an agreed sum on each member of staff. An employee leaving such employment can usually arrange to commute his benefits to a personal insurance on terms suitable to his own requirements.

growth (economics). New capital resources in an organisation provide the capacity for expansion, either through expanding existing markets (new products or advertising), or by diversifying – extending into new areas or by the takeover of another business organisation. *External growth* is the increase in profit resulting from the acquisition of other businesses; *internal growth* is generated from a company's successful trading from existing resources.

guarantee. An agreement undertaken by product manufacturers to indemnify customers against faulty goods over a limited period of time.

guarantee, company limited by. *See* LIMITED LIABILITY.

guarantor. A person who undertakes to be responsible for the liabilities of another.

guillotine and decollator. Designed to meet the continuous stationery requirements of the computer operation. The cutting system removes any trace of perforation on standard computer forms; following trimming, the decollator will separate duplicated sets of forms (invoices, statements, etc.) into sets of individual forms.

guillotine closure. A form of closure of a meeting or debate (rarely used outside the House of Commons) in which a time limit is fixed for debate on each section or stage of a Bill. When the time limit expires, discussion ceases, whether the business is concluded or not.

H

hammering. Announcement of the failure of a STOCK EXCHANGE firm. A compensation fund is maintained by the Stock Exchange to recompense investors should a member firm fail to meet its obligations.

Hang Seng Index. The most frequently quoted index of shares on the Hong Kong Stock Exchange.

Hansard. The official, printed reports of the proceedings and debates of the Houses of Parliament.

hard copy. Copy on paper of information held on word processors or computers which is produced directly on printers linked to the machines.

hard disk (computers). A disk which is made of rigid material, such as aluminium; it may be fixed or exchangeable.

hardware. The physical components of a computer system. These include input and output devices, the central processing unit (CPU), and any auxiliary storage devices.

Hatton Garden. Site of the London diamond market where many independent traders have their offices. It is close to the offices of the Central Selling Organisation (CSO) whose companies sort, value and sell rough diamonds to the world's major diamond-cutting centres and industries.

hawkers. Itinerant dealers who carry their goods for sale from place to place.

head hunting (personnel). Searching for and recruitment of personnel, especially at executive level, and often from other firms.

header/heading (word processors). A short piece of text or other information that appears at the top of every page in a document.

Health and Safety at Work Act 1974. *See* EMPLOYMENT LEGISLATION.

hedging. An attempt by an investor or speculator on the FUTURES (Terminal) MARKETS to safeguard the real value of his investments. The *buyer* of physical goods – sugar, cocoa, or any other commodity – for which there is a futures market (i.e. he has bought them for payment and delivery at some *future* date) will protect himself by *selling* a balancing amount on the same market. The net effect is that whether the commodity value rises or falls, the buyer or seller is assured of a minimum price. A loss on the physical side is offset by a gain on the futures markets – or the other way round. Hedging also takes place on the forward market in currencies.

highly-organised market. Market where the whole range of buying and selling takes place through institutional or other arrangements. The organisation of such markets depends on the rules under which the market operates; examples are those which deal in commodities such as coffee, cocoa or silver, or the Stock Exchange with its numerous special markets in foreign stock, mining, gilts and ordinary shares. In these markets, buyers and sellers are numerous and communication between them rapid; only experts are permitted to deal and the minimum contracts allowed are set at a very high figure.

high street banks. Also known as clearing banks, joint stock banks, or commercial banks. They handle the accounts of millions of depositors through a countrywide network of high street branches.

hire purchase. A hire purchase agreement is an agreement to hire goods for a specified period, with an option for the hirer to purchase the goods at the end. The property does not pass to the hirer until the last payment has been made, therefore he cannot sell while it is still under an HP agreement. The hirer may terminate the agreement, but must allow the seller to take possession, bring the total payments up to 50 per cent of the purchase price, and pay for any damage. The seller may retake goods if instalments are overdue; notice of default requires payment within seven days. After one-third of the purchase price has been paid, the seller cannot recover the goods except by court order. The agreement must contain: a heading – 'Hire Purchase Agreement regulated by the Consumer Credit Act 1974' – shown prominently on the first page; the name and postal address of both trader and customer; a declaration of the cash price; the amount of any advance payment; the amount of credit to be provided; the total charge for credit and the total amount payable by the customer; the timing and amounts of repayments, of credit and credit charges; the ANNUAL PERCENTAGE RATE (APR) denoted as *the APR of the total charge for credit*, statements about the main rights of customers provided by the CONSUMER CREDIT ACT 1974. An agreement must be recorded in a document which embodies all its terms, is signed by both trader and customer, and is readily legible when given or sent to the customer for signature. No right of cancellation exists on a contract made on trade premises. A right of cancellation exists on all contracts signed elsewhere, i.e. doorstep sales, etc. Such a sale will be cancelled if the hirer gives notice within five days of receiving the second statutory copy (or fourteen days if bought from a mail order company). This is the cooling-off period. All agreements are to be signed by both customer and trader or their representatives and the date of signature entered. The customer's signature must be inside a box. The signature of the trader must be outside the customer's signature box; similarly, the signature of any witness and its date must also be outside the customer's signature box. Copies of agreements must be given to a customer – when and how depends on the circumstances in which the customer signs the agreement. Retailers do not usually finance HP sales themselves, but use the services of a FINANCE HOUSE. To the financier this is, in spite of its highly speculative nature, a most rewarding field of investment, yielding higher than average results. This is due to the nominal rate of interest being in fact doubled up by repayment systems, and why due regard should be paid to the annual percentage rate shown. Hire purchase controls are one of the means used by the government to control the economy. They do this by varying the HP deposit and the period of repayment. *See* CONSUMER CREDIT.

hire retailing. A relatively new development: the retailer hires out equipment for use in the hirer's own home or garden. Equipment used for 'do-it-yourself' activities is particularly popular, such equipment being expensive to buy and not frequently used by the amateur. Another area where hire retailing is developing rapidly is in the holiday trade: bicycles, camping and skiing equipment are among items which can be hired.

histogram. A statistical graph in which frequency distribution is shown by means of rectangles.

historic(al) cost. An accounting convention which normally ignores the impact of inflation.

holding company. Essentially a financial institution, the purpose of which is to maintain or gain control of other trading companies by acquiring a majority shareholding in them, and bringing the subsidiary company within the direct influence of the parent company. It is one way of building up a large-scale business, as subsidiaries may supply the parent manufacturing company with particular components; it may also present the possibilities of diversification where there is a fear of decline in any particular market. The term multinational is commonly used to describe a holding company with foreign subsidiaries. The shareholders of subsidiary companies are in the minority; the Companies Acts protect the rights of such minority shareholders by allowing them to appeal to the Department of Trade and Industry against unfair treatment. Where a company is a holding company there must, with every BALANCE SHEET and PROFIT AND LOSS ACCOUNT laid before a general meeting, be presented also: a consolidated balance sheet dealing with the state of affairs as at the end of the financial year of the company and its subsidiaries; a consolidated profit and loss account dealing with the profit or loss for the financial year of the company and those subsidiaries. The financial years of the holding company and its subsidiaries shall, if possible, coincide.

hologram (computers). A photographic system which uses laser light to create a three-dimensional image.

Home Office (HO). Government department responsible for law and order and for all home affairs except those specifically assigned to other departments. Most of the Home Office's responsibilities are limited to England and Wales, but in some matters they extend to Scotland and Northern Ireland. Among the more important duties of the Home Office are the administration of justice, police administration, provision of prison services, control of aliens and naturalisation. The Home Secretary acts as a channel of communication between the Queen and her subjects; other functions include the conduct of elections, community relations, and supervision of the BBC and IBA.

home trade. The buying and selling of goods and services by persons living in the same country. This can involve extractive and manufacturing industry together with commercial services connected with the chain of distribution, through the wholesale and retail markets. 'Home produce' usually refers to such perishable items as milk, butter, cheese, and other fresh foods and vegetables which are bought either direct from the farmer or through farmers' cooperatives. A large amount of produce is sold through the produce markets in London and other large cities. Home trade may be protected from foreign competition by the application of embargoes, quotas and tariffs to imported goods.

horizontal integration (of businesses). *See* MERGERS.

hot money. Funds transferred suddenly from one country to another because conditions on the international money markets make transfer financially advantageous.

household protection insurance. Many insurance companies offer a household policy which generally covers the complete contents of a home against various types of risk. *See* FIRE INSURANCE.

House of Commons. The United Kingdom Parliament legislates (makes laws) by means of Acts of Parliament, and has two chambers. The lower chamber is the House of Commons, the upper chamber the House of Lords. Members of the House of Commons are elected at a general election by voters over the age of eighteen, normally for a parliamentary term of five years. By-elections occur when a member dies or resigns during such a parliamentary term. After a general election the Queen asks the leader of the party which has gained most seats to form a government. The leader – the Prime Minister – then selects ministers who are approved by the Queen; other ministers are also appointed by the Prime Minister who fill the positions below Cabinet rank. Ministers share responsibility for government actions, and also have individual responsibility for the work of their own departments. *See* GOVERNMENT (FUNCTIONS OF), LEGISLATION.

House of Lords. The upper chamber of the Parliament of the United Kingdom, composed of the Lords spiritual (two archbishops and twenty-four bishops of the Church of England), and the Lords temporal. The Lords temporal are those peers holding peerages in Great Britain; some are hereditary peers, but the Crown is enabled also to confer life peerages on both men and women. *See* GOVERNMENT (FUNCTIONS OF), LEGISLATION.

hovercraft. Vehicle particularly effective over water. A cross-channel hovercraft ferry carries cars and passengers between England and France.

hull insurance. The hull of a vessel, which includes the machinery, can be covered against damage or total loss by storm, stranding, fire, collision or other perils of the sea. *Time policies* usually last 12 months; *voyage policies* cover the hull from the port of departure to the port of arrival with no specific time limit.

human relations. Describes the activities of management in attempting to achieve the best possible fit between workers and their jobs. Problems involving morale, teamwork, creativity, introduction of change, etc. are the concern of those working in this field. Employer/employee relationships are of the utmost importance as they are often a source of conflict.

human resources (economics). The labour market is a market where employers can buy human resources and where workers can sell their labour. Labour is one of the factors of production, the others being land and capital. The management of human resources should ensure that the employees of an organisation are used to obtain the optimum benefit for those who employ them.

hypermarkets. Very large establishments with ample parking usually situated outside large towns, offering a tremendous range of consumer goods. Like SUPERMARKETS, their prices are highly competitive.

I

imperfect competition. *See* MONOPOLY.

import broker/commission agent. Deals with goods for foreign exporters on a consignment basis. A consignment in mercantile law means a particular lot of goods sent or consigned to an agent, usually in another country, for disposal on behalf of his principal. The agent makes arrangements for the landing of goods and sees to the Customs formalities; if necessary, he arranges warehousing before selling the goods. When the goods are sold he renders an ACCOUNT SALES to his principal, which details expenses incurred in the transaction, including brokerage or commission (possibly also an additional DEL CREDERE commission). These expenses are deducted from the gross proceeds of the sale and the agent then remits the amount due to his principal.

import documentation. The main documents of the import trade are the BILL OF LADING (or AIR WAYBILL), INVOICE, CERTIFICATE OF ORIGIN, and CERTIFICATE OF INSURANCE. In addition, goods arriving in the UK must be entered for Customs clearance on an 'entry' form.

import duties. *See* CUSTOMS DUTIES.

import licences. If goods are not listed on the schedules of goods which may enter the country without restriction, a licence must be obtained. Such licences may be 'quota' licences, as they restrict imports to a given quota which has been approved.

import merchant. An import merchant usually has connections with a particular country or area, buys goods from manufacturers or growers there, and sells them for his own profit. He may deal on the commodity markets or direct with wholesalers and retailers in this country.

import trade. Trade between nations takes place because, for climatic reasons, a country may not be able to produce all its natural products; on the other hand, it may be able to produce a surplus which it can export. A further reason for trading lies in the international specialisation of labour. Many of the raw materials which are imported into Great Britain are manufactured into goods which are then exported. British imports of *primary products* are mainly bought as BULK CARGOES, e.g. in oil tankers or refrigerated meat carriers. They are handled by the COMMODITY MARKETS, financed, transported and warehoused until required by middlemen, or directly imported by a manufacturing firm which has built up a special link with an overseas supplier. *Secondary products* (manufactured goods) are imported directly by importing organisations or by agents appointed to handle goods in this country. A nation which wishes to import must be prepared to export, but exports must be of the right quality and price to achieve a favourable BALANCE OF TRADE. *See* IMPORT BROKER/COMMISSION AGENT and IMPORT MERCHANT. Imports are controlled by CUSTOMS DUTIES and IMPORT LICENCES; Customs can give the 'most favoured nation' treatment to a particular country or countries. Repayment of duty can be claimed when an import pays duty and is manufactured into a finished product which is subsequently exported. The exporter can then claim the duty back from Customs. *See* INWARD PROCESSING RELIEF. Goods for transhipment – that is, for immediate re-export – which are transferred to another vehicle for onward delivery to an overseas port, are entered on a special 'entry' form and are not liable for duty. Duty is normally payable in advance before 'entry' is allowed. A system of BONDED WAREHOUSES permits landing of cargo on which duty has *not* been paid. *See* BALANCE OF PAYMENTS, INVISIBLE TRADE.

imprest. A sum of money advanced to a person for a particular business purpose; today, the term is mostly associated with petty cash. The cashier starts off the petty cash fund with an amount of money (the 'float') deemed sufficient to cover expenditure for a limited period (usually a week). Records are kept of each item of expenditure and at the end of each period are checked by the cashier who then restores the imprest. This means that the petty cash fund is reimbursed with the amount of money spent during the period, which brings the money left in the cash box to the original imprest again.

incentive schemes. Incentive schemes enable employees to become more effective and so ultimately reduce wage costs. Usually the incentive involves financial reward of some kind, but flexible working hours and a less rigid demarcation between jobs also have an effect on an employee's contribution to the general effectiveness of an organisation. Schemes based on the VALUE ADDED concept offer employees a percentage share of an organisation's created wealth.

income and expenditure account. An income and expenditure account is more than a mere statement of cash transactions; it is credited with all income pertaining to the period whether received in cash or not, and is debited with all expenses; all transactions of a capital nature are excluded. The income and expenditure account is normally used only by clubs and other non-trading societies. Under the Companies Acts it is compulsory for a company registered as not trading for profit to lay an income and expenditure account before the company in general meeting.

income tax. A *direct tax* on personal income, graduated according to the amount of such income. It is a statutory deduction made by employers from salaries and wages (PAYE), and in general is a tax levied on earnings to help meet the expenses of the government. There are two ways in which the government can alter the level of income tax: first, by changing the rate at which tax is charged and, secondly, by altering the allowances (i.e. the tax-free portion of income).

income tax forms. The following forms are the most familiar:
P6 *Notice of amended coding.* Sent by the Collector of Taxes to an employer when the tax code number of an employee has been changed.

P11(New) *Deductions working sheet.* Supplied by the Inspector of Taxes for the employer to record the amount of income tax and National Insurance contributions deducted from the employee's pay. There is a separate form for each employee.

P13 *Emergency Tax Card.* Used if an employee has no code number. When a code number is issued, the record is transferred to the P11.

P14 *End of year return.* A form made out in triplicate at the end of each year by employers for each employee. The top copy is sent to the Collector of Taxes for the DHSS; the second copy is sent to the Collector of Taxes for the Inland Revenue; *the third copy is the P60 Certificate of pay, tax deducted and National Insurance contributions,* and is given to each employee as proof that his income tax and National Insurance contributions have been paid for the year shown.

P15 *Coding claim.* Given to an employee who has no code number, possibly because he cannot get a P45 or has lost it, or because he is earning money for the first time.

P45 *Particulars of employee leaving.* When an employee leaves one place of employment for another, the employee is given a form P45 on which is written the total taxable pay to date for the current year, and the total tax deducted to date for the current year. One copy is sent to the employer's tax office, and two are given to the employee to give to his new employer, who keeps one and sends the other to the employee's new tax office.

P46 *Particulars of first employment.* Form sent by the employer of a person earning money for the first time, to the Inspector of Taxes.

P60 *Certificate of pay and tax deductions.* Made out annually by employers for each employee, and is proof that income tax has been deducted for that year. *See P14 End of year return.*

incomes policy. The aim of an incomes policy is to ensure that incomes do not rise faster than increased wages costs can be absorbed by rising productivity; its object is to curb inflation and avoid unemployment. Incomes policies range from statutory policies (laid down by Act of Parliament) and voluntary policies (social contracts between governments and representatives of the trade unions) to 'market policies' where controls are released and the free play of market forces is allowed to take place.

Incorporation, Certificate of. Sent by the Registrar of Companies to a newly-registered company and is its 'birth certificate' which gives the company a legal personality and allows its shares to be sold to secure the capital it needs. *See* FLOATING A COMPANY.

indemnity. The object of all insurance (except for life insurance and personal accident insurance) is to restore the insured to the position he was in before the event which was insured against took place, i.e. to indemnify him.

indent. Export houses or merchants may receive their orders in the form of an 'indent' from overseas; this requires the exporter to find a supplier for the goods required.

independent trader. *See* SOLE TRADER.

index-linked. Increasing or decreasing proportionately to a rise or fall in an index, especially the RETAIL PRICE INDEX. For instance, 'an index-linked gilt' is stock whose interest and capital change in line with the RPI.

index numbers. A single figure which summarises a comparison between two sets of figures. It is constructed from: a starting point or 'base' year, and a set of figures for the base year and year of comparison. If the index number is to compare a 'basket' of commodities (as in the index of retail prices), an average basket must be computed and the contents 'weighted'. For many purposes, 100 is used as a base, since comparison then becomes much clearer.

index of retail prices. *See* RETAIL PRICE INDEX.

indicator system (Bank of England). A system whereby the central bank adjusts short-term interest rates according to a predetermined formula relating to the growth of the money stock. If the money stock is growing faster than the official target, then interest rates will automatically be increased.

indirect costs. For most costing purposes the term may be treated as synonymous with 'overheads', meaning those expenses which cannot be directly traceable to a cost unit. There are three categories of indirect costs – materials, labour and expenses. Indirect materials consist of 'consumables', used by the production department but not a part of manufacture; indirect labour refers to functional sections of the business such as R & D, administration, sales, etc. The balance of indirect costs is in the expenses incurred by production and these include heating, lighting, rent, rates, insurance and depreciation. These factory overheads are added to prime costs to give production costs.

indirect production. *Mass production* or *production by specialisation*; each worker contributes a part of the whole product. Mass production is a system which seeks to make the greatest number of goods with the least number of workers (cf. DIRECT PRODUCTION).

indirect taxation. Taxes on expenditure such as VAT, car tax, road fund, TV licences, and duties collected by the CUSTOMS AND EXCISE.

induction courses. Induction courses for new members of staff are often provided in large organisations to help new employees get used to the new environment and to see their own work in relationship to that of all other employees in the establishment. By visits to other departments, lectures and films, the new employee can be introduced to the organisation's structure, its products or services, the availability of welfare facilities, health and safety measures, and the operating 'rules of the house'.

industrial action. Action (e.g. a strike or go slow) taken by a body of workers in an effort to force an employer to comply with demands.

industrial life offices (also known as 'home service offices'). Offer most types of insurance cover, including life assurance. The premiums are collected by agents who visit the homes of the insured.

industrial property. Refers to such intangible assets of a business as patented inventions, goodwill, trademarks and copyrights. These non-physical properties can be owned and sold.

industrial relations. The academic study of the rules and procedures which govern employment and the organisations that regulate them.

Industrial Society, The. Society which began its work in 1918 and was granted a Royal Charter on 20 February 1985. It is a self-financing and non-profit-making organisation, is independent and non-party political, and it enjoys the support of employers and trade unions. It is a leading management advisory and training body which works to achieve greater employee involvement – to increase both the effectiveness of organisations and the satisfaction of people working in them. It spreads the good practice needed to achieve this by running courses and conferences and by advising and assisting organisations in all sectors.

industrial tribunals. Courts which fall outside the ordinary court system, and concerned with disputes arising out of a person's employment, such as claims for redundancy payments, equal pay, and complaints of unfair dismissal and discrimination. If the matter is not settled by the industrial tribunal it may be taken to the Employment Appeals Tribunal: this consists of judges and members from both the employer's and employee's side of industry.

industrial unions. See TRADE UNIONS.

industry. Covers all productive organisations; see PRODUCTION.

inelasticity of demand. When the price of a good or service changes and the change in demand is small, demand is said to be inelastic.

inflation. A rise in price levels causing a fall in the value of money; an undue increase in the quantity of money in proportion to buying power, so that if the value of money in circulation is not matched by earnings, the country is said to be suffering from inflation. The government can curb excess demand by increasing taxation and/or reducing public expenditure. Monetarists argue that inflation only occurs because the money is available to permit price increases, but so far there has been no successful formula for permanently reducing inflation. Inflation is a serious threat to investors, since it causes the value of money to fall – the nominal value remains the same, but the real value is diminished. Inflation also distorts the calculation of profit and the valuation of assets.

inflation accounting. During an inflationary period it becomes increasingly difficult to assess the assets of a firm in real terms. Constantly increasing prices mean that all figures need constant adjustment to keep pace with inflation. The cost of depreciation of fixed assets, for example, should keep pace with inflationary prices; stock may increase in value but the increase is not profit. In times of rapid inflation, cash resources lose their value, but borrowed money (because the interest rate does not reflect inflationary rates) remains 'cheap'. It is difficult to measure the value of money at such times, because the valuation of assets and the calculation of profit become increasingly difficult. The Accounting Standards Committee has put forward suggestions to assist accountants to present a true and fair picture of a company's accounts which take into consideration the fact of inflation.

informal organisation. 1. A type of organisation in which relationships and communications are not rigid and restrictive, but which emphasises teamwork and cooperation. The organisation becomes a dynamic and flexible system which uses people's expertise more effectively. Conventional principles and lines of command tend to fall into the background while staff are expected to display more self-discipline and responsibility in their highly flexible roles. 2. 'Informal organisation' may also refer to the informal behaviour of social groups within an organisation which are often in conflict with its aims. Normally, objectives are implemented by the delegation of authority, but pressure put on the organisation by a pressure group within it can often complicate issues. The introduction of new methods by management which do not win the approval of such a group is one illustration.

information retrieval. The process of recovering specific information from a database.

information technology. The acquisition, processing, storage, dissemination and use of vocal, pictorial, textual and numerical information by a micro-electronics based combination of computing and telecommunications. Information is acquired from all the relevant sources; control staff supervise the collection and preparation of data for input into the computer, which then sorts and stores it. Information can be enlarged, edited, deleted or rearranged, and must always be kept up-to-date. Organised files of information – databases – are compiled for reference; usually it is sufficient to view the information on the VDU screen but, if necessary, HARD COPY can be produced on a printer. *Stand-alone workstations* are independent of others and all operations are carried out at the one place. When using 'floppy disks' only the information on the disk being used is 'on-line' – i.e. the information on it can be accessed by the operator. All information held on other disks is 'off-line'. HARD (Winchester) DISKS are available for use on certain microcomputers and offer greater storage capacity, thereby increasing 'on-line' facilities. Some microcomputers are powerful enough to support more than one computer terminal; all share the computing power of the main unit. *Local Area Networks (LANs)*. Independent computers can be linked together via a Local Area Network. This is a communication system usually based in one building, which enables each terminal to access databases, central files, printers, scanners, etc. which are distributed throughout the LAN. Compatibility between the machines is essential. *Wide Area Networks (WANs)* provide intercommunication between specific Local Area Networks. *Public on-line database systems* (information retrieval services/electronic publishing). Information is stored by the provider of the service on a central computer or computers where it is held in organised databases; signals are sent along telephone lines to the subscriber who gains information via a video terminal or microcomputer; a telephone and modem/acoustic coupler are needed to effect communication. The systems permit a two-way service, which means that the user can 'talk' back in simple language, using a remote control handset. *Prestel*, the public viewdata service of British Telecom, has a comprehensive information source; when accessed, information is sent along telephone lines from a central computer. Because Prestel allows the user to communicate with the information source via the host computer, shopping can be done from the home by using a credit card, and hotel and travel reservations can be effected easily and quickly. Prestel subscribers are charged a rental for the use of the service, and Prestel-connected telephone usage is also charged for. Many business groups operate 'closed user groups' within the Prestel service to allow privileged access to confidential or sensitive information to selected users. There are many private information services, particularly in the financial field, which provide immediate on-line information for subscribers. *Teletext.* Unlike Prestel, Teletext information is not sent along telephone lines but over the airwaves. It is broadcast by the BBC and ITV and provides up-to-the-minute information and entertainment on the television screen. The BBC's CEEFAX service covers BBC1 and BBC2; the ITV service is called ORACLE. (*Do not confuse with* TELETEX.)

inheritance tax. Tax which replaced capital transfer tax (Finance Act 1986). The tax is applied to all gifts over a fixed sum, the tax varying according to the sum transferred. The main charges arise in transfers made by an individual on death or within seven years of death.

initial deposit. Sum which a broker requires a client to deposit with him before he starts trading on his behalf in the futures markets.

ink jet printer (computers). Method of printing HARD COPY.

inland bill. *See* BILL OF EXCHANGE.

Inland Revenue. The two sources of Inland Revenue are taxes and stamp duties.

innovation. The exploitation of industrial inventions.

input. *See* COMPUTERS (hardware).

insider dealing (Stock Exchange). The misuse of 'inside' company information which may affect the price of shares; dealing in shares on the basis of privileged knowledge of a company's affairs. The Company Securities (Insider Dealing) Act 1985 prohibits this activity.

insolvency (of businesses). Denotes inability to pay one's debts. The term is for most practical purposes replaced by the term BANKRUPTCY.

institutional investor (Stock Exchange). An institutional investor collects the savings of many people and invests them for the good of the saving public. Banks, building societies, finance companies, insurance companies, investment trusts, local authorities, the national savings scheme, pension funds, trade unions, and unit trusts are all institutional investors. Each institution holds a 'balanced portfolio' – a mixture of SHARES and other securities in both the public and private sector of industry. These 'safe' investments yield a reasonable return.

in-store promotions. When a big retail outlet overseas puts on a 'theme' production and there is a specifically British flavour to the event, with increased sales of British goods as the aim, the BRITISH OVERSEAS TRADE BOARD can often provide support to the store. Taking part in one of these well-organised promotions can help exporters to enter a new market or expand business.

insurable interest. An insurance policy is not a legal contract unless the person insured has a direct *interest* in the matter insured. The insured person cannot improve his position through a loss covered by insurance which can only *indemnify* him, i.e. bring him back to the state he was in before the loss occurred. If the insured himself does not suffer from the loss, he cannot be indemnified.

insurable/non-insurable risks. Insurance rates are based on the probability of the risk which has been insured against actually occurring. If there are statistical records available, the 'probability' of the event can be estimated by an insurance underwriter and the correct amount of the premium worked out. Some eventualities, because there are no records to work on, are non-insurable.

insurance. Insurance provides one of the main commercial services, being an important aid to trade. It relieves traders of the risks involved in developing trade and encourages them in enterprise. The purpose of the contract of insurance is either to indemnify against a loss which may occur if a certain event takes place, or to pay upon some event occurring a sum of money to the insured person. Insurance is a 'pooling of risks'. The success of such an insurance pool depends on adequate contributions (premiums) to cover losses. Insurance companies are institutional investors who invest wisely in a balanced portfolio. The pool must never be allowed to shrink but must grow bigger year by year. It is essential that all claims are paid promptly and in full.

MAIN PRINCIPLES OF INSURANCE

The three main principles of insurance are *insurable interest*, *utmost good faith (uberrima fides)*, and *indemnity*. *Insurable interest.* The insured must be in danger of suffering loss should the thing concerned be destroyed or damaged in any way. *Utmost good faith (uberrima fides).* On the basis of truthful facts, a fair premium is decided. When the proposal form is completed by the person requiring insurance it must contain only the truth; any inaccuracy voids the contract. *Indemnity* means the restoring of someone to the position they were in before the event concerned took place. *Note:* Insurance against death or injury can never be indemnified – it simply provides money called 'benefit' to the injured or to relatives and dependents after the death of the insured. *The principle of contribution* lays down that if a person insures twice or three times for the same risk, the companies concerned must each contribute to the loss a half each or a third each, so that the insured is indemnified. *Subrogation* It is wrong for an insured person to accept an agreed sum in compensation and then continue to have other rights as well. A car that is a 'write-off' may have good tyres, but they belong to the insurance company after the insured person has been indemnified. *Doctrine of proximate cause* When insurance is taken out it covers certain eventualities which must be the *primary cause* of a loss if a claim is to be made against the insurer.

MAIN TYPES OF INSURANCE
Marine, fire, life and *accident*

ARRANGING AN INSURANCE POLICY
A *proposal form* must be completed, and all questions answered honestly. The premium to be paid is assessed on the basis of answers given to the questions on the proposal form, which is the basis of the *insurance contract.* Acceptance by the insurers brings the contract into being; a *cover note* is issued providing evidence of insurance cover. The *insurance policy* is drawn up which gives full details of what has been agreed. *See* LLOYD'S CORPORATION, COMPOSITE OFFICES.

insurance brokers. Agents who undertake to get the best rate from underwriters and carry through the insurance on behalf of their customers. A Lloyd's underwriter will deal only with brokers and cannot be approached by a member of the public.

insurance certificate. *See* CERTIFICATE OF INSURANCE.

insurance claim. When an insured person has suffered a loss against which he has insured, he should complete a claim form, which should be filled in with utmost good faith, i.e. only the truth must appear. The insurer will wish to confirm that the insured peril was the primary cause of the loss, and that liability exists. It must also be ascertained that there were no breaches of the conditions of the policy. When a 'fair' valuation is agreed, the insurance company should pay promptly. Very large disasters which have been covered by several syndicates at Lloyd's may involve the selling of an insurance company's investments to meet the claim.

insurance market. The British Insurance Market is the largest insurance market in the world. Besides LLOYD'S CORPORATION, there are many large insurance companies which offer a very wide range of insurance cover.

insurance of exports. Marine insurance (which now includes aviation) covers cargo insurance, and is largely the concern of the insurance market of LLOYD'S CORPORATION where marine insurance originated in Britain. The EXPORT CREDIT GUARANTEE DEPARTMENT of the Board of Trade provides credit insurance for UK exporters.

insurance of liability. *See* ACCIDENT INSURANCE.

insurance, parties to. In any contract of insurance the first party is the insured person, the second party is the insurer, the third party is any person affected by the contract. (In motor vehicle insurance the third party may be a passenger, pedestrian, or cyclist.)

insurance policy. Document which sets out the terms and conditions of the contract between the person taking out the cover (the first party) and the insurance company or underwriter (the second party). It also shows the value covered, the premium(s) payable, and the date(s) on which payments are due.

insurance premium. The sum of money payable by a policyholder to the insurer for the protection being given. The amount of the premium is calculated from information given on the proposal form, and on past statistical records relative to the proposal.

intangible assets. Assets which do not have a physical identity, such as goodwill, trademarks, copyrights and patents.

intangible goods. Services, both commercial and personal (cf. TANGIBLE GOODS).

integration. *See* MERGERS.

Intelpost. A facsimile transmission service offered by the Royal Mail.

interbank market. The market on which banks borrow and lend large sums of money among themselves.

inter-dealer broker (Stock Exchange). Arranges anonymous deals between GILT-EDGED MARKET MAKERS (GEMMs).

interdependence. All members of society are mutually dependent on each other; producers are also consumers and the relationship is evident. The non-working population is dependent on producers; if there were no dependent sectors (the old, the young, the sick) the need for many services and goods would not exist. Similarly, businesses are interdependent, the producer/consumer relationship again applying.

interest. 1. (finance) The price paid for the hire of money by the hirer, and received by the lender of money. (The same rates do not apply to borrowing and lending.) Interest is a reward paid to lenders for the use of capital. 2. *See* INSURABLE INTEREST.

interest-bearing eligible liabilities (IBELS). The interest–bearing element of ELIGIBLE LIABILITIES.

interest rates. Domestic interest rates printed daily in the press are: the bank base rate; the finance houses base rate; the discount market loans rate; interbank rates.

interest yield (Stock Exchange). The coupon rate related to the market price of a GILT.

interface (computers). A connection between two units of apparatus with different functions.

interim dividend (Stock Exchange). A dividend declared part of the way through a company's financial year which is authorised solely by the directors.

intermediary. A 'go between' in a business transaction.

internal audit. *See* AUDIT.

internal methods of communication. Methods used for all types of communication within the same firm or organisation. These include memoranda, message pads, messengers, circulation slips, paging and public address systems, internal telephone systems. *See also* ELECTRONIC OFFICE.

internal rate of return (IRR). An investment appraisal technique which uses discount tables to compare alternative projects.

International Bank for Reconstruction and Development (IBRD). Commonly called the World Bank. Its function is to assist in the reconstruction and development of member countries by facilitating the investment of capital. The IBRD raises funds by the sale of stock to member countries and from the issue of bonds in the world's financial markets.

International Chamber of Commerce (ICC United Kingdom). Organisation which publishes a range of booklets on payments and documentation for those engaged in international trade.

International Commodities Clearing House (ICCH). Deposits or margins on soft commodity futures contracts are lodged with the ICCH in London, an independent organisation which acts not only as a clearing agent, but as guarantor for deals on the London, Paris and Australian markets.

international company/corporation. A multinational firm which operates outside its own country of origin as well as in it.

International Labour Organisation (ILO). An inter-governmental agency; employers and workers as well as governments take part in its work. Its three major areas of interest are: human resources and economic development; the development of labour relations and social institutions in the labour field; living and working conditions, with special reference to labour legislation, social security and occupational safety and health.

International Monetary Fund (IMF). Established in Washington in 1945, this may be regarded as a cooperative deposit bank. The objectives of the IMF are: to assist nations with temporary balance of payment problems; to provide guidelines for economic policy to nations with a permanent disequilibrium on their foreign trading; to monitor foreign exchange rates. *See* SPECIAL DRAWING RIGHTS (SDR).

international paper sizes. The 'A' series:

A1	594 mm × 841 mm	Large sheets for plans and artwork
A2	420 mm × 594 mm	
A3	297 mm × 420 mm	Legal documents, charts, plans and posters
A4	210 mm × 297 mm	Letters (business and official), legal and technical work, reports, minutes, agendas, literary work
A5*	148 mm × 210 mm	Letters (short business and official), inter-departmental correspondence (memoranda), actors' parts

*A5 paper when used with the shorter edge at the top is known as *portrait*
*A5 paper when used with the longer edge at the top is known as *landscape*

A6	105 mm × 148 mm	Message pads, petty cash vouchers, requisitions, acknowledgment cards
A7	74 mm × 105 mm	Compliments slips, circulation slips, receipts
A8	52 mm × 74 mm	Visiting (business) cards

International Petroleum Exchange (IPE). London futures market for the oil industry.

International Reply Coupon. It is not possible to send a stamped and addressed envelope to anyone abroad or in the Commonwealth. Reply coupons may be bought at the post office and should be enclosed with the letter requiring a reply together with an addressed envelope. The addressee can then exchange his Reply Coupon at a post office for the appropriate stamps of his own country, which he then affixes to the envelope.

international trade. *See* EXPORT TRADE and IMPORT TRADE.

Intervention Board. *See* COMMON AGRICULTURAL POLICY.

intra vires. A legal expression meaning within the power of the person or body concerned (cf. *ultra vires*).

introduction (Stock Exchange). A method of bringing a company to the market. No new securities are issued. Allowed where shares issued are of such an amount and so widely held that their marketability when listed can be assured.

inventory. 1. A list of stock or equipment; a catalogue. *See* ANNUAL INVENTORY and PERPETUAL INVENTORY 2. (North American) The quantity of goods, components, or raw materials on hand in the production process.

investment. A sum of money invested for income or profit; the word also applies to the asset (e.g. property) purchased. Investment in an organisation enables it to expand and so increase production; it is the key to growth of wealth. The amount of money available for investment is determined by the level of spending by consumers on finished goods and services. Investment can take place only when people and organisations save some of their income so that it can be invested to increase production.

investment appraisal. Two considerations must be taken into account when an investment is under review. First, the cost of the projected investment; secondly, the benefits which are expected to accrue. *See* COST BENEFIT ANALYSIS, DISCOUNTED CASH FLOW, INTERNAL RATE OF RETURN, PAYBACK METHOD.

Investment Management Regulatory Organisation (IMRO). Self-regulatory organisation of the Stock Exchange covering those managing the main forms of pooled investment (investment and unit trusts and pension funds).

investment trust. Company whose sole interest consists of buying, selling and holding shares.

Investors in Industry (3i). 3i is owned by nine London and Scottish banks (85 per cent) and by the Bank of England (15 per cent); it is an independent private sector group whose business is the creative use of money. They provide long-term and permanent capital to businesses of all sizes, through innovative investment schemes tailored to meet their individual requirements. For companies seeking advice rather than capital, they have management consultancy, corporate advisory and portfolio management services. Most business is done in the UK but 3i is now established in Europe and the USA, both important UK export markets and sources of technology. The group has a unique knowledge of the small company sector, but invests in businesses of all sizes, from small-scale family firms to major multinational companies.

invisible trade. This involves invisible earnings – the export and import of services as opposed to goods. *Invisible earnings* (exports) make a substantial contribution to the UK's balance of payments; these consist primarily of shipping and banking services, interest on loans and overseas commitments undertaken by insurance in the British insurance market, and tourism (including the arts). *Invisible imports* into Great Britain consist mainly of British government spending overseas, expenditure by British tourists abroad, and additional imports of services.

invoice. In *home trade* this is the bill for payment for goods or services rendered and is sent from the seller to the buyer; it gives details of the goods or services to be paid for, names the terms and any discounts, and shows the method of delivery. *See* TRANSACTIONS. In *international trade* it is the export invoice/commercial invoice; there are certain requirements of an export invoice which do not have to be considered for home market transactions. All the following information should be included: name and address of the supplier and the buyer; date and reference number of the buyer's order; details of packages and individual contents, with package numbers; net gross weights and measurements of packages; total value of invoice (but not including cash discount); details of terms of sale (fob, cif, etc.) and port of destination. *See also* CONSULAR INVOICE.

inward missions. The BOTB can often provide financial support when groups of business people, journalists and others from abroad organise visits to this country to purchase British goods or services.

inward processing relief (IPR) (Customs and Excise). Manufacturers who import goods from outside the European Community, then process and export them, may be able to save customs duty by using IPR; this gives relief from customs duty, agricultural charges, and anti-dumping duty, if certain rules are met. There are two methods available: *Suspension* – where the duty is not paid at import, as long as the manufacturer exports the goods or the products made from them. *Drawback* – where the duty is paid at import and claimed back if the goods or the products made from them are exported. (Drawback is used if there is no established or projected pattern of exports.)

IOU. These documents have no legal properties. The debtor in accepting an IOU is simply taking a written acknowledgement of a debt.

irrevocable credits (letters of credit). Once established, and confirmed by a bank in the exporter's country, an irrevocable credit may not be revoked by the overseas buyer, and therefore offers complete security for the exporter.

Issue Department. *See* BANK OF ENGLAND.

issued (share) capital. *See* CAPITAL.

issuing houses. Some merchant banks are issuing houses and organise the sale of shares for public limited companies. The company will sell its new securities to an issuing house which then offers the shares by an '*offer for sale*' to the public. In general, a PROSPECTUS must be printed in two national newspapers; as the public applies for the shares, the issuing house renounces its rights so that the purchasers become allottees of the company. Copies of the 'offer for sale' must be lodged with the Registrar of Companies. *Placing* is a method of bringing the shares of smaller companies to the market. The issuing house may subscribe for the securities, then invite institutional investors to buy them in block. There is no invitation to the public.

itinerary. A plan or record of a business journey or trip. Itineraries should show the departure and arrival times of trains, flights, etc., the hotels at which bookings have been made, a list of appointments, meetings, etc., together with names and telephone numbers.

J

job analysis. Involves the breaking down of a particular job into the different skills and knowledge required for its performance. Its purpose is to produce a job description or specification for a particular position in an organisation.

job costing. Method of costing that is particularly appropriate for firms such as builders or contractors, where each job or contract is regarded as a separate and distinct unit.

job description/profile/specification. Sometimes given to applicants for a position in a firm or organisation, it lists the tasks involved in the job, and identifies the position of the particular post in the overall organisation. *A job description/profile* is a broad statement of the purpose, scope, duties and responsibilities of a particular job. *A job specification* is a more detailed statement of the physical and mental activities involved in the job.

job enlargement/enrichment. Give employees experience of jobs with different levels of difficulty and responsibility in their own organisation, thereby giving greater job satisfaction and less likelihood of stress.

job evaluation. Determination of the value of a particular job relative to others. One method is to identify the characteristics of a job which are held to deserve payment – skill, experience, responsibility, etc. – and weight these according to their relative importance to arrive at a total points score for each job. The total points will decide where on the job scale the job should be graded and the appropriate salary/wage decided.

'job' production. The production of 'one-off' individual items which do not lend themselves to mass production; often the work is highly skilled and labour-intensive.

job rotation. Allows employees in an organisation to be moved from one job to another of the same level of difficulty and responsibility; it is designed to relieve monotony and boredom.

job sharing. Where two people share the responsibility of a job; hours, pay and benefits are agreed between the employer and the employees.

joint consultation. Joint consultation committees consist of representatives from all levels of an organisation. They provide an opportunity for employers and employees to discuss the impact of policy decisions, and matters relating to welfare, training and discipline.

Joint European Torus (JET). The JET development is the construction near Oxford of one of the most powerful experimental stations in the world. It was launched by the EEC to research the production of energy by nuclear fusion rather than by nuclear fission.

joint stock company. *See* COMPANY and LIMITED LIABILITY.

journal. An accounting book of original entry. The types of entries that would be passed through the journal are correction of errors, sales of worn-out or obsolete assets, the issue of shares or debentures, goodwill valuations, and some adjustments to final accounts.

judiciary. One of the three divisions of government, the others being the Cabinet (the executive) and the legislature. The judicial function is to interpret the laws passed by Parliament, and the law courts provide the framework for the enforcement of the law.

justification (word processors). The process of inserting tiny spaces between letters in a word, or between words themselves, to make the last letter of each line appear at the right margin.

K

kangaroo closure. Method for controlling debate used in the House of Commons, where the chairman of a committee is empowered to 'jump' from one amendment to another, omitting those he considers to be repetitive or of minor importance. This saves time by cutting unnecessary discussion.

Keynesian policies. Keynes believed that the economy was not self-regulatory, and that it was up to the government to intervene with fiscal measures to ensure the level of aggregate demand. Government injections of extra purchasing power would maintain full employment and prosperity.

kilobyte (computers). A unit of measurement of memory or disk storage capacity. It equals 1,024 bytes or characters.

kitemark. The British Standards Institution approval mark which indicates that goods have been made to its standards.

Kondratieff curve. The term applied to long-term swings in economic activity named after its nineteenth-century discoverer. Kondratieff claimed that over a period of 50 or 60 years one could find evidence of a long general upswing in the economy followed by a similar decline.

L

labour (human resources). Factor of production which covers the productive services rendered by human beings; the man hours worked in production of all kinds, using man's ingenuity and skill in producing what is wanted by the community. Labour as a factor of production ranges from the work of the unskilled through the various ranks of specialists to the highest professional experts. All are producers doing all kinds of work which has to be paid for.

labour turnover. A measure for assessing the stability of a workforce. It is calculated by comparing staff replacements with the average number of full-time staff over a set period. Although labour turnover will vary from industry to industry and with the prevailing economic climate, a high relative labour turnover is considered damaging to a firm. It means increased costs in recruiting and training new staff, loss of efficiency while they are learning new duties, and often means low morale among other workers when staff keep leaving. If a problem exists, a check on working conditions and pay structures may suggest a solution; attention should also be paid to selection procedures and training programmes.

lading, bill of. *See* BILL OF LADING.

laissez-faire. 1. A doctrine opposing government interference in economic affairs. 2. *See* LEADERSHIP STYLES.

land. Land is one of the three factors of production (the others being labour and capital); the reward received by the factor land is commercial rent. In economics, land is also understood to include not just the land itself but all its geographical features and its products, such as minerals and forests, agricultural products, the seas and the products of the seas, rivers and lakes, water supplies and the gases of the atmosphere; in fact, all the natural resources of the earth. In common with all resources, they demand the best price which can be obtained on the market.

Land Register. A national register of titles to land.

large-scale production. Large-scale production is sometimes thought to be undesirable as it tends towards monopoly; it also faces central management with ever-widening and less accessible areas to control. Nowadays, with computerisation, it is much easier to run a large-scale enterprise and inevitably successful firms will get larger. The 'economies of scale' which attend such large enterprises still exist and may be summarised as follows: the ability to effect bulk transactions; the use of expensive work-study and O & M techniques, possible only in large organisations, which produces a more efficient use of human resources and machinery and better production planning; the diversification of output, markets, sources of supply and processes of manufacture which help to maintain satisfactory output when breakdowns occur in any area, including the spreading of resources to reduce vulnerability.

laser printer (computers). Type of printer which uses a combination of laser, computer and photocopying techniques.

last in, first out (LIFO). In valuation of stock, LIFO implies that goods were part of the initial delivery and would be valued as such.

launder. To convert money which has been obtained illegally into a form where it can be used legitimately.

law, classification of. The principal sources of English law are legislation and the principles worked out in decided cases in the courts (judicial precedent or case law). *Public law* involves: administrative law; constitutional law; criminal law. *Private law (civil law)* involves: company law; family law; law of contract; law of succession; law of torts; law of trusts. In 1972 the UK joined the European Community and thereby added a new source of law to those already existing. European law covers very few subjects, but if it is different from English law, it prevails over it.

law of demand and supply. *See* DEMAND AND SUPPLY, LAW OF.

law of diminishing returns. *See* DIMINISHING RETURNS, LAW OF.

lead time. The time between the initiation and the completion of a new production process.

leadership styles. Styles of leadership in an organisation can be classified as follows: *Authoritarian (autocratic)* – where managers, supervisors and foremen order subordinates to perform tasks; it produces little feedback. *Democratic style* – which encourages worker participation and feedback. *Laissez-faire* (from a French word meaning 'let alone') – allows the workforce to operate with little control. It encourages workers to make their own decisions.

leasehold land. A tenure of land by lease. As the name implies the tenure has a definite date of ending (cf. the indefinite end of a *freehold* estate).

leasing. If a business is expanding, or if it finds it necessary to replace outdated capital equipment, cost has to be considered. Leasing is a possible solution; it is simple, efficient and inflation-proof, and a flexible form of medium-term finance. The equipment is selected by the firm that requires it, and this firm negotiates the purchase terms with the seller. The financier – usually a merchant or commercial bank – will then place the order, and the firm requiring the equipment will lease the goods from the bank for an agreed period. The bank will claim the capital allowances and any regional development grants from the government, and this is passed on to the leasing firm in the form of reduced rentals. Usually the rental is fixed at the outset, so the firm's budget is not pressurised by increases in interest rates, tax changes, or inflation, since the rental payments will be coming out of future earnings. Leasing can be the most economical way of financing new capital equipment without laying out capital. Most large leasing organisations are members of the Equipment Leasing Association (ELA).

ledger. The principal book of accounts required for a proper record of all the transactions of a business. In theory the ledger is one book, but in practice it is convenient to divide the book into several volumes – the sales ledger, purchase/bought ledger, and the general (nominal) ledger.

legal aid. A system under which those whose means are insufficient to enable them to pay for legal representation may have their legal costs paid wholly or in part from public funds (Legal Aid and Advice Act 1949).

legal rights. Legal rights stem from the COMMON LAW; a legal estate is a right to hold land that the common law will recognise.

legal tender. Under the law of legal tender, a creditor cannot refuse payment of a debt in notes and coins of the realm. Any debt may be settled by payment in notes, which are legal tender up to any amount. The £1 coin is also legal tender to any amount. Other limits to legal tender are as follows:

Up to £20 may be paid in 50p coins
Up to £10 may be paid in 20p coins or crowns (25p)
Up to £5 may be paid in 5p and 10p coins
Up to 20p may be paid in 1p and 2p coins

legislation. The legislative function of the government is performed by the Queen in Parliament; the UK Parliament legislates (makes laws) through its two chambers – the House of Commons and the House of Lords. A bill may be introduced in either House of Parliament, passed by both Houses, and formerly assented to by the Crown. Sometimes delegated powers of legislation are conferred on local authorities and statutory undertakings to make rules such as by-laws, which come under the general heading of delegated legislation. Legislation regulates and controls society, implements the fiscal policies of the government, and creates, repeals, revises or reforms the law.

lender of last resort (Bank of England). It sometimes happens that those who have deposited money at the DISCOUNT HOUSES demand immediate payment; this may leave the discount houses 'short' because they will probably have lent their borrowed money for three months or even longer. They endeavour to obtain money from every source available, but if they fail are forced to turn to the Bank of England – the lender of last resort – and pay at a high rate of interest which will probably involve them in a loss.

letter of credit. Document in the form of a letter given by a bank to a client. It serves to introduce the client to that bank's branches or agents, to whom the letter is addressed, and authorises them to make payments in favour of the client up to the amount stated in the letter of credit. On the back of the letter, columns are ruled for details of the payments made, and after payment of the last amount the letter of credit is returned to the issuing bank. An importer may arrange to pay the exporter by means of a letter of credit. The importer sends a letter of credit with his order, and the exporter can then collect payment by presenting the signed bill of lading to his bank. This is a common method of settlement, but denies the period of credit possible where payment is made by means of the bill of exchange. There are three principal categories of letters of credit: The *unconfirmed irrevocable letter of credit* is opened through an overseas bank and *not* confirmed by a bank in the country of the exporter. Such a credit can only be cancelled or revoked with the consent of the exporter and does provide the exporter with a certain measure of protection. The *irrevocable and confirmed credit* is also opened through an overseas bank but *is* confirmed by a bank in the exporter's country, thus ensuring that the exporter is paid promptly on presentation of the specified documents. The *revocable credit*, which can be revoked at any time by the overseas buyer, is rarely used.

letter of indemnity. Request to a company's registrar to issue a replacement stock or share certificate when the original has been lost, destroyed or stolen. In it the holder undertakes to indemnify the company for any loss incurred as a result of issuing a duplicate document; most companies require this undertaking to be countersigned by a bank or insurance company.

letter of renunciation (stocks and shares). Form attached to an allotment letter which is filled in should the original holder wish to pass his entitlement to someone else.

leverage. *See* CAPITAL GEARING.

liabilities, current. The current liabilities of an organisation can include trade creditors (for goods supplied), expense creditors (for services supplied), and bank overdraft.

liability. 1. When a dispute occurs which is taken to law the courts decide which person or organisation represented in the case is liable (i.e. responsible) for any wrongful act. 2. *See* LIMITED LIABILITY.

liability, insurance of. *See* ACCIDENT INSURANCE.

licensed deposit-takers (LDTs). Institutions licensed by the BANK OF ENGLAND to take deposits from the public. Licensed institutions and recognised banks (together with a few other institutions) make up the monetary sector.

life assurance. The term assurance is often applied especially to *life* as distinct from fire and other classes of insurance, but in fact the words assurance and insurance are used indiscriminately. Death or physical injury cannot be indemnified – life assurance policies provide benefits rather than compensation. The aims of the various policies vary; they may cover the death or retirement of the insured, or provide for dependents. In certain cases, building societies may insist that a mortgage be backed by life assurance, so that in the event of the mortgagor's death dependents own the property without further repayments.

Life Assurance and Unit Trusts Regulatory Organisation (LAUTRO). A self-regulatory organisation of the London International Stock Exchange.

light pen (computers). Photoelectric device that is pointed at a VDU to create or identify characters, symbols, etc. for input into a computer.

limited company. *See* COMPANY.

limited liability (of companies and partnerships). Both public and private limited companies have limited liability, which means that the personal liability of the owners is restricted to the amount of each investor's stake in the company – they have limited liability for the company's debts. *Company limited by share* means that the extent of the member's risk is limited to the amount of his shareholding (all companies quoted on the Stock Exchange are in this category). *Company limited by guarantee* may or may not have share capital. The guarantee consists of an undertaking by members to contribute up to a stated amount in the event of winding up, such a guarantee being incorporated in the Memorandum of Association. *Limited partners* are accorded the privilege of limited liability. *Unlimited liability* means that in the event of loss all the members would be liable for all the debts which have been incurred, and would have to sell their private possessions to repay the debts.

limited partner. *See* PARTNERS.

line and staff organisation. Organisation where instructions are passed along lines in a hierarchy (LINE MANAGEMENT – which can be illustrated by an hierarchical chart), but which also employs specialists in an advisory or consultative capacity; these specialists support the whole organisational structure but have no authority over it.

line graph. By using distinctive lines, many different statistics can be shown on the same graph; such a graph is suitable for depicting fluctuations and trends.

line graphics (word processors). A feature of some word processors whereby boxes can be put around text, and horizontal and vertical lines drawn.

line management/organisation. Where an organisation is classified into successively subordinate grades (a hierarchy) which can be illustrated by an hierarchical organisation chart. Instructions are passed along lines in the hierarchy which also shows the formal relationship between departments. Authority and responsibility are passed downwards, accountability upwards.

line printer (computers). A printing unit connected to a computer or word processor.

line-spacing (word processing). The number of lines in a vertical inch of paper, normally 6 single spaces. Line-spacing can be set for single, double, half or one-and-a-half spacing.

liner (cargo). Nearly all cargo liners take loads from major ports and have a few cabins for passengers; most passenger liners are now cruise liners used for holidays at sea.

liner conferences. The International Chamber of Commerce, which represents liners' customers, approves the system of liner conferences which charge a steady rate for carrying cargo, unlike 'tramps' whose freight rates fluctuate with supply and demand. As long as customers are 'regular' customers, rebates are allowed, and the service provides security and reliability.

liquid assets. *See* ASSETS.

liquid capital. *See* CAPITAL (TYPES OF).

liquid (capital) ratio. *See* ACID TEST RATIO.

liquidation. A company may cease to exist by winding up or liquidation. The appointed liquidator proceeds to realise the assets and pay off the creditors, after which the company is dissolved and ceases to exist.

liquidity. The ease with which a firm can convert its assets (such as debtors and stock held) into cash. The following is a list of liquid assets (in descending order of liquidity): cash; current account deposits at banks; other bank deposits and deposits at non-bank financial intermediaries (NBFIs); short-term securities (bills and bonds) which can be sold for money on organised markets (note that the price of securities tends to fluctuate); long-term securities; physical assets such as property and machines which may be sold, though the prices they fetch may be very uncertain.

liquidity ratio (banking). Early bankers observed that only about 8 per cent of their customers' funds were likely to be demanded in cash at any time (the *cash ratio*) (which left them free to lend the remaining 92 per cent at interest). In order to meet any sudden demands for cash, bankers keep a further 20 per cent of their deposits in 'near-cash' investments which can be turned back into cash immediately. These investments plus the *cash ratio* form the bank's *liquidity ratio*, which is about one-third of the bank's total deposits. (With depositors' interests in mind, laws and regulations have been drawn up to ensure that banks, under the supervision of the Bank of England, are run by competent trustworthy people who do not take excessive risks with their depositors' money.)

list processing (word processing). A feature of most word processors which allows a list of variable information to be created and automatically included within a standard piece of text. For example, when a list of names and addresses is created, together with a reminder notice, the system automatically includes the name and address in the notice, and produces a letter for each individual.

listed company (Stock Exchange). A company that has obtained permission for its shares to be admitted to the International Stock Exchange's *Official List.*

listing particulars (Stock Exchange). Details a company must publish about itself and any securities it issues before these can be listed on any stock exchange in the European Community.

litigation. The carrying out of an action in law. The process of carrying on a judicial contest.

Lloyd's brokers. All business is brought to Lloyd's insurance market by Lloyd's brokers who represent the public and who obtain for their clients the best insurance terms available.

Lloyd's Corporation (Lloyd's of London). The London insurance market. The Society of Lloyd's was first incorporated by Act of Parliament in 1871, and is controlled by an elected committee of twelve members. The actual insurance is effected by UNDERWRITERS. It is the modern practice for them to work in syndicates, sharing the risks they insure; they may not be approached by members of the public – a Lloyd's broker is the middleman who acts as an agent between the public and the underwriters. Traditionally, Lloyd's is noted for marine insurance (which now includes aviation), but in fact it carries on business in all classes of insurance, though the bulk of insurance in Britain is transacted through the large composite companies.

Lloyd's List. Published daily; in it is recorded all the shipping information available on a worldwide scale. It is Lloyd's own and London's oldest daily newspaper. In addition to general shipping news, it gives arrivals and sailings of merchant vessels throughout the world besides coverage of marine and aircraft casualties.

Lloyd's Register of Shipping (Lloyd's Shipping Index.) This gives full descriptions of 20,000 ocean-going vessels, current voyages and latest reported positions; also the classification of ships according to their strength and efficiency for carrying cargo.

Lloyd's syndicates (insurance). A syndicate is a combination of firms for some common purpose or interest. The Lloyd's syndicate system developed from an old-time practice whereby an UNDERWRITER would 'write a line' on behalf of others. Members of a syndicate take no part in the mechanics of underwriting, which is left to the syndicate's professional manager, who corrects an imbalance on his books by REINSURANCE. A Lloyd's member is not confined to one syndicate, and often works in both the marine and non-marine sectors.

Lloyd's underwriters. Members of Lloyd's Corporation who alone may accept insurance risks in Lloyd's insurance market. They must be elected and prove their financial ability to the satisfaction of the committee of Lloyd's. Most of the members are private individuals who accept unlimited liability; they guarantee that the required amount of money will be available for an insurance risk. They are formed into LLOYD'S SYNDICATES – groups of a few to several hundred individuals – which are represented at Lloyd's by underwriting agents who accept insurance risks on behalf of members of their syndicates. All business is brought to Lloyd's by brokers who obtain for their clients the best terms available in the competitive market.

loan. 1. Bank loans may be made for a specific reason and for an agreed length of time. Interest is paid on the loan, repayment of which may be by instalments or a lump sum. Collateral security may be asked for by the bank for the duration of the loan. To be granted a bank loan, the client need not necessarily be already a customer of that bank. 2. DEBENTURES – loans to a company which can be bought and sold on the Stock Exchange. These are fixed-interest loans made to a company and are issued with specific terms regarding interest, capital repayment and security, and are usually redeemable on a set date.

loan capital. Money a company has borrowed, either on mortgage or by the issue of DEBENTURES.

Loan Guarantee Scheme. This government scheme does not provide money for businesses but removes part of the risk for traditional lenders. If a business fails, the government reimburses the lending bank 70 per cent of its advance.

loan stock (Stock Exchange). Stock bearing a fixed rate of interest. Unlike a DEBENTURE, loan stocks may be unsecured, i.e. not backed by any of the company's assets.

local authorities/local government. Local authorities or councils are given the power by a number of statutes to administer many services in their own areas; local government is supervised by the Department of the Environment. There are three levels in the local authority system: parish councils, borough/district councils, and county councils. They can finance business activities by issuing municipal stock or by raising loans; they may also receive government grants for their projects.

location of organisations. When deciding on a location an organisation will seek the most economic site. *Primary industries* are of necessity located at the source of the product. *Manufacturing (secondary) industry* must consider its proximity to raw materials, energy and labour; transport costs can be relatively high if they are incurred – especially in supplying the market. Proximity to the centre of a good transport network is essential. *Service industries* must be available where required and have little choice in the location of their businesses. The government influences firms by offering attractive regional grants and loans to firms who will locate (or relocate) in areas of high unemployment.

loco price. The price of goods as they lie in the seller's warehouse, or some other specified place, at the time of sale. In cases where packing is necessary, the buyer has to bear the extra cost of this, and he has likewise to pay the cost of transport to his own warehouse.

logic (computers). That part of the central processor responsible for internal processing of the data.

logic-seeking (computers). A characteristic of printers which effectively skip over any blank spaces in text, thereby achieving much faster printing speeds.

Lomé Convention. An agreement between the European Community and African, Caribbean and Pacific states. Besides providing financial assistance, the European Community is almost entirely open to exports from the sixty developing countries which are parties to the convention.

London Bankers' Clearing House. *See* CLEARING BANKS.

London Commodity Exchange Group. Terminal or '*futures*' markets in 'soft' commodities – cocoa, coffee, sugar, rubber, vegetable oil, soya bean meal and wool – are operated on this exchange, which also provides a centralised market for all kinds of cereals produced in Britain.

London Discount Market Association (LDMA). *See* DISCOUNT HOUSES.

London Foreign Bond Market. Although most issues of foreign bonds are listed on the STOCK EXCHANGE or on a continental bourse, dealing is mostly by international dealers and largely takes place over the telephone.

London International Financial Futures Exchange (LIFFE). London market for speculative and hedging transactions in currencies and financial securities.

London Metal Exchange (LME). The primary function of the LME is to provide a protective mechanism against price fluctuations for producers, merchants and users of metal – copper, lead, zinc, nickel, aluminium and silver are all traded. This mechanism is the terminal market where sales and purchases can be covered by HEDGING which attracts speculators. In the past, 'ring trading' – members stood around a chalk circle drawn on the floor and conducted their business by 'open outcry' – was confined to copper and tin; now grading has been extended to a range of metals which makes it possible for ring trading to take place, but the ring now consists of a circle of curved benches. In the LME the buyer and seller are directly responsible to each other for carrying out the deal as agreed.

London Options Clearing House (LOCH). With a TRADED OPTION the buyer and seller each has an option with the LOCH, a special corporation controlled by the Council of the STOCK EXCHANGE. A traded option has a market price which can be traded from day to day, and has a life of up to nine months; it can be bought and sold throughout its period of currency.

longs/long gilts (Stock Exchange). Gilt-edged securities without a redemption date within fifteen years.

loss leader. An item sold at a loss by a retailer to attract other custom.

Lutine bell. Bell which was salvaged from HMS *Lutine* (which sank in 1799 with a cargo of gold bullion which has never been recovered), and which is now in Lloyd's of London. The bell is now rung mainly for ceremonial occasions but used to signal news about overdue vessels. One stroke may still be sounded for bad news and two strokes for good news.

M

M0 (m-zero), M1, M2, M3, etc. *See* MONEY STOCK.

machine language (computers). A programming language consisting of instructions in binary code, with which a computer works.

macroeconomics. The study of the aggregate flows of expenditure between households and firms, and through the financial markets; the overall working of, and interconnections between, the markets in goods, in factors, and in finance (cf. microeconomics).

mail order. There are three main types of mail order business. The most familiar is the very large mail order firm which sells through expensively produced catalogues, operating through agents (usually housewives) who receive a commission. One of the attractions of such buying (mostly of clothes and other non-durable goods) is that customers are allowed to buy on credit – usually over 20 weeks – the basis of the transaction being a credit-sale agreement. These large firms combine the roles of wholesaler and retailer, thereby gaining the profits of both functions. A further financial advantage is that they operate from premises which need not be easily accessible and need not, therefore, be situated in 'prime' or expensive sites. In addition, by dealing in very large quantities they enjoy the economies of bulk buying. On the other hand, these large mail order companies have enormous postage bills and pay all their agents a commission. They are also particularly vulnerable to bad debts. The second method of selling by mail order is by advertising in the daily press and magazines; this is done by manufacturers, wholesalers and retailers. The advertisement requires a direct response from the buyer, who is thereafter kept on the advertiser's mailing list. A third method is by the use of a mailing list. A firm may send advertising literature through the post to selected addresses – their names being usually obtained from a mailing list which a supplier has bought.

mailbox systems (computers). *See* ELECTRONIC OFFICE.

mail-handling equipment. *See* ELECTRONIC OFFICE.

mainframe computers. Extensive corporate systems which meet the needs of very large multi-user organisations.

man specification. *See* PERSONNEL SPECIFICATION.

management. An organisation's policy decisions must be put into effect by those in management, and those in management must not only be good organisers but also possess the qualities of leadership. All managers are experts in a particular departmental function, be it marketing, finance, personnel, production or office administration; managers must implement policy decisions by planning, coordinating and organising their departments to obtain an optimum result, working at all times within budgetary controls. 'Reporting back' – for example, in the case of a limited company to the managing director – is a managerial function which is extremely important. It is from departmental reports that top management is able to assess whether policy decisions are being implemented and how successful they are.

management accounting. The production of financial information for use by management in planning, decision-making and forecasting (budgeting). Management is concerned with frequent and detailed operating results of all aspects of a firm's activities.

management buyout. A group of managers within a large industrial company set out to own a whole (or part) of the business they run and then to operate it as a separate entity. Buyouts are usually financed by VENTURE CAPITAL supplied by a member of the British Venture Capital Association. See INVESTORS IN INDUSTRY (3i).

management by objectives. A management approach which begins with a broad statement of what a company seeks to achieve over a planned period, its aim being the improvement in company performance and the motivation, assessment and training of its employees. It makes the company's goals the concern of every manager.

management information systems. A central, formalised system (commonly computerised) for providing an organisation's management with the information they need to make decisions.

management styles. *See* AUTHORITY.

managing director (MD). The Articles of Association usually give authority to the board of directors to appoint a managing director who, after the chairman, is the most important member of the board. As the chief administrative officer, he has the responsibility of running the organisation according to the decisions made by the board.

mandamus. A command issued from a higher court to a lower court.

manifest. A shipping document which lists all the different packages and items of freight on board a particular vessel.

manpower planning. Forecasting how many and what kind of employees the organisation will have need of in the future – or possible reductions of the workforce. Considerations are the company's policies regarding recruitment, training, promotion, redundancy and retirement; also labour costs and provision of office and factory space for the workforce.

manuals. Booklets which set out the established practices of an organisation, providing a reference for employees. They can cover a wide field, and may include detailed instructions on routine tasks, such as the way in which company letters should be displayed.

manufacturing account. In the case of a manufacturing business, this account contains the items relating to the complete cost of manufacture – the costs of raw materials, direct labour and direct expenses, together with factory overheads.

manufacturing industry. The second tier of production, involving the use of the raw materials of primary production in the production of manufactured goods; it changes the form of raw materials. It requires materials, power and labour; choice of location is often dictated by their ready availability. Manufacturing industry also covers all building and constructive work.

margin. Money put up as security that a contract will be fulfilled. A margin is usually deposited with the clearing house of a COMMODITY EXCHANGE.

margin call. If the market moves against an investor after he has entered into a FUTURES contract, the broker will ask him to provide more money to top up the deposit payment to cover his loss and maintain the deposit at the original percentage level. A margin call is normally made when one quarter to one half of the original deposit has been lost.

marginal costing. A technique for ascertaining the marginal cost of a product, i.e. the amount by which aggregate costs are changed if the output is increased or decreased by one unit. In marginal costing, *fixed expenses* do not form part of the marginal cost, as they are incurred irrespective of the volume of output.

marginal propensity to consume (MPC). A disposition to spend on consumption any increase in income, expressed as a fraction of the increment.

marginal propensity to save (MPS). A disposition to save any increase in income, expressed as a fraction of the increment.

marginal revenue. The increase in total revenue to be achieved by selling one further unit of output.

marginal utility. The term 'utility' means the satisfaction which, at a given time, is derived from a good or service. The utility derived from the last unit purchased by a consumer is known as marginal utility. The law of diminishing marginal utility is based on the principle that the more a person possesses of a particular commodity, the less satisfaction he will derive from a further increase. The law states that as a general rule the marginal utility of a commodity will diminish with every increase in the supply of the product. Money is considered to be an important exception.

marine insurance. Mostly transacted by LLOYD'S UNDERWRITERS, it is of particular importance to shipowners. Apart from hull, cargo and freight insurance, which are treated separately under their own headings, the shipowner is faced with many risks against which he can insure. These include events which may result from his own or his employees' negligence; examples are collision with other vessels or shore installations, injuries to those on board, and water pollution. An FPA (free of particular average) policy covers only against total loss; a WPA (with particular average) policy covers against all risks (aar).

market. 1. The market system assumes that prospective buyers and sellers satisfy their needs by the PRICE MECHANISM, particularly if there is a choice of identical products. 2. A place where buyers and sellers are in contact with each other. The main categories of market are as follows (each type shown is treated fully under its own title): retail trade; wholesale trade; the commodity markets; Baltic Mercantile and Shipping Exchange; the financial markets: discount market, Eurocurrency market, foreign exchange, Lloyd's insurance market, money market, and the Stock Exchange; produce exchanges. There are many different methods of dealing (*see* challenging, private treaty, ring trading, 'open outcry'). *See also* 'SPOT' DEALING and FUTURES.

market forces. *See* PRICE MECHANISM.

market-maker. An International Stock Exchange *Member Firm* which is obliged to buy and sell securities in which it is registered as a principal, at all times.

market mechanism. The market mechanism (system) assumes that prospective buyers and sellers satisfy their needs and wants by the mechanism of price, particularly if the products are identical. *See* SUPPLY AND DEMAND (LAW OF).

market(ing) mix. The marketing strategy of an organisation covering the types of product manufactured, pricing, marketing, promotions, advertising, etc, and the methods of distribution.

market overt. Open or public market.

market price. The short-term equilibrium price on the market which equates demand and supply.

market research. Supplying information to manufacturers and wholesalers about consumer market trends. Data may be collected by observation, mailing, questionnaires, telephone, or interview. *See* MARKETING.

market segment (marketing). An identifiable sector of the market to which special marketing strategies are applied.

marketing. Discovering what the customer wants and selling it to him. The results of this research are applied to product (or service) design, production planning, post-production storage, distribution, delivery to wholesalers/retail outlets/customers, advertising and, finally, successful sales.

The public image of the organisation and its products or services is fundamental to the marketing function. *Market research and analysis* is concerned with present and future needs of users, monitors present and potential competition in the field, and consumer trends and preferences. *Desk research* consists of analysing in-house information over a previous period, so that trends and tendencies can be identified; it also involves the analysis of statistics published by official bodies and trade associations, and should reveal the potential market and size of the market for a projected product or service. *Field research* involves actual entry in the field in which the research is interested, SAMPLING the opinions of customers and clients first-hand. Many organisations undertake such market research on behalf of other businesses. *Planning.* Goods must be available in the right form and of the right quality; this is the function of secondary production (manufacturing). They must also be available at the right price, time and place; this is the function of tertiary production employing commercial services. Cooperation and coordination between research and development, basic engineering, production control, financial control, sales and promotional functions are essential to the successful marketing of a product, and the changing nature of demand makes it necessary for these coordinated functions to be constant factors during the life of a product. Specialised marketing activities include branding and packaging, merchandising, pricing, physical distribution, selling, advertising (large organisations make use of the services of advertising agencies), public relations and provision for after-sales service.

marketing boards. These were established in the 1930s by the Agricultural Marketing Acts which empowered ministers to set up marketing boards for agricultural produce, but they were only to be established on the initiative of independent farmers themselves. Marketing boards may be empowered to buy all produce from farmers, and have been associated with guaranteed prices and production grants.

marketing stimuli. The main stimuli which will influence a potential buyer of goods are: the product itself as having utility; attractive packaging; a fair price; advertising; and the buyer's attitude, particularly towards branded goods.

markup. Usually a percentage of the cost price, added to the cost price, to produce the selling price of an article.

mass production. The manufacture of goods on a huge scale by automation. Standardisation, simplification, and specialisation (division of labour) are essential to its success. To produce most goods at the lowest costs, the production lines should be kept going continuously.

mean. The average, or mean, of a group of numbers is the *sum* of all the numbers divided by the *number of numbers* in the group.

median. The value in the middle position of a series of values.

mediums/medium gilts. Gilt-edged securities with a redemption date between 7 – 15 years ahead.

medium-term financial strategy (MTFS). The collective term for the Conservative government's plans for monetary public spending and tax policies. The MTFS was introduced in 1980 and has involved the setting of targets and projections for monetary growth, public spending etc. for a number of years ahead.

meetings (committee). At the ANNUAL GENERAL MEETING of an association, club or society, a committee is elected to deal with the running of the organisation. Members of a committee attend regular meetings at which the activities of the organisation are discussed and decisions taken. The three *elected officers* of such committees are; the *chairman* who is responsible for the proper conduct of a meeting. All speakers should 'address the chair' – they must get permission from the chairman before they speak to the meeting. The *secretary* who is responsible for notifying members of the time, date and place of the forthcoming meeting, and also for the preparation of an agenda after consultation with the chairman. After the meeting the secretary writes up the minutes which are either distributed to the committee members before the meeting or read to the members at the next meeting. All correspondence is dealt with by the secretary; the *treasurer* who is responsible for all financial aspects, and prepares the financial report and accounts.

Before a meeting can commence a *quorum* must be present; this is the minimum number of persons necessary for the transaction of business at a meeting. The number is established when the constitution (or standing orders) of the association, club or society are drawn up. Within an organisation there may be a variety of committees, usually meeting at regular intervals. The general rules for committee meetings apply, but the secretary should be thoroughly conversant with the procedures applying to the particular committee and any 'rule of the house' which should be followed.

meetings (of limited companies). Company 'general meetings' of shareholders are of three types: *The statutory meeting.* This must be held not earlier than one month and not later than three months after the company is entitled to commence business. Its purpose is to inform members of the state of the company's affairs, and to give shareholders an opportunity to discuss any matter concerning the formation. *The annual general meeting (AGM)* of a limited company must be held at least once a year in addition to any other meetings in that year, and not more than fifteen months must elapse between one AGM and the next. If a company fails to hold an AGM, the DTI may call or direct the calling of a meeting. Matters generally dealt with at the AGM are: declaration of a dividend; presentation of the accounts and an auditor's report; submission of the directors' report (under the Employment Act 1982, this must include a statement showing how employee participation has been developed in the organisation); election of directors; appointment of auditors and fixing of their remuneration. *Extraordinary general meeting (EGM).* In addition to the AGM and any other general meetings of members, a company may hold an EGM at which the special business set out in the notice convening the meeting may be transacted. Other company's meetings may be held – e.g. meetings of a class of member, meetings of debenture holders, meetings of directors, and meetings relevant to winding up.

megabyte (computers). A unit of measurement of disk storage capacity, being 1,024,000 bytes or characters (i.e. 1,000K).

member firm. A trading firm of the International Stock Exchange, who may act as an agency broker on behalf of clients or as a market-maker.

Memorandum of Association (limited company). After obtaining clearance from the Registrar of Companies that the proposed name for the company is acceptable, the promoters join in signing, among other documents, the Memorandum of Association. This sets out: the proposed name for the company which must have after the name the word 'limited' for a private limited company, or PLC for a public limited company; the address of the company's registered office; the objects of the company; a statement that members' liability is limited; the amount of nominal share capital and its division into shares of fixed amounts; in the case of a company limited by guarantee a statement that each member undertakes to contribute to the assets of the company in the event of winding up (but not exceeding a specified amount).

memory (computers). A set of electronic components in which data is stored. Also known as immediate access store.

merchandising. A marketing term that describes the promotional activities (excluding media advertising) that are designed to stimulate purchasing at the point of sale. There are numerous forms employed in the marketplace; these include gift coupons, free samples, premium offers, competitions, and special in-store displays.

merchant. Middleman who trades on his own account.

merchant bank. The term merchant bank is properly applied only to the members of the Accepting Houses Committee – finance houses whose primary business is the finance of overseas trade, but which also raise capital for industrial expansion, and generally take care of mergers and takeovers and the needs of commercial and industrial companies. Some merchant banks are also 'issuing houses' which organise the sale of shares for public limited companies. The Gold and Silver Bullion Markets are operated by merchant bankers, who are also very active on the Foreign Exchange Market, especially in the issue of Eurobonds.

merge (word processors). To combine units of text, or to append one document to another, to form a new document.

mergers (of businesses). Firms agree to amalgamate to achieve rapid expansion. *Horizontal integration* involves the merging of firms which have an identical market, in order to gain greater geographical control. *Lateral integration* is the combination of firms with fairly similar markets. A *conglomerate merger* – a combination of firms with similar markets to achieve diversification – usually involves all the firms in the group with a common 'holding company'. Holding companies may also achieve *vertical integration*: by taking over the companies which supply raw materials or components *(backward vertical integration)*; or by taking over markets/retail outlets *(forward vertical integration)*.

merit good. Product or service provided by the government or local authorities to the community on a non-commercial basis according to their merit or need. Health and education are examples (cf. private good, public good).

merit rating. *See* STAFF APPRAISAL.

metal exchange. *See* LONDON METAL EXCHANGE.

method study. The critical examination and recording of work techniques with a view to developing and applying easier and more cost effective methods.

methods of dealing. There are four methods of dealing on the COMMODITY MARKETS; these are by auction, challenging, private treaty, and ring trading which are all explained under their own headings. *See also* 'OPEN OUTCRY'.

methods of payment. Prompt payment in cash or cash with order are recognised methods of payment. PROMISSORY NOTES and BILLS OF EXCHANGE are promises to pay by a certain date and are legally binding; they are therefore regarded as fairly secure methods of payment. The *clearing banks* offer current account customers the following payment facilities: banker's draft, bank giro credit, cheques, credit transfers, direct debits and standing orders. A banker's credit card is another method of payment, but not restricted to current account customers. *Girobank* also offers banker's drafts, Girobank cheques, Girobank payment services, direct debits, standing orders, and transfers to its current account customers.

(*Transcash* is a method of paying money into a Girobank current account to clear a debt if the payer does not have such an account himself.) The *Post Office* offers postal orders for the payment of small debts, and an international payments service. The *Royal Mail* offers a Cash on Delivery (COD) service. Many *building societies* now offer cheque systems. *See also* LETTER OF CREDIT, OPEN ACCOUNTS and ELECTRONIC FUNDS TRANSFER.

microcomputer. A general term describing personal computers which are mostly single-user.

microeconomics. The study of the 'small' elements of economics – individual buyers, sellers and firms (cf. macroeconomics).

microelectronics. A branch of electronics that deals with or produces miniaturised electronic circuits and components.

microfiche. Used in microfilming, these are single sheets of film which can hold a large number of individual documents.

microfilm/micrographics. *See* ELECTRONIC OFFICE.

microprocessor. A term which properly describes the single chip containing the central processing unit, but which is also used to mean the complete microcomputer system.

middle price (Stock Exchange). The price halfway between the two prices shown in the International Stock Exchange's Daily Official List under 'Quotation', or the average of both the buying and selling prices offered by the MARKET-MAKERS. The prices found in newspapers are normally their estimate of the middle price.

middleman. A commercial intermediary or wholesaler who acts between producers of primary products (such as perishable foodstuffs) and the retailer, or between manufacturers and the retailer.

minicomputer. Smaller than a mainframe computer, this will support a limited number of users at the same time.

minimum capital. *See* CAPITAL (TYPES OF).

minimum lending rate (MLR). In 1981 the Bank of England suspended its practice of setting the MLR formally every Thursday. Now it does on occasion designate the rate, which is the minimum rate of interest at which the Bank would normally lend to the discount houses.

minority shareholders. The right to make decisions concerning a company's affairs rests with those holding the majority holding power. If the majority support the directors there is nothing the minority can do about it, but provision is made for the protection of minorities where the majority rule operates against them unfairly; this can happen in the case of shareholders in a company which has merged or been taken over by another.

minutes. The written record of business transacted at a meeting, prepared by the secretary. As minutes may be required as evidence in a court of law they must give a precise account of the proceedings. The chairman usually signs the minutes at the subsequent meeting after their accuracy has been verified.

Misrepresentation Act 1967. The Misrepresentation Act established that innocent, negligent or fraudulent misrepresentation invalidates a contract.

mixed economy. Mixed economies – such as that of the United Kingdom – have a mixture of public and private enterprise.

mnemonics (word processors). A memory aid; as applied to word processing, it is a code consisting of a few characters, which instructs the word processor to carry out a certain task.

mobile shop. Usually selling groceries, bread, fruit, vegetables, meat, etc. they are of particular benefit to those living in outlying areas.

mode. The most frequently occurring value in a set of data.

modelling. In its broadest sense, a model is a representation of a real-world situation. It may be three-dimensional, or simply a verbal or mathematical expression describing a set of relationships in a precise manner. A model can be useful in explaining or describing the behaviour of a system or it can be used to predict actions and events. The chief advantage of using models is that they permit an alternative course of action to be evaluated before a possible risk is taken. Also they provide a formal and structured description of a complex problem. *Computer modelling* includes everything from models of the economy to financial forecasts and computer simulations used in training.

modem. An electronic device which converts data from a form understandable by a computer into a form that can be transmitted via a telephone line, radio signal, etc. and that reconverts data so received to allow communication between distant computers.

monetarism (economics). A school of thought which emphasises the importance of controlling the growth of the money stock. Monetarists believe that the rate of growth of the money stock should be reduced over time in order to eliminate inflation.

monetary authorities. The collective term for those responsible for monetary policy – usually this means the government department responsible for financial policy and the central bank. In Britain the monetary authorities are the TREASURY and the BANK OF ENGLAND.

monetary base. The banks' deposits, or balances, with the central bank. The monetary base can also be defined to include cash held by either, or both, the banks and the public.

monetary base control. Method of monetary control in which the central bank seeks to control the growth of the money stock by regulating the growth of the monetary base.

monetary demand. The level of overall demand for goods and services in the economy measured in terms of money. Monetary demand means the same as expenditure or money income.

monetary policy. Regulation of the monetary system designed to contribute toward the objectives of economic policy. The basis for monetary policy is the belief that such things as the stock of money in circulation, or the level of interest rates, have important effects on the development of the economy.

monetary sector. In Britain this is composed of recognised banks, licensed deposit-taking institutions, National Girobank, the trustee savings banks and the Banking Department of the Bank of England. Broadly speaking, the money stock in Britain includes cash held by the public plus the deposits of the public with the monetary sector.

monetary systems. As soon as a market develops with frequent exchanges of standard commodities, a measure of value becomes necessary. Many commodities – shells, tobacco, all the common metals – have been used for this purpose; these have given way to a standard abstract unit of exchange – money – which means that goods can be priced to a monetary scale and exchange of goods and services effected between parties where a coincidence of needs and produce does not exist. *Bank money*. In modern economies the main means of payment are cash (notes and coin) held by the public, and bank deposits. The depositor can withdraw cash up to the value of his deposits, or transfer them to someone else by writing a cheque. Because bank deposits can be exchanged for goods and services in this way they qualify as a means of payment. It is important to note that not all bank deposits are a means of payment. This is true only of those deposits which can be transferred directly in exchange for goods and services, that is, current account deposits. Other non-current account deposits are not a means of payment and should not be counted as 'money', although they can either be withdrawn in cash or transferred to the customer's current account with little delay, and are almost as convenient when it comes to purchasing power. It is not just banks that accept deposits that can be withdrawn with little delay. In Britain most of the deposits with the building societies can be withdrawn at any time. These, with the current account deposits with banks, are important examples of 'liquid assets' or liquidity. Broadly speaking, it can be said that an asset is more liquid the more swiftly it can be converted into the means of payment and the more certain (or less variable) its monetary value.

monetary targets. Targets for the growth of the money stock.

money. The main functions of money are: a specialised means of payment; a store of value; a unit of account; and a standard of deferred payments. The properties of money are stability of value; durability, divisibility, transferability, and recognisability.

money incomes. These are the actual amounts of money earned; *real incomes* refer to the actual goods and services which can be purchased with those incomes. In times of inflation, a static income means that over a period of time fewer goods and services can be purchased.

money market. The BANK OF ENGLAND, the DISCOUNT HOUSES, and commercial and merchant banks provide a market where large sums of money (or wholesale funds) are borrowed and lent for relatively short periods.

money market instruments. These are Treasury Bills, eligible local authority bills, eligible bank bills, certificates of deposit, and gilt-edged stock. ('Eligible' signifies that the bills have been accepted initially by 'eligible' banks – those whose bills are eligible for rediscount at the Bank of England.)

money market intervention. The Bank of England intervenes in the money markets in order to set very short-term interest rates. It does this mainly through intervention in the bill market by buying and selling MONEY MARKET INSTRUMENTS.

money stock/money supply. Money stock can be defined in various ways. Central banks have to decide which monetary aggregates are important for policy purposes, and in terms of which aggregates they should express their targets.

M0 (M-zero). Equals notes and coin in circulation with the public *plus* banks' till money and banks' balances with the Bank of England. (M0 is a measure of the 'monetary base'.) *M1* equals notes and coin in circulation *plus* private sector non-interest-bearing sterling 'sight' bank deposits, *plus* private sector interest-bearing 'sight' bank deposits (i.e. deposits which can be withdrawn at any time). (M0 and M1 are described as 'narrow money'.) *M2* equals M1 *plus* private sector interest-bearing retail sterling bank deposits *plus* private sector holdings of retail building society shares and deposits and National Savings Bank ordinary accounts. *£M3* (to become M3) equals M1 *plus* private sector sterling time bank deposits, *plus* private sector holdings of sterling bank certificates of deposit. *M3c* equals *£M3(M3) plus* private sector holdings of foreign currency bank deposits. *M4* equals *£M3(M3) plus* private sector holdings of building society shares and deposits and certificates of deposit, *plus* building society holdings of bank deposits and bank certificates of deposit, and notes and coin. *M5* equals holdings by the private sector (excluding building societies) of money market instruments (bank bills, Treasury bills, local authority deposits), certificates of tax deposit and national savings instruments (excluding certificates, SAYE and other long-term deposits). (M3, M4 and M5 are described as 'broad money'.)

Monopolies and Mergers Act 1965. This set up the Monopolies Commission which investigates those mergers likely to operate against the consumer's interest – i.e. if, by the merger, 25 per cent of the market would be controlled by one supplier. Under the *Fair Trading Act 1973* the Commission was renamed the Monopolies and Mergers Commission, and now includes services as well as goods. The Commission conducts enquiries and investigations into the organisation's pricing policies, profit record and general practice of any firm or industry referred to it. Its recommendations will then be a matter for the Minister to take action upon and secure improvements to ensure fair trading.

monopoly. A firm which has more than 25 per cent of the production of a particular product or service under its control. When such a producer dominates a market, then market forces play a smaller part in the price decisions, and 'imperfect competition' exists. *See* previous entry.

monopoly rights. Granted by the Crown to an inventor who patents his idea. Patent rights can be sold, or another party granted a licence which allows use of the invention.

monopsonist. Single buyer. Organised employers are monopsonists – single buyers of labour. (*Note:* A monopolist is a single seller.)

monorail. Monorail transport systems have been built to carry passengers on elevated tracks through cities, e.g. the line between Tokyo and its airport.

monospacing (word processors). Method of printing in which each character printed takes up the same amount of space horizontally, irrespective of the size of the character (cf. proportional spacing).

monthly statement. All businesses make a practice of balancing their debtors' accounts at regular intervals, usually monthly. At the end of each month a statement of account is made up and sent to each debtor, setting out his/her dealings with the firm during the month just passed.

'Account customers' do not pay cash for each transaction, but are able to avail themselves of short-term credit.

moratorium. A legally authorised delay in the performance of an obligation or the payment of a debt.

mortgage. A building society or a bank can offer loans of money to prospective home buyers by means of a mortgage. The borrower of the money is the *mortgagor*; the lender is the *mortgagee*.

mortgage debenture. A limited company's DEBENTURE which is covered by a particular part of the firm's property, which will be sold in order to repay the debenture holder in the event of difficulty.

mortgage security policy. In certain cases, building societies may insist that a mortgage be backed by life assurance, so that in the event of the mortgagor's death dependents own the property without further repayments.

motion (meetings). A proposition put forward for discussion and decision at a meeting.

motivation. 1. (marketing) Research into motivation – to find the reasons why people react as they do – has been successfully applied in the area of marketing to product design, package design, advertising, public relations, servicing and pricing. 2. (personnel) In the personnel field, job design, pay, benefits, consultation, participation, and negotiation have all been influenced by the results of research into human behaviour. *See* INCENTIVE SCHEMES.

motor vehicle insurance. *See* ACCIDENT INSURANCE.

mouse (computers). An alternative to the keyboard as an input device, it moves the cursor around the screen.

move (block) (word processors). To remove a block of text from one location and re-position it at another. The block is deleted from its original location.

multi-access (computers). A system that allows several users to access simultaneously.

multilateral clearing. *See* CLEARING BANKS.

multinational company/corporation. A company with productive facilities in more than one country, but under the ownership based in one country only. It may be a holding company with foreign subsidiaries.

multi-user system (computers). A system with sufficient power to support more than one computer terminal.

multiple store. A group of similar shops operated by one large-scale retailer, with numerous branches. Such organisations can be operated by manufacturers to sell their own goods, or they may produce some of the commodities they sell, but also offer a wide range of other consumer goods.

multiplier. An economic concept that describes the effect of changes in investment on consumption and income. A small change in investment can exert a magnified effect on income and hence on employment and consumption. The size of the multiplier effect depends on the MARGINAL PROPENSITY TO CONSUME. Where this is high, the multiplier will be high since the additional spending released into the economy will generate a knock-on effect among subsequent consumers.

municipal undertakings. Commercial enterprises can be operated by borough and district councils. Examples of these are swimming baths, bus services, leisure centres and theatres. Finance for trading purposes is raised by the issue of municipal/local government stock and from loans; some are financed from the rates or from the government's rate support grant.

mutual insurance offices. These offer insurance to members who have mutual interests, such as belonging to a particular trade or profession. These *mutual organisations* are able to apply their income to the mutual benefit of the policy-holding owners.

N

naked debentures. Debentures which carry no charge on a company's assets.

name of limited company. This must not be the same as that of any other company. It must be followed by the word 'limited' (for a private company) or PLC (for a public limited company). The usual procedure is to gain clearance from the Registrar of Companies before flotation so that the proposed name is known to be acceptable.

National Audit Office. Independent body charged with ensuring that the taxpayer gets value for money.

national bank. The central bank of a country, in the UK the Bank of England.

National Consumer Council. Set up by the government in 1975 to give a vigorous and independent voice to consumers in the United Kingdom, it represents the interests of consumers when they buy or use goods or services. Its brief includes some special obligations: to watch over the interests of inarticulate and disadvantaged consumers – people on low incomes, for example; and to promote advice services for consumers nationwide. It takes a particular interest in supplies of goods or services where competition – and therefore consumer choice – is limited.

National Debt. In developed countries the government often borrows money from the people in order to finance its expenditure, particularly in times of war. It pays interest on the money and may give a date of repayment. Nowadays the borrowing is for permanent public works ('productive' loans) and various schemes have been mooted over the years to bring about a reduction of the debt. The National Debt is administered by the National Debt Commissioners who, among other things, invest deposits from the ordinary account of the National Savings Bank (under the NSB Act 1971) in government securities. Marketable government stock comprises more than 70 per cent of the National Debt.

National Economic Development Council (NEDC). Part of the 'Neddy' organisation. The Council brings together representatives of government, management, the trade unions and other interests to assess economic performance and opportunities for improving it. The NEDC meets quarterly, under the chairmanship of the Chancellor of the Exchequer and other Secretaries of State. There are eighteen NEDC sector groups and working parties covering different parts of industry or working on practical industrial issues. Sectors covered include agriculture, tourism and leisure, engineering, electronics, construction, pharmaceuticals and textiles. Working parties are studying packaging, the supply chain, innovation and finance for industry. The NATIONAL ECONOMIC DEVELOPMENT OFFICE provides the secretariat for the NEDC and its sector groups and working parties. It plays a key role in promoting change and the ways in which obstacles to growth may be overcome.

national expenditure. Very broadly, the total expenditure of citizens and firms, government departments and local authorities. *See* NATIONAL INCOME.

National Girobank. The national banking system operated from the post offices, offering a competitive service to that of the clearing banks. It enjoys no special privileges and has to compete in the market place with other banks; it is to be privatised.

national income. This relates to the total income of the members of the community, and is the addition of incomes from employment and self-employment, the gross trading profits of companies and surpluses of public corporations and other public enterprises, and rent. *See* NATIONAL EXPENDITURE and NATIONAL OUTPUT, the figures for each of which, broadly speaking, equal the figure for national income.

National Insurance (NI). This is a form of direct tax, payment of which is shared between employers and employees. The money is raised specifically to fund the National Health Service, the National Insurance Fund and the Redundancy Fund. NI is a statutory deduction from salaries and wages and the money is used by the government to provide many cash benefits. These include payments to the unemployed, the sick and those permanently unable to work. Retirement and widows' pensions, together with maternity and child allowances, are funded in this way. The amount of contributions paid is related to the amount of money earned, and the money, when deducted by the employer, is entered on the Deductions Working Sheet and is subsequently sent, with the INCOME TAX that has been deducted, to the Income Tax Office. All school-leavers are issued with their personal National Insurance number which remains the same throughout life. It is essential that the number is retained for reference.

National Loans Fund. This records the government's lending and borrowing. Money invested by the public in savings certificates, premium bonds, and the yearly plan savings scheme are authorised under the general borrowing powers conferred on the Treasury by the National Loans Act 1968 to be paid into the National Loans Fund, from which all payments (including premium bond prizes) are met.

national output. This is the total production of consumer goods and services, plus the total of producer goods, created by all the industrial firms of the nation in one year. Figures are collected on a 'value added' basis to avoid counting them twice. A deduction from this figure for industry's net interest payments on their borrowings will give the Gross Domestic Product at factor cost.

national savings.

NATIONAL SAVINGS BANK

There are two National Savings Bank accounts:

A *Savings Bank ordinary account* may be opened with £5 or more at any Savings Bank Post Office, which will issue a bank book in which transactions are recorded. An *investment account* may be opened with £5 or more at any Savings Bank post office. All withdrawals are subject to one month's notice in writing. Payments on demand are not allowed.

NATIONAL SAVINGS CERTIFICATES

These are issued for different amounts and on different terms from year to year. They can be cashed at a few days' notice, but have to be kept to maturity to gain the full amount of interest.

PREMIUM BONDS

A government security for which winning bond numbers are selected each month. The only essential difference between these and other forms of small savings is that instead of earning interest the bonds carry, after a qualifying period, a chance of winning a tax-free prize.

YEARLY PLAN

National savings scheme for regular savers which offers guaranteed returns on the investment with tax-free interest.

national standard shipping note. An ALIGNED DOCUMENT which can be used by exporters and forwarding agents when delivering cargo to any British port, container base or other freight terminal.

nationalisation. The taking into state ownership and public control of the means of production, distribution and exchange in an industry.

nationalised industries/public corporations. Each of these is set up by an Act of Parliament to carry out the duties entrusted to it by Parliament. A minister is appointed to achieve general control and direction when the national interest demands it. A board is appointed by the minister which is responsible for the management of the industry; it recruits its own staff and is not run by the Civil Service. An annual report and the annual accounts must be presented to Parliament, which gives the House an opportunity to discuss the industry's work if it seems necessary. The accounts are investigated by the Public Accounts Committee. Any surplus in trading belongs to the state, but is mainly 'ploughed back'. In the event of a loss, the state bears the liability. Each nationalised industry has a consumer council which represents the users of the product or service, and which deals with complaints.

natural monopolies. In the industrial and commercial fields certain goods and services are by their nature monopolies. Examples are gas, electricity and water supply.

natural resources. Primary products from the earth's fields, rivers, lakes, seas, forests and mines, and gases such as 'natural gas'.

naturalisation. The admission of a foreign national to citizenship of a country.

near-cash. Money in a form which is easy to convert into cash: current and deposit accounts, building society and savings bank accounts.

'Neddy' organisation. *See* NATIONAL ECONOMIC DEVELOPMENT COUNCIL.

negotiable instruments. Any document which it is possible to pass into the possession of another person is a 'negotiable instrument'. Most cheques are negotiable; when they pass into the possession of another they should be endorsed (signed on the back). BILLS OF EXCHANGE are also negotiable.

negotiation (industrial relations). A conflict between employers and employees, especially in relation to salaries/ wages and conditions of employment, is often resolved through collective agreements reached through negotiation. If problems remain unresolved, parties may seek independent arbitration (*see* ACAS), and employees can resort to an INDUSTRIAL TRIBUNAL.

nem con. An abbreviation of *nemine contradicente* – Latin for 'no-one dissenting'. When a vote is taken at a meeting and no member votes against the motion – though some members abstain from voting – it is said to be carried *nem con.*

net asset value. The value of a company after all debts have been paid, expressed in pence per share.

net capital formation. The total amount of capital assets which a country has created over a given period, less depreciation of capital assets for the same period.

net national product. The Gross National Product (GNP) after the figures for depreciation have been subtracted from it.

net pay. The amount of pay received after all DEDUCTIONS FROM SALARIES/WAGES have been made. Also called 'take-home pay'.

net present value. Discounted cash flow (DCF) techniques recognise that *present* cash in hand is worth more than cash received at some future date. *Discount tables* can be used to ascertain how cash flows can be discounted at a rate which reflects the cost of capital.

net profit. All the expenses associated with running a business (the overheads) must be deducted from gross profit to give the net profit figure.

net turnover. 'Turnover' refers to the total value of the sales of a business. If goods are returned to a trader they are 'sales returns'. *Net turnover* is therefore turnover minus the figure for returns; this is often referred to as 'sales less returns'.

net worth. The net worth of the business to the owner; the total assets of a business less the total liabilities.

network. A system of interconnected microcomputers.

network analysis. *See* CRITICAL PATH ANALYSIS.

new issue. A company coming to the International Stock Exchange market for the first time.

new issues market. *New issues* may represent the first issue of SHARES by a new company or the issue of additional stock by an established company. ISSUING HOUSES undertake the administration of new issues; they will buy them from a company, reselling to the investing public at a profit. Large issues are usually underwritten – issuing houses arrange with large institutional investors to accept responsibility for a part of a new issue, and will only be called upon to take up their undertaking if the issue is not fully subscribed by the public.

new shares (Stock Exchange). Shares newly issued by a company; usually indicates that the shares can be transferred on Renounceable Documents.

new time (Stock Exchange). 'New time' dealings may be done by special arrangements in the last two days of an ACCOUNT, and settled as if they had been effected during the following account.

Newly Industrialised Countries (NICs). Many Far Eastern countries come into this category; they have successfully competed with older industrial nations in shipbuilding, the motor industry, microelectronics, coal and textiles, and have contributed to economic decline in the UK, especially in the North, Wales and in Scotland.

Nikkei Index. A share index of the Tokyo Stock Exchange.

nil paid. A new issue of shares, usually as a result of a RIGHTS ISSUE, on which no payment to the company has yet been made.

Nine Elms. The site of the London Produce Market dealing in fruit, flowers and vegetables which has transferred from Covent Garden.

no par value (NPV). *See* PAR.

nominal accounts. These represent the expenses, gains and losses of a business.

nominal capital. *See* CAPITAL.

nominal ledger. *See* GENERAL LEDGER.

nominal price/value. *See* PAR.

nominee name. Name in which a security is registered that does not indicate who the BENEFICIAL OWNER is.

non-bank financial intermediaries (NBFIs). Financial institutions none of whose liabilities are a means of payment.

non-insurable risks. *See* INSURABLE/NON-INSURABLE RISKS.

non-profit-making organisations. With these units the ownership rests with the members – for instance, of a club or cooperative society. Any money 'made' is a surplus, and is not referred to as profit.

non-shop retail outlets. Shops form an overwhelmingly large proportion of retail outlets, but some retailing is effected away from 'shop' premises. Examples are automatic vending machines, door-to-door salesmen (these sometimes represent manufacturers and eliminate both the wholesaler and the shop), mail order, mobile shops and street markets.

non-trading companies. Under the Companies Act 1948, it is compulsory for a company registered under the Act as not trading for profit to lay an income and expenditure account before the company in general meeting. Some clubs, benevolent and similar institutions come into this category.

normal profit. The concept of normal profit in economics describes a hypothetical figure considered to be the minimum level of return necessary to induce an entrepreneur to remain in an industry.

North Atlantic Treaty Organisation (NATO). The treaty was signed in 1949 in Washington by the USA, Great Britain, Canada, France, Belgium, the Netherlands, Luxembourg,

Norway, Denmark, Iceland, Italy and Portugal. By it the USA associated herself with the Western European countries in security arrangements for their common or mutual defence against possible aggression.

'not negotiable'. A special crossing added to a cheque as an additional safeguard to protect the legal title of its true owner. *See* NEGOTIABLE INSTRUMENTS.

note issue. The Issue Department of the Bank of England issues bank notes as required by the public. The currency of the UK is no longer backed entirely by gold but also by government securities and other assets; it is a *fiduciary issue*.

numeric (word processors). A type of field or character that can only contain or specify a numeral.

numeric keypad (computers). A small keyboard which has keys with only the numerals on it.

O

objects clause. The objects clause in the MEMORANDUM OF ASSOCIATION establishes the purposes of the company and what it may do to achieve its objectives.

Occupational Pensions Board. Provided a company pensions scheme at least matches the benefits, an employer can opt out of the earnings-related part of the state scheme, but he cannot withdraw his employees from the basic part. Many thousands of firms with schemes approved by the Occupational Pensions Board have contracted out. Others use the company scheme to supplement the state provisions.

Occupier's Liability Act 1957. States that occupiers of property have a duty to ensure that visitors will be safe when visiting the premises for a permitted purpose. Adequate warnings can free the occupier from liability, but visitors themselves have a duty to take care. The law does not expect the occupier to safeguard a trespasser's interests.

off-line (computers). All information in storage – i.e. not under the control of the CPU – and which cannot therefore be directly accessed.

offer for sale (shares). *See* ISSUING HOUSES.

Office of Fair Trading. A government agency set up by the Fair Trading Act 1973, whose job is to keep watch on trading matters in the UK and protect both consumers and business-men against unfair practices. To do so the Office works very closely with local trading standards departments and advice agencies, especially in the following areas: the fitness of traders who provide credit, or hire goods, to individuals; en-forcement of the safeguards which consumers have under the Consumer Credit Act; resolution of disputes which con-sumers may have over the accuracy of information held on them by credit reference agencies (*see* CREDIT SCORING); collect-ion of information about trading practices; if they are considered to be unfair, the OFT may suggest changes in the law or other remedies. *Encouraging competition.* Lack of com-petition in business may be against the public interest. The

Director General has a duty to keep a watch on monopolies, mergers and other trade practices which may be restrictive or anti-competitive. He provides guidance for traders. *Monopolies, mergers, and anti-competitive practices* can be referred to the Monopolies and Mergers Commission. *Restrictive trade practices* may be referred to the Restrictive Practices Court. The OFT cannot take up people's complaints, but a local consumer adviser at a Citizens Advice Bureau, Trading Standards/Consumer Protection Department or Consumer Advice Centre is best able to help with these problems. Firms or individuals help the OFT in its work involving monopolies, restrictive trade practices, and anti-competitive practices by sending any details of such practices direct to the OFT.

Offices, Shops and Railway Premises Act 1963. *See* EMPLOYMENT LEGISLATION.

Official List (Stock Exchange). The major of the Stock Exchange's three markets for UK shares; a list of the companies which are allowed to trade on this market. The Stock Exchange's *Daily Official List* is the list of official prices published each day.

Official Receiver in bankruptcy. The DTI official who carries out the collection and distribution of a bankrupt's property.

OFGAS (Office of Gas Supply). The gas industry's 'watchdog'.

OFTEL (Office of Telecommunications). The telecommunication 'watchdog'.

oil and oilseeds market. Market dealing on the Baltic Exchange in primary commodities which yield vegetable oil, and also in the 'cake' left over after the extraction of oil which is used to feed cattle and poultry. Further commodities dealt in are linseed, castor seed, soya beans, groundnuts and cotton seed.

oil tankers. Cargo ships built to carry oil and oil products. These large bulk carriers are too large for many ports to handle; 'outports' with refining facilities – such as at Milford Haven – have been specially designed to accommodate such carriers. The largest are very large crude carriers (vlccs) which operate from the oil-producing countries to Europe, North America and Japan. Freight rates per tonne for return journeys are based on the 'Worldscale' system which is operated in US dollars.

oligopoly. A situation in which there are few sellers, and a small number of competitive firms control the market; it approaches monopoly, and is a major incentive to form 'cartels' – firms forming a 'ring' to preserve their own positions by mutually agreed output, price and marketing arrangements. In the UK the Monopolies Commission seeks to control such situations.

Ombudsman. In 1967 the House of Commons appointed a 'Parliamentary Commissioner for Administration' – the Ombudsman – who investigates complaints of maladministration by government departments, brought to his notice by MPs on behalf of their constituents. (Maladministration covers delay, neglect, incompetence or prejudice.) Complaints concerning the running of nationalised industries do not come within the ambit of the Commissioner's work, nor do complaints against individual policemen, though the Ombudsman may deal with complaints against a police authority. In addition to the Parliamentary Commissioner, the Local Government Act 1974 established a Commission for Local Administration in England and another for Wales, to investigate complaints about injustices suffered as a result of maladministration in local government. Ombudsmen have been appointed to ensure particularly that maladministration in local government and the Health Service is kept to a minimum. *Ombudsman schemes* exist in a number of industries, including banking, insurance, the law, building societies and unit trusts.

on-line (computers). Information immediately accessible to the user because the disk is under the control of the computer (cf. OFF-LINE). (Large, public, on-line databases are known as *electronic publishing.*)

open accounts. *See* EXPORT FINANCE (SHORT- AND MEDIUM-TERM).

open cheque. An uncrossed cheque which can be cashed over the counter of the bank on which it is drawn.

open cover agreement. *See* CARGO INSURANCE.

open market operations. One of the BANK OF ENGLAND'S measures for controlling the money supply is by its operations on the open market. TREASURY BILLS and other money market instruments are sold to the DISCOUNT HOUSES to remove a surplus of money on the market. They are bought back to relieve a shortage, and to prevent the discount houses having to seek help from the Bank of England ('the LENDER OF LAST RESORT'). The Bank of England also borrows money by the issue of gilt-edged securities on the STOCK EXCHANGE. These operations help to implement the government's policy; by selling such stock the government siphons money out of the system; to put money back, it can buy back stock in the same market.

open outcry. In some of the London COMMODITY MARKETS where 'ring trading' takes place, the bids and offers are shouted across the ring (open outcry) so that all are aware of the prices prevailing.

open reference. This is a type of personal reference which is not sent to any particular person or firm. It is dated and addressed 'To whom it may concern'. A copy of such a testimonial may be sent to a prospective employer.

operating capability. The total of goods or services which a business can supply with its existing services, over a given period of time.

operating cycle. A measure of the time which will elapse between the first purchase of raw materials or goods for process or resale and the receipt of payment after they have been sold.

operating statement. An accounting report produced for the purpose of control or communication. Each type of expense – wages, salaries, materials, rates, etc. – can be shown, the difference between budgeted and actual cost can be identified and, if necessary, procedures modified.

operating systems (computers). The systems software which acts as an interface between the computer hardware and the applications software.

operating targets (Bank of England). In order to achieve its intermediate targets, a central bank brings its influence to bear on key conditions in financial markets, such as money market interest rates or the banks' central bank balances.

operational research (OR). Describes a series of techniques – of which CPA (critical path analysis) is one – which assist managers in planning and decision-making. Many OR techniques are computer-based.

opportunity cost. 'Opportunity cost' or 'alternative cost' expresses the cost of a commodity, not in money, but in the terms of the alternative forgone. In making business decisions it is necessary to weigh up the opportunity costs of the alternative uses of resources.

optical character recognition (OCR) (computers). Entails the marking of source documents with specially shaped characters which can be recognised by the computer.

optical mark recognition (OMR) (computers). Entails the marking of source documents with pencil (as in multiple-choice examination papers) which can be recognised by the computer.

optimum firm. A firm operating at a scale which gives it the lowest unit cost possible.

optimum population. The population of a country which will combine exactly with the available natural resources and the average stock of capital to give the highest possible output of goods and services per head of population.

option (Stock Exchange). The right (but not the obligation) to buy or sell a share at a set price within a set period.

order cheque. A cheque which can be negotiated by endorsement to a third party.

ordinary shares. *See* SHARES.

organisation and method (O & M). The application of time and motion assessment to office procedures by systematic analysis of office methods. Simplification and improvement can be achieved in most clerical practices by the use of O & M.

organisation chart. An attempt to portray the responsibilities (areas of activity) and relationships in an organisation or part of an organisation, such as an office. Large charts can give very little detail; more information can be obtained if a smaller area is analysed.

Organisation for European Cooperation and Development (OECD). Now serves to bring Europeans, Americans and

Canadians together. The headquarters is in Paris. Its aims are: to achieve the highest sustainable economic growth and employment and a rising standard of living in member countries, while maintaining financial stability, and thus to contribute to the development of the world economy; to contribute to sound economic expansion in member as well as non-member countries; to contribute to the expansion of world trade on a multinational, non-discriminatory basis in accordance with international obligations. The Council produces statistical and economic publications and cooperates with other international bodies.

Organisation of Petroleum Exporting Countries (OPEC). Members of this organisation cooperate to fix oil prices in a cartel, which seriously hampers a free market in the commodity concerned.

organisations. These notes apply particularly to large organisations which are established to meet a need in society and to achieve certain goals; examples are businesses, governments, international institutions. They have status, objectives, rules and structures. They may be *productive* and produce goods or services in the public or private sector, or *non-productive* such as legal institutions (courts of law, etc.), trade unions, and churches. All such organisations aim to employ resources to the best advantage; they must be directed and controlled successfully; they are accountable to those who provided the means to bring them into being; they must perform within the law.

original entry, books of. *See* BOOKS OF PRIME ENTRY.

output (computers). The process of communicating the results of the computer's processing, usually through a printer or a visual display unit.

outward missions. These are often supported by the British Overseas Trade Board and enable the prospects for the sale of goods and services to be explored at first hand. CHAMBERS OF COMMERCE and TRADE ASSOCIATIONS are often responsible for their organisation.

outward processing relief (OPR) (Customs and Excise). Describes a relief from Customs duties which applies to Community goods sent outside the Community to a third country for process and subsequent reimportation. *Triangulation.* This procedure allows compensating products to benefit from Customs relief when imported into a member state other than that from which the goods were exported.

over capitalisation. The situation which arises when a firm has bought too many fixed assets and left itself short of working capital.

overdrafts. *See* BANK CREDIT.

overfunding (government). Sales of government gilt-edged stock to the public results in money leaving the commercial banks to pay for them. When the government deliberately sells more gilt-edged securities – i.e. more debt – than is necessary, it is overfunding in order to counteract the rise in private bank lending.

overhead expenses (overheads). The general expenses of running a business, including rent and rates, heating, lighting, etc. *See* COSTS (FIXED).

overseas agents. One method of selling on overseas markets is by the employment of overseas agents who are 'home nationals' and able to understand the complexities of trade in their own countries. The Overseas Status Report Service of the British Overseas Trade Board will help to assess the suitability of suggested agents.

Overseas Projects Fund. The Projects and Export Policy (PEP) Division of the BOTB brings together all the various government support measures for large international projects. The PEP is divided into sectors according to the type of industry.

overseas sales base. Goods can be sold abroad by setting up an overseas base. This is a typical activity of many international companies who have resources not available to the small exporter. The British Overseas Trade Board offers help and advice.

overseas seminars. The British Overseas Trade Board supports these by help with costs and organisation, and travel grants for seminars outside Western Europe. The scheme enables British companies to bring their products or services to the attention of a specific audience.

Overseas Status Report Service. The British Overseas Trade Board will provide impartial reports on the trading capability and commercial standing of possible agents. These will be drawn up by the Commercial Department of the relevant British Embassy or diplomatic post and will complement a financial report from the enquirer's bank or commercial enquiry agency.

overseas trade. *See* IMPORT TRADE, EXPORT TRADE, BALANCE OF TRADE.

over-the-counter (OTC) market (in securities). Not a part of the International Stock Exchange but run by a group of dealers who specialise in the shares of smaller companies.

overtime (salaries and wages). Covers time worked beyond the regular hours, and usually carries a rate of pay higher than the basic rate, e.g. time-and-a-quarter (the basic rate plus one quarter of the basic rate, per hour), time-and-a-half, double time. Higher rates of pay also apply to those working unsocial hours. *Time in lieu* means that in some cases 'time off' is given instead of payment. A person working on a Bank Holiday may be paid his normal rate for the day, but instead of extra payment will be given a day off with full pay at a later date.

overtime ban. Industrial action by workers who will only work during normal working hours.

overtrading. If a firm leaves itself short of working capital by dealing beyond the limits of its available liquidity, it is said to be overtrading.

own account transport. Owners of a business can effect deliveries by road by the use of their own fleet of vehicles (own account transport). This gives complete control over drivers and operations, vans can be used for advertising, and vehicles can be available for other uses. Disadvantages lie in the fact that return loads are difficult to organise and garaging and maintenance can prove to be expensive. Alternative methods are by the use of leasing (a contract hire fleet) or making use of the services of a public haulier.

own brand/own label goods. Goods offered for sale under the label or trade name of the retail distributor (e.g. a chain store).

owner's risk (OR). Goods may be sent 'owner's risk', in which case the carrier is only responsible for damage caused by the deliberate neglect of his employees or their dishonesty. Rates are lower than those for 'company's risk' (CR).

ownership of organisations. The type of business unit which will describe a particular organisation can be determined by identifying who provided the capital (the owner) and who receives the profits. *The sole trader* owns his own business and takes the profits. *Partnerships* are owned jointly by the partners, who take the profits. Both *private and public limited companies and holding companies* are owned by the shareholders who receive the profits in the form of dividends. *Cooperative societies, friendly societies and clubs* are owned by all the members, who can decide how best to use any money that is made. All organisations in the public sector are publicly or 'socially' owned; the public fund them and should benefit from them.

P

packaging. Costs must be incurred in the packaging of goods, and the form of packaging should contribute favourably to the total marketing operation. Prepackaging – i.e. packaging before distribution to retail outlets – aids identification, and is associated with the branding of goods. Packaging should protect against transport and other damage, and present a good and attractive 'image' which helps to identify a competitive product.

pagination (word processors). The process of breaking up text into units that will fit on a given size of page, by inserting page breaks.

paid-up capital. *See* CAPITAL (TYPES OF).

pallets. A platform or tray for lifting and stacking goods, used with a fork-lift truck, and having a double base into which the fork can be thrust. Pallet loads can be deposited in a container and provide very economical lifting operations.

paper market. *See* COMMERCIAL PAPER.

paper sizes. *See* INTERNATIONAL PAPER SIZES.

par. The nominal value of a security (always taken as £100 in fixed-interest stocks). By British and Irish company law, a company must set a *par* value on its ORDINARY SHARES. In some countries, shares can have *no par value* (abbreviated NPV).

pari passu **(Latin).** Equal in every respect: used to describe new issues of SHARES in relation to those already in issue.

Parliament. The legislative function of the constitution is performed by the Queen in Parliament. Parliament, which makes laws, consists of three components: the Queen, the Lords and the Commons. Acts of Parliament have to be approved by all three. The government translates its policy into Bills which, having been approved by Parliament (the government usually has a majority) and having received the Royal Assent, become Acts of Parliament or Statutes. Private members are allowed time to introduce their own Public Bills.

participating preference shares. *See* SHARES.

participation (of employees in the running of an organisation). The Bullock Report of 1977 recommended that employees should take part in the policy decisions of a firm, and some countries of the European Community have enforced this by law. The Employment Act 1982 stipulates that where there are more than 250 employees, the directors' report must contain details of moves made during the year to develop and improve employee participation in the management of the company. Part ownership of a company through owning some of its shares (some large organisations run such schemes) enables workers to identify with the company's objectives and contribute to the general good of the firm; this leads to greater efficiency.

partners. At least two but not more than twenty people, known as partners, may share in the ownership of a firm. Partners receive all the profits and are liable to meet fully any debts incurred to the full extent of their share in the partnership, and their private fortunes. *Limited partners.* By the Limited Partnership Act 1907, the liability of a partner for the debts of the firm may be limited to the amount of his fixed stake in the business, but in exchange for this limited liability he is required to remain a dormant or 'sleeping' partner, and to take no part in the management of the business.

partnership. Partnerships are unincorporated associations suitable for commercial and professional services such as doctors, solicitors, decorators, etc. It is not lawful to have more than twenty partners in a partnership or ten in the case of a banking business. The Partnership Agreement, often called the Articles of Partnership, is a formal agreement, mainly regulated by the Partnership Act of 1890. All the terms of partnership, other than those contained in the Act, must be stated in the agreement. All matters are settled by a simple majority; each partner is allowed 'drawings' which are really profits taken in advance. The Articles of Partnership must be maintained; if the nature of the business is to change, all partners must agree to it. Once a firm is liable under the contracts entered into by a partner, all the partners are jointly liable. Books of account must be kept at the principal place of business and each partner has access and the right to copy them. The advantages of partnerships are that they are simple to establish, make more capital and better management available, and personal contact with clients or customers makes for a keener interest in the business. Among the disadvantages are the risks of dissolution, and liability in the event of a failure in the business. There is a certain limitation of size, and the actions of one partner being binding on all partners can cause problems.

part-paid stock. Some government stocks require that the investor pays only part of the subscription money on application, the remainder being payable in a series of instalments.

passenger liners. Nearly all cargo liners take cargo to and from major ports and have a few cabins for passengers; most passenger liners are now cruise liners used for holidays at sea.

patents. More correctly *letters patent* – documents in which the Crown vests a subject with special rights and confers on him the sole right to make, use and vend an invention for a limited period of time. Such a grant creates a monopoly in favour of the patentee. Patent rights can be sold, or another party can be granted a licence allowing him to use the invention. Applications for patents are processed by the Patent Office in London (Department of Trade and Industry).

pay (salaries and wages). Factors which determine the level of salaries and wages offered are: supply and demand of the type of labour required; the difficulty of the job – the amount of intelligence, experience, knowledge or skill required; whether the working conditions are pleasant or unpleasant; the cost of living; government intervention; and, additionally, in the case of promotions or transfers within a firm, the proficiency, merit, and length of service of the employee concerned.

pay as you earn (PAYE). The system used in Britain to collect INCOME TAX from the employee as he earns his money. The amount due is collected from employees' earnings each pay-day and sent by employers to the Tax Office.

payback period. A method of investment appraisal which compares the cash cost of the initial investment with the annual cash inflow which it will generate, and measures the time taken for the initial cost to be recovered. By using this method the assessment and comparison of different projects can be quickly computed, and the investment programme most likely to produce the quickest return more easily evaluated.

payment by results (salaries and wages). The employee receives a basic rate of pay plus an additional emolument based on productivity beyond a standard required.

payments. *See* METHODS OF PAYMENT.

payroll giving scheme. Government scheme which gives employees the opportunity to obtain tax relief on regular donations to charity by permitting their employers to deduct the money directly from their pay packets. Because it is deducted gross there is no need for the Inland Revenue to become involved.

pedlar. Salesman who travels and trades on foot. A certificate must be obtained before a person can trade as a pedlar; this is normally issued by the Chief of Police of the area for which it is required.

penalty clause. A clause in a contract which states (usually) that the work will be completed satisfactorily by a certain date; failure to do so will involve financial penalties. Penalty clauses may refer to other elements, apart from time.

pension funds. The large amounts of money collected for occupational pension schemes are invested in STOCKS and SHARES to produce the regular payments promised upon retirement. As institutional investors the pension funds are a very powerful force in the stock markets. These pension funds are in no way connected with the state pension, which is financed out of employers' and employees' National Insurance contributions.

per procurationem (pp or per pro). In business, authority is sometimes given to certain officials to sign on behalf of another. When signing *per pro*, the signature should appear *below* the name of the person taking responsibility for the letter.

perfect competition/perfect market. In a perfect market there are many buyers and sellers, none of whom is such a large dealer that he can influence the price. The price which is charged in a perfect market is determined by the interaction between consumers and the most efficient suppliers. The market mechanism sets the price and determines how much is supplied. For perfect competition to exist, products should be homogeneous (i.e. identical) and there must be no barriers or restrictions on entry into the market by any firm as a result of governmental or any other type of intervention.

performance bond. Guarantee that a contract will be completed in a satisfactory manner; failure to do so means that the guarantor (usually a financial institution) will have to pay compensation to the organisation who initiated the contract.

perpetual inventory. A stock procedure that involves checking small sections of stock at regular intervals throughout the year. The book figures are checked against actual stock count and any discrepancies reported for immediate investigation. Although it may take more time overall than a one-off stocktake, it avoids the upheaval associated with the latter, and it is also claimed to discourage pilfering and fraudulent stock entries. It also highlights slow-moving stock items and problems over damage or deterioration. *See* STOCKTAKING.

personal accident policies. *See* ACCIDENT INSURANCE.

personal accounts. The accounts of a firm's dealings with other persons or firms (cf. REAL ACCOUNTS)

personal allowances (income tax). In the UK the amount of income – based on status (e.g. whether a man is married or not) – that is free of taxation.

personal credit agreements. A consumer credit arrangement with a bank, finance house, moneylender, credit union or other institution. Such an agreement for the purchase of consumer *goods* can be a credit sale, conditional sale, or hire purchase agreement. *See* CONSUMER CREDIT ACT 1974.

personal equity plan (PEP). Launched by the 1986 Budget, this allows small investors to put £400 per month into equities, or unit and investment trusts, and earn income and capital gains tax relief.

personal loans. Bank loans (from the commercial banks) are normally made to customers to enable them to purchase a particular item, such as a car.

personal portable pensions. Employees of companies which run their own pension schemes are usually expected to join, but may, since 1988, make their own pension arrangements should they wish to do so. Such personal pensions are portable – they can be taken from job to job.

personal reference. A testimonial from a person who has been given as a referee by an applicant for a post. It is sent direct to the employer who has requested it. Where personal references are asked for, the referee's permission to use his name should be obtained in advance.

personal services. Part of tertiary production, these are services rendered by producers who are not concerned directly or indirectly with material production, but whose services are necessary in so far as they 'service' the workforce and ensure its efficiency. Examples of such services are those provided by doctors, teachers, the police, army and navy, and those who provide entertainment. (The services offered by COMMERCE also form part of tertiary production.)

personnel management. The Institute of Personnel Management provides the following definition: Personnel management is that part of management concerned with people at work and with their relationship within an enterprise. Its aim is to bring together and develop into an effective organisation the men and women who make up an enterprise and, having regard for the well-being of the individual and of working groups, to enable them to make their best contribution to its success. In particular, personnel management is concerned with the development and application of policies governing: human resources – planning, recruitment, selection, placement and termination; education and training; career development; terms of employment and working conditions; methods and standards of remuneration; formal and informal communication and consultation both through the representatives of employers and employees and at all levels throughout the enterprise; negotiation and application of agreements on wages and working conditions; procedures for the avoidance and settlement of disputes. Personnel management is also concerned with the social implications of change within organisations, methods of working, and their effect on the individual.

personnel specification. Interpretation of the job specification in terms of the kind of person suitable for the job, physically, mentally, and temperamentally.

persuasive advertising. Uses techniques which may be harmful if, as a result of them, consumers buy anything dangerous or antisocial.

petrocurrency. The currency of an oil-producing nation.

petty cash book. An account of a sum of money from which small cash payments are made. A *petty cash voucher* must be prepared for every payment. Petty cash is usually run on the imprest system, which means that it starts off with a 'float' (imprest) and no matter what is spent out during a week or other set period, that sum is returned to it so that the total in the cash box is again equal to the float.

physical distribution. *See* DISTRIBUTION.

pica. A size of type giving ten characters to the inch (25 mm).

picket. A group set to watch and dissuade from working those who go to work during a strike. This is legally acceptable if it is by employees at their normal place of work, former employees connected with the dispute, or a trade union official accompanying a member of the union involved in the dispute. *Secondary picketing* – i.e. picketing at a workplace other than a worker's own – is illegal.

pictogram/pictograph. A chart which uses symbols to represent statistical data instead of figures, lines, etc.

pie chart. A method of presenting statistics. A circle (representing a whole amount) is divided into separate proportional sectors.

piecework. Work paid for by the number of units produced and not by the amount of hours worked. Wages are not allowed to fall below a minimum flat rate.

pipelines. Modern oil and natural gas trunk pipelines have three basic functions: to transport crude oil from oilfields to ocean terminals, and from ocean terminals to refineries or, where no sea voyage is necessary, from oilfields direct to the refinery; to carry refined products from refinery to tanker terminals or to large consumers or to local distribution depots; to transport natural gas from the fields to local distribution centres or direct to large consumers.

pitch. A measure of character spacing, i.e. the number of characters that are printed in a horizontal inch; measured in characters per inch (CPI).

placings (shares). *See* ISSUING HOUSES.

planning permission. Under the Town and Country Planning Act 1971, planning permission must be sought for all proposed developments, including changes of use of land or premises, and the construction or alteration of buildings, roads, etc. There is a right of appeal to the Secretary of State against local planning decisions and, in important cases, public enquiries are held.

plant. The buildings, machinery, etc. employed in carrying on a trade or an industrial business; a factory or workshop for the manufacture of a particular product.

plotter (computers). A machine used for drawing plans and diagrams.

'ploughing back'. Using the profits to buy new equipment, premises, or any services which will enable the firm to expand.

point of order. An interruption of a meeting by a member drawing the chairman's attention to some irregularity in the proceedings.

point-of-sale advertising. *See* ADVERTISING.

policy. 1. (insurance). *See* INSURANCE POLICY. 2. An overall plan embracing general goals and procedures which affects all aspects of an organisation. The policy provides a guide to the decision-making which will implement the policies.

Policyholders' Protection Act 1975. In the event of an insurance company going into liquidation, customers are protected by this Act, which provides that up to 90 per cent of the company's liabilities will be met out of a levy on other companies, and 100 per cent if the insurance is compulsory. Policyholders' interests are also under the constant surveillance of the Investment Protection Committee of the British Insurance Association.

poll tax. *See* COMMUNITY CHARGE.

pollution. Many waste products are harmful and it costs money to make them safe. Industrial development often produces pollution and much of the waste is disposed of without any attempt being made to render it harmless. Often it cannot be detected without scientific apparatus. The United Nations Environment Programme (UNEP) monitors the environment globally, and the European Community is conducting massive investigations into pollution of every kind. In the UK the Deposits of Poisonous Wastes Act makes the dumping of poisonous materials illegal. The United Nations Food and Agriculture Organisation monitors the impact of pesticides on food products.

pooling of risks (insurance). An insurance pool is the money contributed (in the form of premiums) by all the policy-holders; it is kept in a central fund from which those contributors who suffer loss can be indemnified. In the case of injury to life or limb, indemnity cannot be effected, and the sufferer – or his dependants – receive cash benefits instead. An insurance pool must fulfil three obligations: the money collected from premiums must be adequate enough to indemnify those who suffer loss; the pool should never be allowed to shrink, but should, by careful investment, increase in size; claims should be met promptly and in full.

population. Population changes may involve an increasing population or a decreasing population, or changes in the average age of the population. Any change has economic implications, especially when the ratio between working and non-working people is considered. At the present time, children stay at school longer than they used to and people are living longer; both groups have to be sustained by the working population whose numbers are declining. Statistics obtained in the government census which is taken every ten years are used to provide accurate information on the economic and social conditions of the population, and also as a basis for the government's social and economic policies. *The distribution of population* refers to the number of people in each age group. The main divisions are 0 – 15 years, 16 – 64 years, and 65+. The relative size of the 16 – 64 group indicates the main source of the working population. *The dependency ratio* is the ratio of the dependent population (the young and the old) to the working population.

port rates schedule. Paid by a shipper to the relevant port authority for handling cargo.

portfolio. Collection of securities owned either by an individual or an institution.

ports. Terminals for ships, providing access for passengers and cargo. Most ports are also road and rail terminals, enabling easy transhipment, particularly of containerised cargoes. The facilities a port provides depend largely on the type of shipping catered for. Milford Haven (an 'outport' serving oil tankers) is vastly different from the container port at Tilbury. There are certain requirements for a port to be successful: it must be sheltered – either by artificial building or by the endowment of nature; it should have the right depth of water for the type of shipping served – if necessary, maintained by dredging; it should supply everything that ships need while on a voyage – food, oil, water, electricity; it should have labour and machinery for loading and unloading, and commercial services to deal with all the documentation involved with international trade; it should provide good communications with other forms of transport – road, rail, air, etc.

FREEPORTS

A freeport is an enclosed zone within or adjacent to a seaport or airport inside which goods are treated for customs purposes as being outside the customs territory of the country.

Post Office (government department). The Post Office now controls: all inland postal services in Great Britain (letters and cards, newspapers, parcels, express services, registration and recorded delivery services); all overseas post (air and surface mail – letters and postcards, small packets and parcels, registration, insurance and compensation); postal orders, inland telegraph and international payments. The following are also available at Post Office counters: National Girobank services; National Savings Bank services; government stock and securities on the National Savings

Stock Register; savings certificates; premium savings bonds; Yearly Plan National Savings scheme; payment of state pensions and allowances.

poste restante. Letters and parcels to be called for may be addressed to any post office (except a town sub-office). The words 'To be called for' or 'Poste restante' should appear in the address.

pre-entry form. A declaration to the Customs authorities giving details of goods which are to be exported.

preference shares. *See* SHARES.

preferential form. The International Stock Exchange allows companies offering shares to the public to set aside up to 10 per cent of the issue for applications from employees or, where a parent company is floating off a subsidiary, shareholders of the parent company. Separate application forms, usually pink in colour – hence the nickname 'pink forms' – are used for this.

premium. 1. (insurance). The sum of money payable by the policy-holder to the insurance company or UNDERWRITERS for the protection being given. It varies according to the nature of the risk and the value of the property insured; the greater the risk and value, the higher the premium. Premiums must be paid when due or the policy will lapse. 2. (Stock Exchange). Premium is the amount by which a security is traded above its original price. If the market price is lower, the difference is a *discount*.

premium bonds. *See* NATIONAL SAVINGS.

prepayments. When the payment period for business expenses such as insurance, rent and rates does not coincide with the accounting period, an adjustment must be made to the books to show any amounts paid in advance as an asset to the firm. The purpose of these adjustments is to produce an accurate set of final accounts for the period under review.

pressure group. A group of people organised to influence public policy, and especially government policy, for a specific purpose. Formed to promote the common economic interests of its members, or to fight for particular causes, it makes use of the following: membership of decision-making body (such as a trade union sponsoring MPs); publicity via the media; demonstrations and marches; strikes; lobbying members of Parliament. The following are examples of pressure groups: trade unions, political organisation, BBC, ITV, the press, conservation lobby, anti-noise and anti-pollution groups, shareholders of companies.

Prestel. *See* INFORMATION TECHNOLOGY.

price/pricing. In practice, the build-up of price consists of the cost element and a mark-up on that cost; it is a way of expressing how much a good or service is worth, as measured by the quantity of goods and services that one unit of the good or service can be exchanged for. The relationship between the prices of different goods is determined by the relative demand for the various goods, and by the amount of each good available and the ease with which the supply can be altered. For any one good the price will tend to be the level where supply equals demand; normally an increase in price will cause demand to fall and, conversely, a fall in price will cause demand to rise – i.e. market forces prevail. If a change in price leads to a large change in demand, then the demand is described as elastic; a small change in demand is said to be inelastic. If perfect competition exists, the price for identical articles will be the same in all markets.

price differentiation/discrimination. *See* VARIABLE PRICING.

price/earnings (P/E) ratio. The current share price divided by the last published earnings (expressed as pence per share). It is used as a measure of whether a share should be considered expensive.

price elasticity. *See* ELASTICITY.

price index (of retail prices). *See* RETAIL PRICE INDEX.

price mechanism. The mechanism by which supply and demand are balanced is referred to as the 'price mechanism' or 'pricing'. If supply increases while demand remains constant, prices will fall; if demand increases while supply remains constant, prices will rise. These movements restore the balance between supply and demand. Organisations must respond to movements in demand by a complete marketing strategy.

prices and consumer protection. *See* RESTRICTIVE TRADE PRACTICES.

prices and incomes policy. The aim of such a government policy is to curb inflation and to avoid unemployment. *See* INCOMES POLICY.

primage. In addition to the declared freight charges, shipping companies sometimes impose a supplementary charge known as 'primage', originally designed to cover the cost of handling and stowing the cargo.

primary market (Stock Exchange). The sale of new stocks and shares to the public and financial institutions. *See* GILT-EDGED MARKET, ISSUING HOUSES.

primary production. The first stage of production involves the production of goods made available by nature in mines, oilfields and quarries (the extractive industries), and goods produced in the forestry, farming and fishing industries. Many of these materials proceed to secondary production where they are manufactured into PRODUCER or CONSUMER GOODS.

primary research (market research). Also known as field research, this is the process of finding out new facts directly from source. It is normally undertaken by selecting a representative sample of a population and asking carefully chosen questions, after which the results are analysed.

prime costs. Costs which are essentially incurred in the purchase or preparation of an article for sale, made up of the direct cost of new materials, direct labour, and direct expenses.

printer. Device which can print computer information on to paper; computer printout is known as *hard copy*.

prior charges. *See* DEBENTURES.

private automatic branch exchange (PABX). An internal/external telephone system.

Private Bills. Private Parliamentary Bills can be defined in broad terms as being for the benefit of a person or body, e.g. local authorities and public utilities. Private members' Bills are, in fact, PUBLIC BILLS.

private branch exchange (PBX). An internal/external telephone system where all calls go through the switchboard.

private corporations. All private and public limited companies are corporations in the private sector.

private enterprise. *See* BUSINESS UNITS (private sector).

private good. A good (or service) which benefits a particular individual or group of individuals rather than the whole community (cf. MERIT GOOD, PUBLIC GOOD).

private investors. Individuals who use their money for investment, usually on the Stock Exchange, as opposed to institutional investors such as banks, building societies, etc. who collect the savings of many people and invest them for the good of the saving public.

private law. *See* CIVIL LAW.

private ledger. In sole trading and partnerships the private ledger may be used to contain the capital account, drawings account and the trading and profit and loss accounts and balance sheets for each period.

private limited company. *See* COMPANY and LIMITED LIABILITY.

private sector. That part of the British economy which covers, in general, the production of goods and commercial and personal services by privately-owned organisations. *See* BUSINESS UNITS (private sector).

private treaty/deal. On the Stock Exchange, the Baltic, Foreign and Corn Exchanges, and the insurance markets, dealing is by 'private treaty' on a one-to-one basis.

privatisation. Transfer of ownership from the public to the private sector. When privatised, nationalised industries acquire the status of a public limited company (PLC).

probate price. The price used in valuing shares for taxation purposes. It is calculated on the QUARTER UP principle.

process costing. Method of cost accounting generally employed when a standard product is being made which passes through a number of distinct sequential processes towards completion, as in the manufacture of paper, flour, chemicals or cement. The object is to trace and record costs for each distinct stage, to obtain the average cost per unit for each accounting period.

process inwards relief/outwards relief. *See* INWARD PROCESSING RELIEF and OUTWARD PROCESSING RELIEF.

produce exchanges. Wholesale produce markets exist in most large towns and cities. The famous London markets are at: Billingsgate – fish (now in the West India Dock Road); Nine

Elms – flowers, fruit and vegetables (this used to be at Covent Garden); Smithfield – meat; Spitalfields – like Nine Elms, but in the East End of London.

producer. A member of the working population who exchanges his skills or knowledge for a wage, salary or earnings.

producer goods. Capital goods; plant, buildings and machinery; raw materials and partly finished goods which are all necessary for the production of CONSUMER GOODS.

product. A thing produced either by nature or a natural process, or that which is produced by any action, operation or work, especially a saleable or marketable commodity.

product differentiation. The distinctive packaging of branded goods which enables consumers to differentiate between similar products.

product liability. As part of the framework of consumer law, the European Council of Ministers in 1985 produced a directive on product liability (to be implemented by 1988), the intention being to impose strict liability on manufacturers for damage caused by defective goods. Under the UK's Consumer Safety Act 1978, safety standards were set for toys and oil heaters, among other products. The Food and Drugs Act 1955 makes it a criminal offence to sell food unfit for human consumption.

product life-cycle. A marketing term which describes the life expectancy of individual products. Sales of a product appear to follow a typical pattern: introduction, growth, maturity, saturation of the market, and decline. It is essential that marketing and production departments are aware of the position of any product in this 'life-cycle' so that a corporate decision may be made as to its future, and to ensure that new products can be introduced appropriately for the business to remain vigorous.

product mix. The range of products which a company offers for sale. Ideally, their production involves total use of financial, manufacturing and manpower resources.

production. Achieved by combining land, labour and capital in the creation of utilities and the economic activity which serves to satisfy human needs by creating material goods or by providing a service. No rational owner of economic resources will use them to produce a service or commodity for which there is no demand. Production includes the activities of all those occupations which are engaged, directly or indirectly, in adding utility to man's natural resources. There are three classes of production: The *primary stage* involves the production of goods made available by nature in mines, oilfields and quarries (the extractive industries), and goods produced in the forestry, farming and fishing industries. *Secondary production* uses those things produced at the primary stage to manufacture more sophisticated products. *Tertiary production* comprises the service industries, both personal and commercial. A further classification divides into: *Direct production* – the satisfying of a person's wants without help from any other person. *Indirect production/mass production* – the manufacture of goods on a huge scale by automation; standardisation, simplification and specialisation are essential to its success. *See* CYCLE OF PRODUCTION.

production costs. *See* COSTS.

production planning. Production (manufacturing) involves the buying-in of raw materials and components in the right quality and quantity, at the right place and time, and at a favourable price, and their consequent utilisation in the manufacture of a good or goods. Production planning is effected by a closely coordinated strategy involving the marketing, accounting, engineering and production departments of an organisation. Production management has overall responsibility and control over all aspects of physical production, including quality control.

production unit. The plant where production takes place. Size is dictated chiefly by the technological factors involved in production.

productivity. The production or increase in wealth or value brought about by the full utilisation of the capacity of the workforce. An increase in productivity occurs when output increases without an increase in costs, or when output is maintained but costs decrease.

profit. There are two rewards for the use of capital – interest and profit. Profit is that part of production paid to the investor for bearing the risks of losing his capital. Generally speaking, profit is an increase in the value of assets. *Profit can be utilised* to permit further growth – in the same industry by 'ploughing back' or on distribution to shareholders it can be invested in new industries. Profits can also be used to pay higher rewards to the factors of production. (Note that the interest due on loans to businesses must also be paid out of profits.) Profit-seeking has played an important part in economic progress, particularly in free enterprise systems. It can only be earned where a firm produces goods which consumers both want to buy and are willing to pay for. The possibility that losses may be made is a spur to efficient low-cost production. Abuses of the profit system can be controlled by legislation, or taxation can be used to redistribute incomes.

profit and loss account. A summary of the resources a firm has acquired and how they have been allocated during the financial period. Together with the BALANCE SHEET, this account must by law be filed annually with the Registrar of Companies for public scrutiny. (*See also* APPROPRIATION ACCOUNT.) (Profit and loss does not show the rate of flow of revenue income; delays are not apparent and do not indicate any period where cash flow problems may have been experienced.) If a firm makes sufficient profit after tax, then some money can be 'ploughed back' into the organisation through a reserve fund.

profit margin. The difference between a company's profit before tax and its sales revenue.

profit-related schemes. Incentive schemes for the workforce based on the 'value added' concept offer employees a percentage share of an organisation's created wealth.

profitability. Financial gain or profit.

profitability test. A measure of management performance.

$$\text{Profitability } (\%) = \frac{\text{Profit before interest and tax}}{\text{Total assets}} \times 100$$

pro forma invoice. An invoice sent to a customer who will pay cash for goods rather than being allowed credit. Payment is made on or before receipt of the goods. It is sometimes used when trading with customers who have temporarily exceeded their credit limit. A pro forma invoice is also sent with goods 'on approval' or on a 'sale or return' basis. It gives a description of the goods and prices, but is not sent in this case to show the recipient that a charge is being made.

program (computers). A set of instructions written by a programmer, designed to enable the computer to perform some specified task. Programs are the computer's 'software'.

programme evaluation and review technique (PERT). A network analysis technique. If time is being considered, the objective is to find the operation with the least idle time; if cost is under consideration, the objective is to find the solution which will cost the least.

programming language (computers). A special language, such as BASIC, COBOL or PILOT, in which a program is written so that the computer can understand it.

progress chasing/progressing (*also* expediting). The process of expediting orders to eliminate bottlenecks or production stoppages.

prohibition. A judicial writ prohibiting a lower court from proceeding in a case beyond its jurisdiction.

Projects and Export Policy Division (PEP). The PEP division of the British Overseas Trade Board deals with large international projects. The PEP is divided into industrial sectors and offers experience in coordinating every aspect of government assistance.

promissory note. Unconditional promise in writing, signed by the promiser, to pay on demand, or on a fixed or ascertainable future date, a definite sum of money to, or to the order of, a named person. It is a NEGOTIABLE INSTRUMENT.

promoters (of limited companies). Anyone may register a company with the Registrar of Companies, and so 'promote' it. Anyone who undertakes to form a company with a definite object in mind and who takes the necessary steps to accomplish that object is a promoter. *See* FLOATING A COMPANY.

promotions. A marketing term involving advertising and public relations; promotions can include special offers, point-of-sale offers, and exhibitions.

property. Something which an owner has the exclusive right of possessing, enjoying and disposing of, or the subject of such exclusive rights (the things themselves). *Industrial property* comprises the non-physical properties of companies which can be bought and sold – goodwill, trademarks, patents and copyrights.

property insurance. *See* ACCIDENT INSURANCE.

proportional spacing. A method of printing in which each character printed takes up only the space it needs, rather than a fixed amount of space as in mono-spacing (e.g. the letter *i* needs less space than the letter *m*).

proposal form. *See* INSURANCE.

prospectus (of limited company). An advertisement giving details of a company and inviting the public to buy shares in it. A copy of the prospectus must be lodged with the Registrar of Companies before the public are invited to subscribe, and must always be available for inspection at the company's registry.

protectionist policies. Many devices may be used to protect a country's home trade and industries. These include: *embargoes* which prohibit the import of particular goods; *quotas* which limit the amounts of particular goods which may be imported; *tariffs* which impose a duty (customs duty) on certain goods entering a country.

proximate cause. *See* INSURANCE.

proxy. A person empowered by a SHAREHOLDER to vote on his behalf at company meetings.

proxy card. The form supplied by the company by which the shareholder appoints his proxy, the person who is to vote on his behalf.

prudential controls (Bank of England). Controls designed to ensure the stability and health of the banking system. These include measures to ensure that banks have sufficient shareholders' funds (to protect depositors against losses) and sufficient LIQUID ASSETS (to meet deposit withdrawals and other commitments).

psychometric testing. Measurement of mental capacities and attributes by psychological theory and techniques.

Public Accounts Committee (government). Committee empowered to scrutinise the accounts of nationalised industries.

Public Bills. These are introduced to Parliament by a Member of Parliament (usually by a minister unless it is a private member's Bill). *See* PRIVATE BILLS.

public borrowing. *See* PUBLIC SECTOR BORROWING REQUIREMENT (PSBR).

public company. *See* COMPANY and LIMITED LIABILITY.

public corporations. Independent bodies set up by statute or, as in the case of the BBC, by a charter issued under the Royal Prerogative, to carry out the duties entrusted to them by Parliament. The nationalised industries and local government departments are public corporations.

public enterprises. Cover municipal undertakings and nationalised undertakings. Municipal undertakings are commercial enterprises which can be operated by borough and district councils. Examples of these are swimming baths, bus services, leisure centres and theatres.

public expenditure. Government expenditure is made up of: *capital expenditure* on new fixed assets, such as schools, hospitals, roads, etc.; *current expenditure* – the 'running costs' necessary for schools, hospitals, the armed forces, etc.; *transfer payments* – money contributed by taxpayers and paid out in unemployment, sickness, child and retirement benefits, and subsidies such as those on council housing; *wages and salaries* to civil servants and others in the public sector.

public finance/income. The sources of public finance are: *direct taxes* – personal (INCOME TAX), including NATIONAL INSURANCE, CORPORATION TAX, INHERITANCE TAX, CAPITAL GAINS TAX; *indirect taxation* – VAT, CUSTOMS AND EXCISE DUTIES, MOTOR VEHICLE DUTY, RATES.

public good. Product or service provided by the state for the benefit of all. Defence is an example (cf. MERIT GOOD, PRIVATE GOOD).

public law. Involves administrative law, constitutional law and criminal law, details of which are to be found under their own headings.

public limited company (PLC). *See* COMPANY and LIMITED LIABILITY.

public ownership. All organisations in the public sector of the economy are publicly or 'socially' owned. *See* BUSINESS UNITS (public sector).

public relations (PR). Defined by the Institute of Public Relations as the 'deliberate, planned and sustained effort to establish and maintain mutual understanding between an organisation and its public'. In Britain, public relations have now become generally accepted. Their value is fully appreciated in industry and has become an acknowledged part of both central and local government. Members of the Institute of Public Relations are employed by institutions; some are staff members of individual companies whose job is concerned with the interests of their employer. PR ensures that the public and press are kept informed of an organisation's activities and intentions.

public sector. All organisations in the public sector of the economy are publicly or 'socially' owned. *See* BUSINESS UNITS (public sector).

public sector borrowing requirement (PSBR). The size of government borrowing during the current year.

public sector debt replacement (PSDR). When government income exceeds expenditure in a year.

public utilities. Business organisations providing public services, such as electricity, transport, etc.

publicity. 1. Paid advertising. 2. Public attention, not necessarily giving a good profile.

pull/push marketing strategies. When it is possible to bring direct pressure to bear on a potential customer (e.g. by a salesman) it is a *push* strategy. Where it is better for advertising and promotion to be used – such as for groceries – it is a *pull* strategy.

purchases ledger. *See* BOUGHT LEDGER.

purchasing. Department responsible for buying all the goods required by a factory or business; this includes raw materials, component parts, consumables, and often capital equipment. The job of a buyer can be summed up as purchasing the right goods, in the right quantity, at the right price at the right time.

pure competition. In perfect or perfectly competitive markets, prices are fixed in an atmosphere of 'pure competition'; in such markets the price adjusts to that level which equates demand and supply.

put option (Stock Exchange). An option to sell SHARES at an agreed price at a future date, whatever happens to the market.

Q

qualitative guidance. 'Requests' by the central bank asking the banks to give priority to lending to certain sectors of the economy and to restrain lending to other sectors.

quality control. Tests to ensure that standards of quality are being maintained should take place at all stages of production.

quango (quasi-autonomous non-governmental organisation). An autonomous body set up by the British government and having statutory powers in a specific field.

quantity discount. A discount allowed to a purchaser for buying in bulk.

quarter up. The price used in valuing SHARES for taxation purposes. It is calculated on the 'quarter up' principle, that is, instead of taking the middle price in the official list, the difference between the two prices given under 'Quotations' is divided by four, and this amount added to the lower one.

quasi-governmental body. Organisation which is neither a private business nor has been elected, whose function it is to implement or further government policy.

quasi-judicial bodies. Examples are land tribunals, rent tribunals and industrial tribunals, who resolve civil conflicts outside the formal judicial process.

quasi-rent. If the supply of any factor is inelastic (i.e. it is fixed at a certain quantity), that factor will be enabled to demand more than normal rewards. *See* ECONOMIC RENT.

Queen and Parliament. Examples of some of the most important duties of the monarch are: appointment of the Prime Minister; summoning, proroguing and dissolving of Parliament; giving the Royal Assent to all Bills passed by the House of Lords and the House of Commons, thereby converting them into Acts of Parliament; appointing the judges – acting on the advice of the Prime Minister and the Lord Chancellor; granting a free pardon (on the recommendation of the Home Secretary) to those found guilty by the courts and who have subsequently been shown to be innocent.

questionnaire. A prepared set of written questions for purposes of compilation and comparison, used especially in MARKET RESEARCH.

quick assets. The assets of a business which are made up of cash, and of investments such as securities and short-term deposits, which can quickly be turned into cash.

quick ratio. *See* ACID TEST RATIO.

quorum. The minimum number of persons required to be present at a meeting in order that business may be validly transacted.

quota licences. Allow entry into the country of a specific quantity of a certain type of good; the country of origin is usually named. Quota licences restrict the import of goods by either a volume quota or a value quota.

quota sampling (statistics). This uses groups of individuals each representing the same numerical mix (i.e. a mix of age, sex, ethnic group, etc.); each sample so selected reproduces those characteristics in the same proportion as they are present in the total population.

quoted company (*also* listed company). A company whose shares are listed and traded on the STOCK EXCHANGE. If a company wishes to have the advantages of a regulated market in its securities, it must conform with company law and must sign the Stock Exchange Listed Agreement, after which it is known as a 'listed company'.

R

race relations. Under the Race Relations Act 1976, the Commission for Racial Equality is empowered to investigate cases of racial discrimination, and has a duty to promote education in the field of race relations and to improve the public attitude especially where it concerns equality of opportunity.

random access memory (RAM) (computers). Sometimes called the read/write memory, this is the temporary memory where data, instructions and results are stored temporarily, and where they can be referred to and altered.

random sample. A part of a statistical population selected in such a way that every item in the population has an equal chance of being included; it produces unbiased data.

rate of exchange. *See* EXCHANGE RATE.

rate of return (on capital investment). The ratio between net profit and capital employed. (Capital employed is the fixed assets plus working capital.)

rate of turnover. The number of times the AVERAGE STOCK is sold during the trading period:

$$\text{Rate of turnover} = \frac{\text{Turnover}}{\text{Average stock}}$$

rate support grant. Assistance (grant) given by central government to local authorities which is received in addition to their own revenue raised from rates. *Rate capping* is a limit on the amount of money which the government will allow local authorities to raise through the rates, thereby curtailing their expenditure.

rateable value. Supposed to reflect the rentable value of a property, and is the value on which local rates are assessed and charged.

rates. Rates provide about one-third of the income of local authorities; they are taxes based on the RATEABLE VALUE of a property, the amount being decided by individual local authorities. Water authorities also obtain revenue from water rates which again are based on the rateable value of properties. A COMMUNITY CHARGE is to replace the rates system in Scotland in 1989, and in England and Wales in 1990.

ratio analysis. The relationship between the profit and loss account and the balance sheet can be clarified by the use of financial ratios: *for tests of liquidity, see* CURRENT RATIO, ACID TEST RATIO, and DEBT COLLECTION PERIOD; *for tests of profitability, see* RATE OF RETURN ON CAPITAL INVESTMENT and PROFITABILITY TEST.

rationalisation. The application of the most efficient methods in production, distribution and transport.

raw materials. The essential materials and commodities for manufacturing processes, usually taken to include the products of all the extractive industries, together with those of forestry, farming and fishing; primary production is involved with making use of the natural resources of a country. Britain has to import large quantities of raw materials which are brought in mostly as primary products and as bulk cargoes, in purpose-built vessels such as oil tankers and refrigerated meat carriers. They are handled either by the COMMODITY MARKETS in the City of London, financed, transported and warehoused by middlemen until required, or directly imported by a manufacturing firm which has built up a strong link with an overseas supplier.

read only memory (ROM) (computers). This is the permanent memory, the contents of which remain static.

real accounts. Accounts relating to the assets of property (business assets) such as plant and stock.

real incomes/wages. 'Money wages' refers to the actual income earned by the worker. Real wages refers to the actual 'basket of goods' (and services) which he can purchase with it. In times of INFLATION, money wages may rise, but in fact will often not enable workers to buy as many goods or services as before.

real value. The actual (real) value of a share varies with supply and demand, and the extent to which profits have been ploughed back since the share was issued. (The nominal value of a SHARE – the value named on it – is retained throughout its life.)

recall (word processors). To transfer text stored on a disk to the word processor's memory, so that editing or other processing can be done on it.

receipts and payments account. A summarised cash account which is adequate for small organisations to present to their members as a yearly financial report.

receiving order. An order putting a receiver in temporary possession of a debtor's estate, pending bankruptcy proceedings.

recognised banks. Institutions recognised as banks by the BANK OF ENGLAND. Recognised banks and licensed deposit-takers (together with a few other institutions) make up the monetary sector.

reconciliation statement. *See* BANK RECONCILIATION STATEMENT.

record (word processors). A set of related data items, treated as a unit.

records management (word processors). A feature of some word processing systems whereby the word processor can be used to create, edit, store, sort and select, and print information that is not necessarily related to text. Maintaining lists of customers and their details is an example.

recruitment (of staff). The process whereby a job vacancy is filled. In the first place a job specification is compiled, and a suitable candidate found by any of the following methods: appointment of a person already employed by the company; through a candidate's enquiry at the workplace; through contact with schools, colleges, trade unions, Jobcentres or Careers Offices; through a private employment agency or by advertising. After consideration of the information obtained from application forms and CVs, a short list of candidates is extracted. These are interviewed and in some cases tested for ability (e.g. shorthand-typists). If a suitable candidate is selected, the offer of employment is made.

redeemable preference shares. *See* SHARES.

redemption date. The date on which a security is due to be redeemed by the issuer at its full face value. The year is included in the title of the security; the actual redemption date is that on which the last interest payment is due. It is the end of the life of a 'gilt', when the government repays £100 to the owner.

redemption yield (gilt-edged stock). The interest rate related to the return at the REDEMPTION DATE.

reducing balance method. *See* DEPRECIATION.

redundancy payments. The Employment Protection (Consolidated) Act 1978 requires employers to pay compensation to certain employees laid off or put on short time, or dismissed as redundant because the work they are doing is no longer necessary or has ceased to exist. The amount of the payment is related to pay, length of service and age. A Redundancy Payments Fund is financed by surcharges on the employers' contributions to National Insurance.

re-export. Imported goods which are to be re-exported or are for transhipment are entered on special 'Entry' forms by the Customs authorities and must be exported within one month; no Customs duty needs to be paid. Primary products embodied into manufactured goods for export are free from Customs duties.

reference. A *file reference* is the title shown on a file which identifies its position in the filing system. It can consist of any combination of letters or figures. Business letters often bear the file reference as a *letter reference*, which should be quoted on all correspondence dealing with the matter. *See also* OPEN REFERENCE and PERSONAL REFERENCE.

registered trademark. *See* TRADEMARK.

Registrar of Companies. The Registrar of Joint-Stock Companies registers companies formed under the Companies Acts. *See* FLOATING A COMPANY.

Registrar of Government Stocks. The BANK OF ENGLAND is responsible for the registration of government stocks, the stocks of nationalised industries and public boards. It also pays dividends on such stocks when they become due.

registration of business names. If the name of a sole trader's business is other than his own name it must be registered under the Registration of Business Names Act 1916. Partnership names and the names of limited companies must also be registered.

reinsurance. Insurance companies limit their liability on a risk to a reasonable amount. Where a proposal in excess of that limit is made it is dealt with by reinsurance, the excess being offered to other companies. Some companies only deal in reinsurance business offered to them by companies undertaking direct risks.

renounceable documents. Temporary evidence of ownership of SHARES; each includes full instructions on what the holder should do if he wishes to have the newly-issued shares registered in his own name, or if he wishes to renounce them in favour of somebody else; action must be taken by a specified date.

rent. 1. Money or other periodic payment made for the use of land, buildings, etc. (Part of the general expenses of a business – fixed costs – as distinct from the direct cost of producing an article.) 2. The term 'rent' has a special meaning in economics – it is the payment made for the use of the factors of production whose supply is inelastic (i.e. cannot be increased with ease). Land is a prime example because it is a factor of production which is in inelastic supply to changes in price. There are other examples of factors which cannot be easily reproduced even if earnings rise, e.g. any natural ability which a person may possess.

rent tribunals. The Rent Act 1965 set up local Rent Assessment Committees to fix 'fair rents' and made intimidation and harassment of tenants illegal. Landlords, tenants or the local authority may apply to these rent tribunals to have the rent of property fixed.

reply coupon. *See* INTERNATIONAL REPLY COUPON.

reports. The furnishing of reports is a necessary function of management. Special reports are called for to investigate a special field of activity; in such reports the terms of reference should be clearly stated and the reports should include recommendations or suggestions.

resale price maintenance. Under the Resale Prices Act 1976, manufacturers cannot compel retailers to charge a certain price for their goods.

research and development/research and technology. The Department of Trade and Industry encourages and provides information and support for collaborative research schemes – research and development conducted jointly by more than one organisation. Industrial and commercial firms, universities and polytechnics, independent research and development organisations and government research laboratories can all be involved. The Department offers grants towards the cost of a collaborative project. The benefits of collaboration are not confined to this country; there are also opportunities in Europe.

reserve requirement (Bank of England). Obligation on banks (or other institutions) to invest a specified minimum percentage of their deposits in specified assets.

reserves (company). A company creates reserves when it retains and reinvests the profits in the business; reserves for general purposes serve to strengthen the financial position of a business. Such reserves become a part of the capital of the company.

reserves (gold and foreign currency). Today, Britain's gold reserves represent only part of the face value of the country's issued currency. Another part is reflected in the amount of foreign currency it holds. *See* EXCHANGE EQUALISATION ACCOUNT.

residual value. The amount for which a fixed asset can be sold at the end of its working life.

resolution (meetings). A resolution is the acceptance of a motion or proposal that has been put to the vote and agreed by the necessary majority at a meeting.

'Resource'. An independent organisation jointly sponsored by the British government and the British Standards Institution. It aims to promote technical cooperation in key overseas markets in the fields of standards, quality, metrology, testing, and the way these practices are applied to industrial and agricultural development and technology areas.

resources. A stock which can be drawn on to satisfy a want. Any attempt made to satisfy a want must make use of three classes of resources (the factors of production): *land* – natural resources; *capital* – the resources of tools and equipment; *labour* – human resources.

responsibility of organisations. All organisations owe a wide social responsibility to their employees, the community and the natural environment. This is often enforced by laws regarding employment and protection of the environment (such as planning constraints); PRESSURE GROUPS also play their part.

restrictive practices (labour). Practice by members of a trade union which limits the flexibility of management, particularly in relation to the allocation of certain forms of work.

restrictive trade practices. If a number of firms making or selling a particular product, or providing a commercial service, agree to fix prices, divide up the market, or restrict supplies, this agreement must be submitted beforehand to the Office of Fair Trading. It is then placed on a register, open to public inspection. The Restrictive Practices Court is then asked to rule whether the agreement is against the public interest and, if so, to ban it.

retail banking. Banks with a branch network who deal with the public. *Retail deposits* are the moneys of individuals and companies deposited with such banks.

Retail Consortium. A trade association which speaks on behalf of retailers generally.

retail price index (RPI). Each month a figure is calculated which is officially described as the index of retail prices. This index (which replaced the old cost of living index) measures the changes in the prices paid for the goods and services on which the great majority of householders spend most of their money. The index is widely used in discussions on wage claims, and in some industries wages vary with it automatically. Also, the government uses the index to measure the effects of its policies. It is compiled on the basis of recommendations made by a committee on which employers, trade unions, cooperative societies, shopkeepers, housewives and others are represented. The index of retail prices is produced every month.

retail trade. That part of commercial services which provides the last link in the chain of distribution where goods are sold to the final consumer. Its function is to sell goods; to break bulk and prepare goods for resale; to arrange hire purchase if necessary; to provide after-sales service if necessary; and to act as a liaison between consumer and wholesaler/

manufacturer. *Types of retail shop:* mobile shop, unit trader, department store, multiple shop, tied shop, self-service store, supermarket and hypermarket. *Types of non-shop retail outlets:* mail order, street market, door-to-door salesman, automatic vending machine.

retailer/wholesaler cooperatives (voluntary chains). In order to compete with the large supermarket chains, associations of small retailers have been set up – SPAR and MACE are examples (SPAR stands for Society for the Protection of the Average Retailer). By joining forces and buying in bulk – i.e. by controlling their own wholesaling and warehousing – these associations afford the opportunity to small retailers to buy at more favourable prices, and to pass the advantage on to the consumer.

retained profits. That part of the profits of a company belonging to the holders of the EQUITY, but not distributed by way of DIVIDEND. Also known as *retentions.*

return. The profit from labour, investment or business.

return on capital employed. This percentage figure is essential if a businessman is to know how his business is faring:

$$\frac{\text{Return on capital}}{\text{employed}} = \frac{\text{Net profit}}{\text{Capital employed at start of year}} \times 100$$

returns inward/returns outward. When a customer returns goods (for which he has received an invoice) because they are either damaged or unsuitable, these are 'returns inwards' and the customer is sent a credit note. When the business returns goods ('returns outwards') which have already been invoiced to them, they should receive a credit note from the supplier.

returns to scale. When an increase in size of a production unit results in a more than proportional increase in output, there are increased returns to scale.

revenue. The total income of an organisation for a given period.

revenue expenditure. When a company spends money but does not obtain a permanent asset, the expenditure is termed revenue expenditure. It covers the day-to-day operating costs of an organisation, such as rent, rates, insurance, salaries, wages, repairs and maintenance, licences, petrol and oil.

revenue reserves. Reserves created by ploughing back profits into the business. They may be either special reserves for particular purposes, or general reserves held back for the equalisation of dividends as between good and bad years.

revocable credits. *See* LETTER OF CREDIT.

revolving credit. *See* BUDGET ACCOUNT (2).

rewards to factors. The factors of production are land, capital and labour. The economic rewards for each of these are: land – *rent*; capital – *interest/dividend* is paid to the investor for the postponement of his own consumption, and for allowing his capital to be used by entrepreneurs; profits are paid to the investor for the risk of losing his capital. labour – *wages/salaries.*

rider (meetings). An addition to a motion. Unlike an amendment, a rider can be put either before or after the motion is voted upon.

rights issue. When a company whose SHARES are already listed makes a further offer of shares for sale, the Stock Exchange requires that these be offered to existing shareholders in proportion to their existing shareholdings, usually at a preferential price. (A 'one-for-three' rights issue means that a shareholder is offered one new share for every three held.)

ring trading. In some commodity markets, 'ring trading' is carried on. In the LONDON METAL EXCHANGE, members sit on benches arranged in a circle (it used to be a chalk ring drawn on the floor) and there are 'rings' for various metals, each metal being traded twice a day. A dealer in the LME ring calls out his bids and offers to the 'ring' by 'open outcry' so that all can hear the price.

risk capital. The shareholding of a company in ordinary shares (equity). *Ordinary shareholders* share in the company's risks and rewards, and own the *risk capital.*

risk management. The anticipation, prevention and action taken against any risk which threatens the workforce, property or profits of a company. All risks have commercial implications: some risks are insurable (fire, theft, floods and factory accidents); but commercial risks (losses due to poor marketing or changes in consumer tastes) are also the concern of risk management.

road transport. Provides door-to-door delivery, offering many specialised vehicles – bulk haulage, containers, tankers for liquids, etc. Vehicles can take the best routes available and there are computerised routes for heavy vehicles made available to drivers. Though slower than rail for journeys over 200 miles, the advantages of door-to-door consignments are often allowed to outweigh this consideration. Because the actual use of the roads is free, hauliers' capital requirements are reduced. Among the disadvantages of road transport are the heavy social costs borne by the congestion and pollution it generates. Running costs are heavy, as petrol costs are particularly vulnerable to international pressures and taxation. Motorways provide the answer to many road transport problems. A further consideration is the effect of the existence of a motorway on the location of industry, and the availability of labour.

roll on/roll of (RORO). These ships (ferries) are designed to allow road vehicles to embark and disembark without unloading.

round tripping. The process whereby bank customers borrow from the banks and then redeposit the funds in the money markets at a higher rate of interest.

royalty. Payment to an author, composer, etc. for every copy sold or every public performance. A firm that licences an overseas company to produce its patented products 'under licence' abroad can earn 'royalties' on sales, which moves the licensing firm into the invisible exports field. Royalties may also be paid to owners of mineral rights for their use.

S

salaries and wages. Earnings paid by employers to employees for specified services. *Salaries* are usually quoted as a yearly figure (*per annum*), paid in twelve equal parts (per calendar month) or thirteen equal parts – four-weekly (per lunar month). *Wages* are usually weekly payments, sometimes based on an hourly rate. Salaries and wages may be paid in one of the following ways: in cash, by cheque, through credit transfer (bank giro), or through the Girobank payment service.

sale and leaseback. The selling of the leasehold of a property owned by a business to a financial institution, which thereafter leases the property back to the company for its occupation and use. The purpose is to release some of the capital for use in the business.

sale and repurchase agreement. Purchase of bills by the BANK OF ENGLAND from the DISCOUNT HOUSES with an agreement that the discount houses will buy the bills back on an agreed day. On occasion the Bank has also conducted sale and repurchase operations in gilt-edged stock with the CLEARING BANKS.

Sale of Goods Act 1979. *See.* CONSUMER PROTECTION.

sale or return. Goods 'on sale or return' are those sent to a person or firm on the understanding that they may be returned to the supplier if unsold, usually by a specified time. *See* PRO FORMA INVOICE.

sales accounting. When a sale on credit is made, an INVOICE is sent to the customer. A retained copy forms the basis of bookkeeping entries relating to the transaction. The invoices are initially listed in the sales record (sales daybook) and debited to the customer's account. At the end of the month the sales book is totalled and the total credited to the sales ledger (or sales account). At the end of the year the twelve monthly totals in the sales account give the total sales for the year for transfer to the trading account.

sales analysis. The breakdown of sales figures to judge performance and further evaluation and control. Results illustrate the size of the individual orders which make up the total volume for the period; the geographical distribution; the types of customers and outlets.

sales budget. The forecast of sales is difficult to assess in view of possible underlying and seasonal trends. Large businesses usually use mathematical forecasting techniques based on the analysis of figures for past trading.

sales force. Besides the basic function of selling, salesmen may also be employed in display and service activities, and should be trained in product and market knowledge, selling skills and administration. Geographical areas regarded as 'difficult' should be given only to experienced staff to cover. Salesmen may be paid by a prearranged salary, a salary plus commission, or by commission only. A bonus award may be paid.

sales ledger. A volume of the LEDGER set aside for the personal accounts of customers.

sales revenue. The net sales of a business – the total sales less discounts and returns.

sampling. Taking a sample of a statistical population whose properties are studied to gain information about the whole can provide useful data in market research. Large-scale sampling is expensive but it has been found that for many purposes adequate information can be obtained from carefully selected samples. *See* QUOTA SAMPLING, RANDOM SAMPLING.

SatStream. British Telecom International's communication system via satellite. A direct office-to-office communications link, SatStream is a high-speed digital circuit that is provided directly via satellite, bypassing public switched networks. A customer in the UK is connected via a high grade digital circuit to a satellite earth terminal on BTI premises which will be directed towards the appropriate satellite. Customers can also have a small dish satellite earth terminal on their own premises. While most users acquire SatStream for communications to a single location, it is also possible for the signal to be received at any number of points within the satellite's coverage. The service is available to North America, Western Europe and India and is being extended. SatStream is designed to enable international companies to transfer large quantities of data quickly, economically, in a wide variety of forms (telephone, telex and data transmission, and a number of specialist services such as video conferencing and broadcast television via satellite), and to a large number of potential destinations. Typical uses are: firms of brokers can have multiple speech circuits between markets; slow-scan and freeze-frame video images can be transmitted for remote diagnostic and trouble-shooting operations; electronic libraries can distribute news and documents to automated offices via bulk data transfer; publishers can use SatStream for remote printing, possibly in a number of centres using the point-to-multipoint option. In remote areas, SatStream can be used to establish temporary telecommunications links using a mobile terminal, bringing business communications to a remote area, such as a construction site. The communication needs of the offshore oil and gas industries can be met by the *SatStream Offshore Service.*

save (word processors). To transfer a document from the word processor's memory to a disk.

save as you earn (SAYE). Several organisations, including building societies, run SAYE schemes, and some employers will make automatic deductions from pay of the amount to be saved and will pay the savings organisations direct.

savings. If people or businesses are not consuming their entire incomes, saving is taking place. If the savings are 'hoarded' they will be non-productive. Most ordinary people save through the institutional investors (banks, building societies, insurance companies, pension funds, etc.) who pass on the savings in the way of investment to entrepreneurs.

scrip issue. *See* CAPITALISATION ISSUE.

sea transport. An efficient mercantile marine force is essential to a nation which depends on international trade for survival. Though air transport almost monopolises international passenger transport, the requirements of the import trade (raw materials) and the export trade (mostly manufactured goods) demand that a large shipping force – including many 'specialist' ships – are available for specific types of cargo. Among these specialist vessels are: *container ships* which, besides carrying large and varied cargoes, offer also the facility of a quick 'turn round' at container ports; *bulk carriers* which carry only one commodity; *oil tankers* – bulk carriers but of enormous size and known as VLCCs (VLCC = very large crude carrier). In addition, to cover the day-to-day and varied requirements of the import and export trades there are: *passenger cargo liners* – cargo ships which cater for a few passengers; and *tramps* (small cargo ships). *See* SHIPPING.

sea waybill. Documentary delays had become a serious problem when the General Council of British Shipping and SITPRO developed the sea waybill. It is not intended to replace the BILL OF LADING where it is necessary for the exporter to retain clear title to the goods until security of payment is assured. Unlike the bill of lading, the sea waybill is not a document of title; it provides a receipt for the goods by the carrier, and evidence of the contract of carriage for the goods as described.

SEAQ. *See* STOCK EXCHANGE AUTOMATED QUOTATIONS SYSTEM.

seasonal unemployment. *See* UNEMPLOYMENT.

secondary market. Trading in 'second-hand' securities on the International Stock Exchange. For NEW ISSUES *see* GILT-EDGED MARKET, ISSUING HOUSES.

secondary picket. *See* PICKET.

secondary production. Utilises those things produced at the primary stage to manufacture more sophisticated products.

securities. General name for all stocks and shares of all types. In common usage, *stocks* are *fixed-interest* securities and shares are the rest, though strictly speaking, the distinction is that stocks are denominated in money terms.

Securities and Investment Board. The City 'watchdog', a private company with regulatory powers assigned to it by the Financial Services Act 1986. It supervises the self-regulatory organisations (SROs), each of which has had to devise a rule-book for approval by the SIB. Different financial activities are covered by: AFBD – Association of Futures Brokers and Dealers; FIMBRA – Financial Intermediaries, Managers and Brokers Regulatory Association; IMRO – Investment Management Regulatory Organisation; LAUTRO – Life Assurance and Unit Trusts Regulatory Organisation; TSA –

The Securities Association. Certain professional bodies whose members undertake investment business (e.g. accountants) can apply to be members of Recognised Professional Bodies (RPBs) instead of joining an SRO, though members have to be authorised to carry on investment business.

security (for loan). *See* COLLATERAL SECURITY.

segmentation (market). *See* MARKET SEGMENT.

selection. *See* RECRUITMENT.

selective credit policy (Bank of England). The use of monetary and credit controls to influence the allocation of credit between different categories of borrowers.

self-regulatory organisations (SROs). *See* SECURITIES AND INVESTMENT BOARD.

semi-manufactures. Among the resources which manufacturers call on to assist in the process of production are semi-manufactures – components for assembly into major installations. They are improved primary products and are classed as producer or capital goods.

sequestration. Seizure (e.g. of a debtor's property) by order of a court.

service industries. Commercial services and personal services together form the tertiary arm of production. Commercial services include: *trade* – retail and wholesale, home trade and international trade; *ancillary commercial services (the aids to trade)* – advertising, banking, communications, financial services, insurance, transport and warehousing. Personal services (direct services) are 'intangible' and given direct from the producer of the service to the consumer. Examples of such producers are doctors, teachers, entertainers, editors and policemen.

settlement day. *See* ACCOUNT DAY.

Sex Discrimination Act 1975. Set up the Equal Opportunities Commission which makes it illegal to discriminate against employees or applicants because of their sex.

share capital. *See* CAPITAL (TYPES OF).

share certificate. The legal document issued to a shareholder certifying ownership of a part of the company concerned.

share groups. *See* ALPHA, BETA, GAMMA, DELTA SHARES.

shared facilities (computers). A general term given to either shared logic or shared resources configurations. *Shared Logic.* A configuration in which a number of word processors are stripped of their disks and control electronics, and instead connected to a central, high-capacity disk unit (CPU). *Shared resources.* A configuration in which two or more word processors share a resource, such as a printer.

shareholder. The owner of a share is a part-owner of a limited COMPANY; the right to vote varies with the type of share held. Shareholders receive a copy of the company's annual report and accounts, and at the AGM of the company those with voting rights elect the board of directors. Shareholders are liable for INCOME TAX on any profits earned.

shareholders' funds. A company's capital which is owned by its shareholders – the share capital plus any reserves.

shares. A limited company must issue shares according to its MEMORANDUM OF ASSOCIATION. The shares of public limited companies may be issued to the public in the following ways: *by a prospectus* which is an advertisement giving details of a company and inviting the public to buy shares in it; *by an offer for sale* using the services of an ISSUING HOUSE; *by a placing* – a system of issuing shares by asking institutional investors to buy up the issue, usually effected by an ISSUING HOUSE. *The nominal value of a share* – the value named on it – is retained throughout its life, but its actual value varies with supply and demand.

TYPES OF SHARE

Deferred shares – also called *founder's shares.* These are shares issued to the original creator of a firm who sells out to a company. The owner agrees to defer any DIVIDEND due to him until the other shareholders have had a reasonable dividend, but he has voting rights. *Ordinary shares* or '*equities*'. The most common form of share – the ordinary shareholders own the company. These shares carry the most risk, but also the best prospects of future growth. Their price is often determined not so much by past results as the expectation of future events. It is the ordinary shareholders who have the right to speak and vote at general meetings of the company. *Preference shares.* These are normally fixed-income shares, whose holders have the right to receive dividends before ordinary shareholders but after debenture and loan stock holders have received their interest. They seldom have voting rights. *Cumulative preference shares* still qualify for dividends passed in previous years, and until these have been paid up to date no payment can be made to ordinary shareholders. *Participating preference shares.* A type of preference share whose holders are entitled not only to a fixed-interest dividend, but also an additional distribution. *Redeemable shares* are those whose terms of issue provide for the company to repurchase them at a stated time. *See* OVER-THE-COUNTER MARKET, STOCK EXCHANGE, THIRD MARKET, PREMIUM, YIELD.

shiftwork. An arrangement whereby one set of production workers takes over from another set to enable manufacturing to continue without a break. Non-stop provision of *services* (police, nurses, Customs, etc.) is usually referred to as day duty, night duty, etc.

shipbroker. A BROKER who represents a shipowner and deals in the sales and insurance of ships; he also arranges cargoes for them.

shipowner's liability. Shipowners have many liabilities, not only in regard to the cargo, passengers and crew, but also in regard to any damage which may be caused by the ship itself in collision with other vessels or port installations, etc. Pollution due to sea contamination is another eventuality which shipowners must insure against.

shipping. The commercial centre of the shipping world is the BALTIC MERCANTILE AND SHIPPING EXCHANGE (the 'BALTIC'). LLOYD'S OF LONDON was originally a market exclusively for marine insurance, and shipping still figures largely in its activities today. An important aspect of Lloyd's work was that it resulted in the development of a world-wide shipping intelligence network, as one of the functions of its agents was to send to Lloyd's shipping, aviation and other news relating to the ports and areas in which they operated. Both the Baltic and Lloyd's contribute greatly to the 'invisible exports' of the BALANCE OF PAYMENTS. *See* SEA TRANSPORT.

shipping and forwarding agents. Agents who carry out the handling, through-transport arrangements, and payment collection for the greater part of exports from the United Kingdom.

shipping conference. *See* LINER CONFERENCES.

shipping documents. *See* EXPORT DOCUMENTATION.

shipping marks. The identification marks put on the cargo containers or chests by the shipping company. Every consignment must bear comprehensive shipping marks, details of which must appear on the invoice. Not only the final destination but also any special handling instructions must be clearly marked. The international signs for 'Keep dry', 'This side up', 'Fragile' and 'Radioactive' are used.

shipping note. A printed form which needs to be completed when goods are shipped. It is submitted to the receiving authority at the docks and lists the ship on which the goods are to be loaded, the marks, numbers, measurements, etc. The SITPRO Standard Shipping Note can be used when delivering non-hazardous export consignments to any British port, container base or other cargo reception point. The SITPRO Dangerous Goods Note should be used if the delivery includes items which are classified as dangerous.

shop floor. 1. The area in which machinery or workbenches are located in a factory or mill. 2. The workers in an establishment as distinct from the management.

shop steward/office representative. The workplace representative of a trade union elected by a group of union members to represent their views to the employer.

short-dated securities/shorts. Government and other stocks with less than seven years to redemption.

short-notice money. Money which bill-brokers borrow from banks, commercial firms, institutional investors, etc. which is repayable in a few days' time.

sight deposits. Deposits (of money) which can be withdrawn at any time.

sight drafts. A 'foreign sight' Bill of Exchange used in a 'D/P transaction' which is payable on sight or on presentation.

silver bullion market. The price of silver is dictated by supply and demand which at any particular time varies from one world centre to another. The price is fixed once a day by a group of merchant bankers; quotations are made in both sterling and dollars.

simplification. The three 'S's' of mass production techniques are simplification, standardisation and specialisation. Simplification is the process of making a manufactured article as simple and functional as possible.

Simplification of International Trade Procedures (SITPRO). A British Overseas Trade Board activity which has produced a revised set of forms to simplify overseas trade procedures. SITPRO provides guidance on customs procedures, and helps to avoid needless delays in payment, especially with letters of credit.

Single European Act. The heads of state or government and the institutions of the European Community have agreed to achieve an open market without barriers by 1992. In view of all the tasks to be accomplished and the obstacles of every kind to be surmounted, this is one of the most ambitious European projects to be conceived in recent years. The Single European Act contains the first amendments to the Treaty of Rome since its adoption in 1957; it entered into force on 1 July 1987. This Act has replaced the original Treaty requirements as regards certain measures which have as their object the establishment and functioning of the internal market. Another major aspect of the Single Act is the new 'cooperation procedure' which allows the European Parliament a greater input to the Community legislative process, in relation to those areas where the procedure applies. The procedure demands closer liaison between both the Commission and the Council with the European Parliament, through the first and second reading of proposals, as they pass from the stage of Commission initiative to Council adoption. The Single Act also sets out a number of amendments to the original Treaties covering such diverse subjects as economic and social cohesion, environment, cooperation between the institutions and political cooperation between the member states. The importance of the Act for the achievement of the internal market lies in the fact that it provides the necessary political impetus and legal framework to achieve a truly unified market by 1992. Above all, the adoption of the Single Act reflects the renewed political will of the Community to halt its economic fragmentation and to complete, within a given time-frame, the aims of the original Treaties. In Britain the Department of Trade and Industry has prepared a set of guidelines – 'The Single Market – Europe Open for Business' – with an action checklist for businesses. The Department has also prepared a large number of fact sheets for their use. More than two million British workers will receive government-funded training over the four years 1988–92 to help industry compete in the Single European Market.

sinking fund. A fund created by setting aside a fixed sum of money each year to provide for the replacement of assets.

SITPRO. *See* SIMPLIFICATION OF INTERNATIONAL TRADE PROCEDURES.

sleeping partner. *See* PARTNER (limited).

slush fund. Fund for bribing (public) officials or for carrying on corrupting propaganda.

Small Claims Court. Cases may be brought in the Small Claims Court by individuals without the need to employ a solicitor. There is a financial limit to the claim being made.

Small Firms Service. Run by the Department of Employment, this is an information and counselling service to help owners and managers of small businesses with their plans and problems. It also acts as an advisory service to those thinking of starting their own business. The service, which operates through a nationwide network of Small Firms Centres, is designed to encourage business efficiency. There is no limit to the type of business the service will help. The Small Firms Service provides information on any business problem; from finance, diversification and industrial training to exporting, planning, technological advances, industrial relations and marketing. The service can put enquirers in touch quickly with the right people in local authorities, government departments, the professions, libraries, chambers of commerce or any other body to help with the problem. It can also identify national and international sources of information that may be needed. If the enquiry is beyond straightforward sources of information, it can be discussed with a Small Firms Counsellor, an experienced businessman who may well have faced a similar situation.

Smithfield Market. The principal London meat market.

social capital. *See* CAPITAL (TYPES OF).

social costs. All organisations should have a sense of responsibility towards the social environment. POLLUTION of the sea and rivers, air pollution, noise, congestion on the roads, or the charging of excessive prices are all antisocial activities whose costs are borne socially – that is, by the public.

social needs. Education, health, welfare, pensions and social security are social services provided for by the government for the good of the public. Many services are also provided by the private sector for which charges are made. The legal profession, insurance, banking, etc. all provide services which are beneficial and necessary for today's society.

societies and clubs. Private organisations, usually run by a committee elected by the members. The annual accounts are normally presented as a RECEIPTS AND PAYMENT ACCOUNT; any surplus cash in hand or at the bank is available for the members to dispose of as they wish.

socio-economic groups. A method of dividing the population into groups based on income and social status, used by market researchers and others when compiling SAMPLES. Groupings are as follows:

Group A – upper middle class	– higher managerial, administrative or professional;
Group B – middle class	– intermediate managerial, administrative, professional;
Group C1 – lower middle class	– supervisory or clerical and junior management, administrative or professional;
Group C2 – skilled working class	– skilled manual workers;
Group D – working class	– semi-skilled and unskilled workers;
Group E – those at lowest level of subsistence	– state pensioners or widows (no other earner); casual or lowest grade workers.

software (computers). Name given to the programs (sets of instructions) that the microprocessor can act on to control the operation of the hardware.

sole trader/proprietor. The small sole trader business is simple to establish and has the advantage that the owner is entitled to all the profits. Other advantages are the freedom of action enjoyed by the owner, the personal incentive which exists, and the personal contact with employees and customers. Disadvantages lie in the uncertain future of such businesses which can fail through no fault of the owner, who suffers the entire loss of his personal fortune if this happens. Also there may be problems of management in so far as the owner must take full responsibility for all decisions, and small businesses often find finance for expansion difficult to obtain. Sole traders, especially small retailers, do manage to survive in spite of the many difficulties at present facing them. *See* RETAILER/WHOLESALER COOPERATIVES, SMALL FIRMS SERVICE .

sound synthesizer (computers). Acting on signals from the computer, this can put sounds together to make words, etc.

source and application of funds statement. *See* ANNUAL REPORT AND ACCOUNTS.

span of control. Refers to the number of subordinates a manager can effectively control. The factors that govern this number are the complexity of the work, whether duties interlock, the degree of self-discipline among the subordinates and the capabilities of the manager.

special deposits. Calls by the BANK OF ENGLAND for institutions in the monetary sector to place balances with the Bank equal to a specified percentage of their eligible liabilities. This is a monetary measure used to take money 'out' of the economy and effectively reduces the amount of money which the banks can lend.

special drawing rights (SDRs). The INTERNATIONAL MONETARY FUND gave to all its members that agreed to accept them an allocation of units, each worth one US dollar. A country wishing to use SDR notifies the Fund that it wishes to exchange some of these units for usable foreign currency. The authorities then designate which countries will make currency available and who will take SDR units instead.

specialisation. The DIVISION OF LABOUR. The means by which mass production – the manufacture of goods on a large scale – is made possible. Each worker becomes a specialist, specialising in his own particular part of the productive process. Specialisation, together with simplification and standardisation, forms the basis of mass production.

specific duties. Customs duties may be specific duties or *ad valorem* duties. *Specific duties* are based on a fixed quantity – i.e. the rate is per unit of weight, volume, measure or number.

speculator. An investor who invests his money in a more or less risky way for the sake of unusually large profits. Speculators are especially active on the highly-organised markets of the City of London, particularly the Stock Exchange and commodity markets. On the Stock Exchange there are three main kinds of speculator – BULLS, BEARS and STAGS; they exert a moderating effect on the market; prices do not rise as high nor sink as low as they might do if they were not active. Speculators on the commodity markets deal in FUTURES and play an important role in balancing supply and demand between the producers (miners and farmers) and the companies which process and sell these products to the public. *See also* LONDON INTERNATIONAL FINANCIAL FUTURES EXCHANGE.

Spitalfields Market. The fruit, flower and vegetable market in the East End of London.

spot dealing/spot markets. On the physical COMMODITY MARKETS, materials are bought at agreed prices on either 'spot' or 'futures' contracts. 'Spot' dealings are for goods already available which are delivered on immediate settlement (in 'spot cash').

spreadsheet (computers). A software system in which large groups of numerical data can be displayed on a VDU in a set format (e.g. in rows and columns) and rapid automatic calculations can be made. They are useful for financial information and are capable of presenting information as a graph.

staff appraisal. The objects of such an appraisal (the judging of an employee's performance and possible ways of improving it) are to discover the training needs, determine the future career, decide on a possible merit pay award, and to motivate the employee.

stag (Stock Exchange). A speculator who applies for shares in a new issue with the intention of selling them at once on the Stock Exchange should they be over-subscribed and, therefore, in strong demand. The price at which he sells will be greater than his buying price.

stamp duty (Stock Exchange). A UK tax levied on the purchase of shares.

standard costing. The process of determining the total cost of a product or service based on a budgeted level of output under standard conditions. It enables actual costs to be compared with the standard yardstick and any variances investigated if they exceed a permitted level.

standard paragraph (word processors). A piece of text which can be a part of many different documents, e.g. a clause within a contract. It is stored on disk, and brought into the text when needed. A collection of standard paragraphs makes up a *library* or *glossary*, and is used in document assembly.

standard shipping note. *See* SHIPPING NOTE.

standardisation. 1. The three S's of mass production techniques are standardisation, simplification and specialisation. Standardisation is the making of standard parts which can be used in many different manufactures. 2. The standards committees of the BRITISH STANDARDS INSTITUTION are drawn from industry, government departments, professional, scientific and technical bodies and consumer groups; they prepare standards issued by the divisional councils in building, chemicals, engineering and textiles. British Codes of Practice are drawn up by a special council.

standing committee. *See* COMMITTEE SYSTEM.

standing order (banking). An order given to a bank to pay a fixed sum of money at regular intervals to a designated payee. It saves repeated drawings of cheques and ensures that payments are not forgotten.

standing orders. The term applied to the rules regulating the conduct and procedure of certain official bodies.

start-up schemes. *See* LOAN GUARANTEE SCHEME.

state-owned concerns/state undertakings. All organisations in the public sector are 'publicly' or 'socially' owned. *See* BUSINESS UNITS (public sector).

state pension. All employed persons are covered by the State Pension Scheme in Great Britain. Pensions above the normal rate are available through the State Earnings-Related Pension Scheme (SERPS), a scheme organised by the employer, or by a PERSONAL PORTABLE PENSION.

statement of account. All businesses make a practice of balancing their debtors' accounts at regular intervals, usually a month. At the end of each period a statement of account is made up and sent to each debtor showing the amounts credited and debited during the period, and the final figure which may be what he owes or a credit balance.

statement of affairs. In the case of a trader who has kept incomplete records of his financial dealings it is sometimes necessary to complete a statement of affairs to give a true financial picture of his business. To prepare such a statement, the following figures have to be ascertained: the value of stock, cash in hand and at the bank; the total sums due from debtors and to trade creditors; the value of any other assets; the value of further liabilities and outstanding expenses; the value of any payments made in advance. A statement of affairs is also submitted by a debtor who has been served with a receiving order (a person who cannot pay his debts and who is insolvent). This lists the debtor's assets and his debts, giving the names and addresses of creditors and how much they are owed.

statement of source and allocation of funds. *See* ANNUAL REPORT AND ACCOUNTS.

statistics. The following are a selection of statistical publications issued by the government and available from HMSO: *Annual Abstract of Statistics; Census of Distribution* – complete analysis of distribution through retail outlets (last carried out in 1981); *Census of Population* (every ten years); *Census of Production* (every five years) – information on manufacturing, mining, quarrying, building, contracting and public utilities; *Economic Trends; Monthly Digest of Statistics* – information collected by various government departments summarised in the *Annual Abstract of Statistics; National Income and Expenditure* (the Blue Book); *Social Trends.*

Statistics and Market Intelligence Library (BOTB). Gives free access to a comprehensive collection of foreign and UK statistics, trade directories, development plans and other published information on overseas markets, including a microfilm database on products and markets.

status enquiry agent. Provides information to suppliers regarding the financial status of buyers.

status line (word processors). A line at the top or bottom of the screen that gives information about work currently being done (specifically things like the cursor position within the text, the length of a page, and any prompts the system may issue).

statute law. A law expressly written by the legislature and therefore an Act of Parliament. All Acts of Parliament contribute to the British Constitution.

statutory. As laid down by a law enacted by Parliament.

statutory declaration of compliance. This is a sworn statement drawn up on the promotion of a company confirming that the requirements of the Companies Acts relevant to registration and 'matters precedent and incidental thereto' have been completed. It is one of the initial documents lodged with the Registrar of Companies for approval before a CERTIFICATE OF INCORPORATION can be issued. *See* FLOATING A COMPANY.

statutory deductions. Refers to the compulsory deductions from an employee's gross pay for income tax and National Insurance.

statutory instrument. Certain Acts of Parliament empower ministers of the Crown to make regulations having force of law on matters of detail. These are statutory instruments and must be laid before Parliament, which can annul them. This procedure is 'delegated legislation'; sometimes power is given to local authorities, public transport undertakings and other organisations to make rules such as by-laws which come under the general heading of 'delegated legislation'.

statutory meeting. *See* MEETINGS (of limited companies).

statutory report. This report must, by the provisions of the Companies Acts, be sent to every member of a public limited company fourteen days before the STATUTORY MEETING and must be filed with the Registrar of Companies. The information must include the following: total number of SHARES allotted and how payments have been made; the amount of cash received for shares; the receipts and payments of the company; an account or estimate of the preliminary expenses; names, addresses and descriptions of directors, auditors, managers and secretary; parts of any modification of any contract which requires the approval of the statutory meeting. The report must be certified by two directors and the auditors.

statutory tribunals. There are over 2,000 special courts called administrative tribunals which have been set up to settle disputes in such areas as rent control and national health insurance. Industrial tribunals deal with a particularly large number of complaints concerned with disputes arising out of employment. These tribunals, though dealing with the laws of the land, cover many aspects of life and are less formal than ordinary law courts. Each tribunal specialises in one type of dispute. *See* ADMINISTRATIVE LAW.

sterling. The pound sterling is the British monetary unit.

sterling area. Today, this consists of the UK, the Channel Isles, the Isle of Man and Gibraltar.

stock. 1. (Stock Exchange). *See* SECURITIES. 2. *See* STOCK IN HAND.

stock control. The function of the stock controller is to ensure that there is always sufficient stock in hand to meet current requirements, and that the replenishment of stock is efficiently organised. The keeping of stock records is vitally important to the correct running of a stockroom; computerisation is an aid to efficiency in this area. The following are important in stock control: there must always be for every item *a full description* (including code number); *a maximum stock level* must be established; this depends on two factors – the amount of this particular item which is used, and the capacity of the stockroom; *the minimum stock level*: this depends on the amount used and the length of time which will elapse between placing an order for fresh supplies and their delivery period; *the re-order level:* this figure is larger than the minimum stock level and depends on the delivery period for the particular item.

Stock Exchange. A highly organised financial market where stocks and shares are bought and sold. Its purpose is to put those who wish to sell securities in touch with those who wish to buy them, so that investments can change hands in the quickest, cheapest and fairest way possible. The general level of prices is decided by the investors who use the Stock Exchange; they create the supply and demand to which the market reacts by offering prices that they hope will be attractive to an equal number of buyers and sellers. To an investor, the buying of stocks and shares is a temporary 'loan' which he may wish to cash at any time; the only way in which he can do this is to sell his shares at the best price he can get for them on the market. On the other hand, the directors of a company regard the money received for shares as a permanent 'loan'; they spend part of it on land, buildings, plant and machinery, transport, etc. The fixed capital which purchased these FIXED ASSETS cannot be turned into cash ('liquified') and cannot be returned to the investor. The investor's reward for his investment is in the form of a DIVIDEND, a share of the company's profits which are divided up between the shareholders. *Types of investment.* The three main types of securities are GILT-EDGED, DEBENTURES and SHARES. A MARKET-MAKER is an Exchange Member Firm which is obliged to buy and sell securities in which he is registered as a principal, at all times. For the most part their dealing takes place in dealing rooms using VDUs and telephones, information being supplied on the SEAQ system (*see* following entry). Dealing takes place on the following sections of the market, and all should be referred to: primary, secondary and third markets; unlisted securities market; over-the-counter market; London Options Clearing House. *See also* BIG BANG. Normally, each Stock Exchange ACCOUNT runs for two weeks (10 working days).

Stock Exchange Automated Quotation (SEAQ). System for UK securities. A continuously updated computer database containing quotations and trade reports in UK securities.

SEAQ is the official information source for trading UK securities and is used by MARKET-MAKERS (*see* previous entry).

Stock Exchange Automated Quotation International (SEAQ International). The Exchange's electronic screen system for non-UK equities displaying quotes from competing MARKET-MAKERS on composite pages.

Stock Exchange Council. Control of the Stock Exchange is vested in a Council which is elected by members.

Stock Exchange Money Broker (SEMB). Firms which lend Gilt Edged Market - Makers (GEMMs) gilts and money.

stock in hand. A store or supply of accumulated goods. Examples of stock are: raw materials awaiting processing into finished products; work in progress – stock which is actually in the production process; finished goods – awaiting sale to customers; stationery and general office stock for use in the business.

stock-in-trade. Everything which is necessary to carry on a business – materials, work in progress, finished products, tools and equipment.

stock valuation. One of the purposes of stocktaking is to support the value of stock shown in the balance sheet by physical verification.

stocktaking. Stockrooms should be checked for stock periodically or have an annual stocktaking at the end of each year. A physical check or count of all stock is made, and the results checked against the figures arrived at by the entries for stock 'in' and 'out' in the stock records. If the stock records have been properly kept, shortages in stock through pilferage, wastage or deterioration may be brought to light. *See* PERPETUAL INVENTORY.

stockturn. *See* RATE OF TURNOVER.

stolport. Airport for short take-off and landing.

straight-line method. *See* DEPRECIATION.

strategic commodities. Arms and ammunition are among items requiring an export licence before they can leave Britain.

street markets. Some local authorities provide special facilities for conducting street markets.

strict liability. A person is strictly liable for a tort committed by himself (cf. VICARIOUS LIABILITY).

strike. A works stoppage by a body of workers made as a protest or to force an employer to comply with demands. *A token strike* involves a short stoppage in support of a claim. *Selective strikes* call out numbers of workers at different locations at different times. *All-out strike* – all members of a union withdraw their labour. If the action is backed by the union it is an *official strike. Unofficial strikes* have no union backing. *Sympathetic strikes* occur when a group of workers withdraw their labour in sympathy with another group who are in dispute with their employer.

structural unemployment. *See* UNEMPLOYMENT.

subpoena. A writ commanding somebody to appear in court.

subsidiaries. A company (the first-named) is deemed to be a subsidiary of another company (the second-named) only if: the second-named company controls the composition of the BOARD OF DIRECTORS or holds more than half of its SHARE CAPITAL; *or* if the first-named is a subsidiary of a third company which is also a subsidiary of the second-named company.

subsidies. Government grants to industries, commercial undertakings, etc. to enable them to stay in business or protect jobs. Subsidies are particularly available to regions designated by the government as being in need of financial support.

succession, law of. Deals with the ways in which the property of a dead person is transferred to the new owners. What is done depends on whether the deceased made a will. If he did, personal representatives called executors or administrators transfer the property; if there is no will, a dead person's effects are distributed according to rules laid down by statute.

suggestion schemes. Many companies have schemes which encourage employees to submit suggestions for improvements in efficiency, safety or welfare. Rewards are offered for suggestions which are adopted. *See* UNITED KINGDOM ASSOCIATION OF SUGGESTION SCHEMES (UKASS).

summary. A summary resembles a precis of a piece of writing or of a report. The following procedure should be followed: *(a)* Before commencing a summary, read through all the material and note the main points. *(b)* Follow the order in the primary material as closely as possible. *(c)* Use indirect speech (the past tense and the third person). *(d)* Read through after completion and ensure that the summary has been written in concise, plain English.

supermarkets. Cut-price, self-service chain stores, offering many different types of goods. Supermarkets (and hypermarkets) are run by large-scale organisations from a centralised head office. They sell many 'own brand' goods and have their own large warehouses.

supply. The supply of any commodity at any given time may mean, in general, the total existing stocks of the commodity wherever they may be (the 'potential supply') or in particular, the quantity available for a particular country or market (the 'market supply'). A more particular meaning of supply in economics is 'the supply of a commodity or service in that quantity of it which entrepreneurs are prepared to make available at a given price in a given period of time'. Two conditions which affect supply are the price of the factors of production and improved methods of production.

supply and demand, law of. The economic statement that the price of a commodity depends on supply and demand means that the price of commodities must be so adjusted whether consciously or unconsciously as to equalise the demand with the supply, and that, in general, the demand increases with a decrease in price, and conversely the demand decreases with an increase in price. Equilibrium price is the price which equates supply and demand. Neither the conditions of supply nor those of demand are sufficient alone to determine the price; in all cases the two sets of conditions are required. The equilibrium between supply and demand conditions depends essentially upon the actions of producers in anticipating the demand.

suspense account. Account in which items are entered temporarily until their proper 'heading' is known. The suspense account is also used when the two sides of a TRIAL BALANCE do not agree. If it is necessary to allow the PROFIT AND LOSS ACCOUNT and the BALANCE SHEET to be drawn up before the two sides have been reconciled, the amount of the difference must be inserted under the suspense account. The procedure is to eliminate the figure in the suspense account as errors are discovered.

suspension. *See* INWARD PROCESSING RELIEF.

syndicate. A group of persons or concerns who combine to carry out a particular transaction or to promote some common interest.

syndicate (Lloyd's). It is the modern practice for Lloyd's UNDERWRITERS to work in syndicates, sharing the risks they insure. The syndicate will normally operate through an underwriting agent (who may be a member of the syndicate). Each syndicate will normally specialise in a particular type of insurance.

synergy. Cooperative action between two or more agencies whose combined effect is greater than the sum of their separate effects; a term used to justify the merging of two business organisations.

systems analysis. Describes the collection, organising and evaluation of facts about a system in order to determine how the necessary operations and procedures may best be computerised and thereby improved.

systems approach. A system is a sequence of activities – a procedure – which is necessary to achieve an objective. A systems approach to an organisation's activities views that organisation as a system made up of many subsystems which interact and interrelate with one another. It must first be proved that the object of each procedure is necessary for the efficiency of the organisation, and then it must be established that all the procedures in question are designed both for speed and efficiency.

systems disk/systems software (computers). A special disk which must be inserted into the system after switching on – it carries the software that makes the computer work, and the operator's first task is to transfer this into memory.

T

takeover. The acquisition by one organisation of the majority of the shares of another company, thereby gaining control of the business.

takeover bid. An offer addressed to the shareholders of a company by an individual or firm to buy their shares at a named price above the present market price, with a view to securing control of the company. A bid which might result in a monopoly situation for a successful bidder may be referred to the MONOPOLIES AND MERGERS COMMISSION.

Talisman. The Stock Exchange's computerised settlement system.

tangible assets. Business assets such as buildings, plant and machinery (cf. intangible assets – goodwill, trademarks, etc.).

tangible goods. Material goods; the opposite of services which are *intangible*.

tap stocks (gilt-edged market). Stock which is not bid for in a gilts issue. It is released on the market in stages by the Bank of England.

tare. The allowance deducted from the gross weight of the goods to allow for the weight of the box, chest, case or container in which they are sent.

target prices. *See* COMMON AGRICULTURAL POLICY.

tariffs. A list of Customs duties to be paid on imports (usually) or exports; they are imposed for protection or revenue purposes.

Tax Tables 'A' and 'B' (income tax). Sets of these are supplied by the Inspector of Taxes to employers for every week (or month if any employees are paid monthly). They are: *Table A.* The amount of *free pay* is shown under every code number for the relevant week or month. This is deducted from *gross pay* to find *the amount of income which has to be taxed. Table B.* This table shows the amount of tax payable for all the amounts of taxable pay worked out from Table A.

taxation. The method of raising the revenue required for public services through compulsory levies. *Direct taxation.*

Personal (income tax), including National Insurance, corporation tax, capital gains tax, inheritance tax. *Indirect taxation.* VAT, Customs and Excise duties, motor vehicle duty, rates.

Technical Help to Exporters (THE) (BOTB). Service run by the British Standards Institution which will give advice on foreign technical requirements.

technological change. All types of organisation have been affected by recent changes in technology. Information technology has meant the more efficient handling of information systems; automation produces goods more cheaply; computerisation of stock records has meant quicker distribution; EFTPOS and similar systems make paying more convenient.

technology. The science of industrial arts which makes possible the best combination of resources to produce the goods and services we need.

telecommuting. An employee working at home from his own computer workstation, sending/receiving information by electronic means via telephone lines.

teleconferencing. *See* ELECTRONIC OFFICE (conferences) and SATSTREAM.

teleprinter. A typewriting device activated by telegraphic signals. Messages typed on the keyboard by the sender are reproduced on the receiver's teleprinter.

Teletext. *See* INFORMATION TECHNOLOGY.

Telex. *See* ELECTRONIC OFFICE (electronic mail).

tender (for contracts). A tender, like an estimate, is an offer to undertake specified work at a given price. It is often used in connection with contracts placed annually by local authorities for the supply of uniforms, stationery, and other necessary supplies. Very large overseas contracts such as the building of hospitals, dams, roads, etc. are advertised in the press and tenders invited.

tender (for gilts and shares). A way of selling to the highest bidder. In an offer by tender, buyers of gilts and shares specify the price at which they are willing to buy.

tender (for Treasury Bills). *See* DISCOUNT HOUSES/MARKET, TREASURY BILLS.

term draft. A 'foreign sight' Bill of Exchange used in a D/A transaction (documents against acceptance of the Bill).

terminal (computers). A device through which a user can communicate with a computer.

terminal (transport). A terminal is situated at the end of a recognised transport route; seaports, airports, bus stations, oil refineries (for pipelines) and railway terminals come into this category. Essentially, terminals need to be also junctions between differing forms of transport, so that easy transfer for passengers or cargoes can be effected to complete journeys; this is particularly true of container traffic in order that road/rail/sea/air transhipments can take place speedily and efficiently. One of the difficulties of siting new airports in remote areas where noise pollution will not affect well-established residential areas is the lack of road and rail communications. The provision of these adds greatly to the capital costs. *See* DISTRIBUTION.

terminal markets. *See* FUTURES.

termination of employment. At common law, either the employer or employee may lawfully terminate the contract of employment by giving reasonable notice, or summarily where one or the other has committed a breach of contract.

terms of payment (trade). Before a business transaction is entered into, it is necessary that the terms of payment are known and agreed by both parties. On the large, highly-organised markets in the City of London and elsewhere the controlling authorities lay down regulations for the settlement of deals made under their control (cf. SPOT and FUTURES markets). Conditions also vary in different industries, and manufacturers, wholesalers, retailers and consumers follow patterns already set. Generally speaking, sales can be cash or credit sales, the length of credit (monthly account, etc.) being by arrangement. Discounts (cash, trade or quantity) and delivery arrangements are agreed before sale.

terms of trade. These are an indication of the exchange rate existing between any two countries for a particular commodity. The terms may favour either country, but a continuing unfavourable balance for one country will force that country to cease dealing in that particular commodity.

test marketing. Attempts to minimise the risk of a new product launch by selling to a carefully selected localised area first. Advertising and sales promotion activity is given the same weight and intensity as they would be if the product were launched nationally. During the test period statistical data about sales, stock levels, reorder levels and reactions of customers and retailers to the product are collected. Any problems which are seen to occur can then be solved prior to a national launch.

The Securities Association (TSA). Self-regulatory association of the Stock Exchange. Represents most of the leading securities houses, foreign investment banks, and encompasses the Eurobond market.

third market. The Stock Exchange's market for small companies, open for those who do not qualify for the *Unlisted Securities Market (USM)* or as a *listed company*.

time-and-a-half. *See* OVERTIME.

time and motion study. The systematic study of work practices with a view to improving the efficiency of workers, especially in industry.

time charters. *See* CHARTER PARTY.

time in lieu. *See* OVERTIME.

time policies. *See* HULL INSURANCE.

times covered. *See* COVER (Stock Exchange).

Topic. The International Stock Exchange's own videotex terminal network. Used for disseminating, among much other information, SEAQ and SEAQ INTERNATIONAL.

tort. In law, a type of civil wrong done to a private person by a private person – a civil wrong which is neither a breach of contract nor a breach of trust. The usual remedy for tort is the award of damages. In general, a person is only liable for a tort committed by himself (*strict liability*) but he may be *vicariously liable* for the faults of another if that person is his servant (employee) if the tort is done in the course of carrying out his duties.

total costs (of production). The addition of fixed costs and variable costs. *Fixed costs* are those which cover rent, rates, interest on loans, and depreciation which an organisation has to pay, even when production is not taking place. *Variable costs* are those which vary with output, such as expenditure on raw materials, fuel, lighting, heating and the wages of those directly engaged in production.

total utility. *See* UTILITY.

touch (Stock Exchange). The best buying and selling prices available in a given security at any one time.

tourism. Despite the fact that the tourist industry in Britain makes a large contribution to the favourable 'invisible' trade figure in the BALANCE OF PAYMENTS, this is counterbalanced by the fact that large numbers of UK residents holiday abroad.

trade. The buying and selling of goods and services; it is an important commercial service and part of tertiary production. Trade covers the home, export and import trades, and retail and wholesale trading. Further details of each can be found under their own titles. In the study of commerce the ancillary commercial systems – the aids to trade – must also be considered. These are advertising, banking, communications, finance, insurance, transport and warehousing.

Trade and Industry, Department of (DTI). Government department; its central aim is to encourage, assist and ensure the proper regulation of British trade, industry and commerce, and to increase the growth of world trade and the national production of wealth. The DTI's Regional Initiative offers selective assistance to investment projects undertaken by firms in Assisted Areas; Regional Enterprise Grants are offered to small firms (with less than 25 employees) to help them expand and diversify. Through its export arm – the British Overseas Trade Board (BOTB) – the DTI offers extensive services to exporters. *See* EXPORT SERVICES.

trade associations. Formed to protect and assist members in the same industry, e.g. the Association of British Travel Agents (ABTA). They will also provide advice and services for their members relevant to their industry, and organise trade missions and participation in trade fairs abroad.

trade bills. *See* BILL OF EXCHANGE.

trade credit. Usually given by a firm to other firms or persons who are regular customers. *See* CREDIT TRANSACTIONS.

Trade Descriptions Act 1968. *See* CONSUMER PROTECTION.

trade discount. The term given to a percentage discount allowed to trade buyers on the list price of goods.

trade fairs abroad. The British Overseas Trade Board (BOTB) can provide an exhibition stand and display aids at reduced rates for exhibiting abroad. There are also travel grants for fairs outside Europe.

trade gap. The difference between the value of imported goods and the value of exported goods. There is an adverse trade gap if the import figure is greater than the export figure.

trade margin. The difference between the buying and selling price of goods.

trademark. Any word or distinctive device warranting goods for sale as the production of any individual or firm; packaging and labels can be trademarks. The proprietor of a registered trademark has a monopoly right in its use.

trade missions. *See* INWARD MISSIONS and OUTWARD MISSIONS.

Trade Promotions Guide. Quarterly supplement of *British Business*, a magazine which gives details of forthcoming events supported by the British Overseas Trade Board, including overseas trade fairs, store promotions, inward and outward missions; information about major UK fairs and exhibitions is also given.

Trade Union Act 1984. Introduced to increase democracy within trade unions by ensuring that elections for positions on a union's executive and decisions to conduct strike action became subject to a secret ballot of the members.

Trade Union and Labour Relations Act 1974. Protects employees against unfair dismissal.

trade unions. Organisations of workpeople, all of whom have something in common – a skill, a trade, an industry, an employer or an occupation. They are formed, financed and run by their members in their own interests, primarily for the purpose of collective bargaining about wages and working conditions, and the provision of educational, recreational and social amenities. Trade unions form an influential pressure group. The objectives of trade unions are: improvement of employment conditions – wages, hours and holidays;

improvement of workplace environment – heating, lighting, ventilation, health and safety; job security; job satisfaction and prospects – personal fulfilment; elimination of boring repetitive work; training and retraining; equal opportunities; income security – protection when work is interrupted by illness, accident, redundancy or unemployment; full employment; redistribution of national income and wealth between labour and capital; a share in planning and control of industry; improvements in the standard of living – in education, health service, housing, pensions and social security benefits; the defence of trade unions' right to operate freely; promotion of equal opportunities. The British trade union movement is a mixture of different types of union – craft, general, industrial, and non-manual.

CRAFT UNIONS

Craft unions restricted membership to craftsmen who had served a proper apprenticeship to the trade, and at the same time limited the number of apprentices. Very few wholly craft unions exist today.

GENERAL UNIONS

Nineteenth-century methods of manufacturing led to the breakdown of many traditional skills and the growth of industries employing semi-skilled labour; workers so employed were not catered for by the original craft unions and began to organise at the turn of the century, mainly in the docks, transport services and gas industry. After World War I, many unions amalgamated and the large *general unions* were formed. The three largest are the TGWU (Transport and General Workers Union), the AEU (Amalgamated Engineering Union), and the GMBATU (General Municipal, Boilermakers and Allied Trades Union – mainly in gas, local government, engineering and boilermaking).

INDUSTRIAL UNIONS

These were formed in the early part of the century with the aim of representing all the workers in a single industry. Examples are the NUR (National Union of Railwaymen) and the NUM (National Union of Miners).

NON-MANUAL UNIONS

These are the 'white-collar' unions and are the most rapidly expanding sector of the trade union movement, reflecting the increase in white-collar occupations since World War II. Examples are ASTMS (Association of Scientific, Technical and Managerial Staffs) and APEX (Association of Professional, Executive, Clerical and Computer Staff).

It may be more relevant to Britain today to make a distinction between 'open' and 'closed' unions, rather than the categories listed above. *Open unions* do not seek to restrict membership entry to one particular occupation, while *closed unions* take their membership from a single occupation.

traded options (shares). Transferable options – right (but not obligation) to buy or sell share at set price within set period.

trades councils. In most areas, trade union branches join together on a voluntary basis to form a local Trades Council (sometimes known as 'Trades Union Council'); a Council is a representative body of delegates from local union branches. The main function of a Trades Council is to provide services to affiliated branches on a wide range of industrial, social and community issues; they also make representations to local authorities and nominate representatives to a number of statutory committees and tribunals. They make the national policy of the Trades Union Congress (TUC) more widely known and understood in their areas, and feed back to the TUC local reactions and opinion; they are the local representatives of the TUC.

Trades Union Congress (TUC). A permanent organisation of trade unions to which all the major unions are affiliated; it puts forward the collective view of the trade union movement on a range of issues such as the economy, education, health, social policy, and international affairs. An Annual Congress, attended by delegates representing the affiliated unions, decides TUC policy. The General Council carries out the decisions of Congress and provides centralised leadership on questions of broad policy between Congresses; it acts as a pressure group to influence government and business decisions. It also promotes research and publicity on behalf of organised labour.

trading account. Used by organisations which purchase goods to resell. It records the turnover (the money raised from sales) and deducts the *cost* of goods sold to give the *gross profit.*

Trading bloc(k). Examples of such trading bloc(k)s are the European Community, EFTA, the British Commonwealth, and COMECOM.

trading capital. *See* CAPITAL (TYPES OF).

trading certificate. *See* FLOATING A COMPANY.

trading stamps. Vouchers in the form of stamps issued by retailers to their customers in accordance with the amount of their purchases, and which can be exchanged for gifts or money. The Trading Stamps Act 1964 provides that stamps should carry their cash value stamped upon them, and that where the customer has accumulated more than 25p worth, they should be redeemable in cash if so desired.

Trading Standards Office/Consumer Protection Department. Offices run by local authorities where, among other services offered, consumer advisers help with people's complaints about such things as faulty goods, or goods or services which are misdescribed. Informative literature published by the OFFICE OF FAIR TRADING is available at these offices.

training. The human resources of an organisation are most important and it is in the organisation's own interests to develop employee skills and knowledge. Skills in teamwork and cooperation are necessary in a changing technological environment. In a large firm a training officer will be a responsible member of the personnel department. He will provide induction courses for new members of staff, and technical and supervisory training in all departments and at all levels.

Training Agency (Department of Employment). Replaces the Manpower Services Commission. Jobcentres and their related services become part of the DOE. The Training Agency is Britain's national authority for vocational education and training. It plays a central role in securing a skilled and adaptable workforce capable of responding rapidly to change; in supporting business competitiveness and economic growth; and in helping to develop to the full the skills of individuals. The Agency has taken over three programmes which have the common theme of increasing the relevance of education to employment: the Technical and Vocational Initiative (secondary education); the partnership with local authorities to develop Non-advanced Further Education; and the initiative concerned with Enterprise in Higher Education. These operate alongside the *Youth Training Scheme. Training provided by employers.* The Agency offers information, advice and some financial support to employers (particularly to small firms) to help them in the training and development of their own workforces. The *Skills Training Agency* provides training to both employed and unemployed people through services based on a network of Skillcentres. The *Training Standards Advisory Service* is a source of independent advice on the quality of its training programmes. The Agency will promote equality of access and treatment for people at a disadvantage in the labour market.

tramp. A small cargo ship which will travel anywhere in the world to make a living. Tramps can be chartered for a voyage (voyage charter) or for a specified time (time charter).

transaction. The word 'transaction' implies a transfer of goods or services from one person to another. Where the transaction involves immediate payment it is a *cash transaction*; where payment is delayed until a later date it is a *credit transaction*. Transactions are usually initiated by the sending of an *enquiry*, or (as in the case of a large contract) by the inviting of *tenders*. An *enquiry* can be sent on a special *enquiry form* if it is for routine supplies, but sometimes it is sent in the form of a business letter. Several likely suppliers are usually circulated by the would-be buyer. *Tenders* are usually 'invited' by advertisement in the press, so that any firm interested in procuring the contract can submit its tender to the advertiser. When enquiries have been received or tenders invited the prospective suppliers send to the possible purchaser: *an estimate* which is an estimated cost for particular goods or services and must be worked out for each enquirer; *or a quotation* which is the price charged by a particular supplier. *Quotations* are often accompanied by *price lists* or *catalogues*; sometimes they are given as *firm offers* which are only available if the order is received by a certain date; *or tenders* are submitted by competing firms who are endeavouring to obtain a particular order or contract. They have usually been invited by large public bodies or local authorities and can involve the building of a dam, hospital or school at home or overseas, tree-felling for a local authority, etc. When the purchaser decides who is to supply the required goods or services he sends an *order* to the chosen supplier. (Contracts are usually drawn up for large works for which tenders were made.) When the goods are ready for despatch an *advice* or *despatch note* is sent to tell the customer that his order has been sent from the warehouse or factory, and the method by which it will be delivered. With the goods when they arrive there should be a *packing* or *delivery note* stating what is being delivered at that particular time. It should be checked to see there are no discrepancies. Often the *delivery note* is signed by the customer and returned to the driver. Sometimes there is a copy for the customer to retain which also acts as an invoice or bill. A *consignment note* covers all the goods delivered at any one time – whether all or part of an order. After delivery the *invoice* or bill is sent. For occasional transactions with a firm this should be regarded as the bill for payment. If there are many and frequent transactions with the same firm, monthly *statements of account*, showing exactly what has happened to the customer's account in the course of a month, are sent. Sometimes a *pro forma invoice* is sent, but this should not be regarded as a bill to be paid like an ordinary invoice. It is sometimes sent with goods 'on approval'. *Credit notes* are sent to credit a debtor with a certain amount and reduce the amount of an invoice. *Debit notes* are an extra charge to the invoice and increase the amount the debtor owes the supplier. *Statements of account* are sent out to account customers each month (or other agreed period) and give a record of all payments to the supplier and debts incurred by him during the month. If the debtor has failed to pay the previous account, or has only partially paid it, the debt is brought forward to the new account and is shown as an *account rendered*. The final figure on the statement of account is the amount owed by the buyer on the last day of the previous month. The cost of goods and services can be reduced by DISCOUNTS. If settlement of a debt is made in cash, a *receipt* is usually given. Receipts for other METHODS OF PAYMENT will be given if asked for.

transfer payments. A transfer payment occurs when taxes are used by the government to pay unemployment benefit, sickness benefit, child benefits and state pensions, or when it uses the money to subsidise council rents. Most transfer payments are made for social reasons.

transhipment. To transfer from one ship to another ship, or to another conveyance, or vice versa. In practice, goods landed in Britain for re-export and for transhipment (transfer to another vessel for delivery to an overseas port) must be exported within one month.

transmission mechanism. The way in which the effects of changes in monetary policy are transmitted through the economy.

transport. A part of tertiary production and an aid to trade; its function is to move goods and passengers geographically. It enables fuller use to be made of the division of labour by increasing the size of the production force and of the market. If the scale of production increases, it increases the wealth of the nation. The extractive industries and service industries have little choice in the matter of location, but the cost of transport is an important factor in the location of manufacturing industry. Besides the four main transport systems – air, rail, road and water – the use of pipelines should also be considered. Their use in the movement of oil and gas has considerably simplified what could present a difficult transportation problem. *See* TERMINAL (transport).

transport documentation. *See* EXPORT DOCUMENTATION.

Transport International Routiers (TIR) (international road transport). A permit for sealed transport vehicles, once inspected and passed by Customs, to pass through European Community frontiers with a minimum of delay.

Treasury. The central department of state which manages the financial resources of the UK and controls public expenditure. The First Lord of the Treasury is the Prime Minister; the Chancellor of the Exchequer as the Second Lord of the

Treasury is the effective head. The main tasks of the Treasury are to collect taxes (effected by the INLAND REVENUE and CUSTOMS AND EXCISE Departments), to regulate spending in other government departments, and to control the national economy. The Chancellor of the Exchequer is responsible for the planning of the BUDGET and the passing of the annual Finance Bill into law. The Department of National Savings is responsible to the Treasury.

Treasury Bills. The means by which the British government borrows money for short periods. The Bill itself is a promise to pay a stated sum within a period not exceeding one year, though normally the period is three months. Bills are issued by the BANK OF ENGLAND, and form the largest part of the government's floating debt; they are offered for tender (sale) on Friday of each week. Treasury Bills are underwritten (almost exclusively) by the DISCOUNT HOUSES which put in weekly tenders for them, the sum total each week being decided by the Bank of England in the light of government needs. The Bank chooses at its discretion which offers to accept and the houses 'buy' them at the discounted rate. When the Bills become due (mostly in three months' time) the Bank 'honours' them (buys them back) at their full value, so that the discount houses gain considerable amounts of money on their loans. Treasury Bills are negotiable and sometimes pass through several banks before being finally honoured.

treasury stock. The official name for GILT-EDGED securities (gilts).

Treaty of Rome. Signed in 1957, it brought into being the European Economic Community of which Great Britain became a member in 1972. In a referendum in 1975 the electorate decided by a majority to remain in the EEC. *See* EUROPEAN COMMUNITY and SINGLE EUROPEAN ACT.

trial balance. Taken in order to see that all the accounts in the LEDGER have been posted properly. It is made before the accounts have been closed for the month or the quarter of the year, and generally is a preliminary for getting out a BALANCE SHEET. The total of the debit balance of all the accounts must equal the total of the credit balances, including the cash and bank balances from the cash book. If the totals of these two columns balance, the account is arithmetically correct.

triangulation. *See* OUTWARD PROCESSING RELIEF.

tribunals. *See* ADMINISTRATIVE LAW.

trustee status. Used with reference to ordinary shares of those companies which meet the requirements of the 'wider range' investments defined by the Trustee Investments Act 1961. Briefly, trustee status means that the company is UK registered, has paid-up CAPITAL of at least £1 million, and has paid a DIVIDEND for at least the last five years.

trusts. A commercial trust is a large financial and industrial combination of firms 'federated' for common policies on price, output, etc, but otherwise independent in domestic matters. The aim of trusts is partly monopolistic. The firms involved in a trust are all in the same or similar industries or industrial chains and are often vertically integrated. Trusts can be distinguished from conglomerates which are combinations of firms covering many diverse industries. Trusts can be investigated under British anti-monopoly legislation if they control 25 per cent or more of the output or supply of a monopoly. *See also* INVESTMENT TRUST, UNIT TRUSTS.

turnover (of a business). The total net sales during a trading period – i.e. the total gross sales less RETURNS INWARDS. *See* RATE OF TURNOVER.

U

uberrima fides. *See* UTMOST GOOD FAITH.

UKASS. *See* UNITED KINGDOM ASSOCIATION OF SUGGESTION SCHEMES.

***ultra vires* (Latin).** 'Beyond one's power of authority.' Legal phrase used particularly with regard to the limitation of the legal or constitutional powers of a person, court, company or corporation. In company law, anything done by a company outside the powers given in the MEMORANDUM OF ASSOCIATION is *ultra vires* and void (cf. *intra vires*).

unconfirmed credits. *See* LETTER OF CREDIT.

underwriters (insurance). *See* LLOYD'S UNDERWRITERS.

underwriting of shares. An arrangement by which a company is guaranteed that an issue of shares will raise a given amount of cash, because the underwriters, for a small commission, undertake to subscribe for any of the issue not taken up by the public. *See* ISSUING HOUSES.

unearned income. Income from investment or property, as opposed to EARNINGS (money received for paid employment).

unemployment. Term applied officially to the condition of those capable of, and available for, remunerative work and registered for, but unable to secure, employment. The demand for labour is directly associated with economic activity, but a state of 'full employment' does not necessarily mean there is no unemployment. Advances in technology often have the effect of reducing the workforce. *Frictional unemployment* is the result of temporary readjustments between the supply of and demand for labour, and may be met by increasing the mobility of workers or by ensuring that the supply of workers in any one place has the qualifications required. *Seasonal unemployment* occurs when work depends on the time of the year. *Structural unemployment* is the result of the demands on an industry slackening. Structural unemployment tends to be regionally restricted. The government employment policy lies in retraining the unemployed and the designation of certain areas as zones where employment is encouraged through tax and rates relief.

Unfair Contract Terms Act 1977. Makes restrictive clauses in a contract inoperable, while others can apply only if they are adjudged to be fair and reasonable. Guarantees can never exclude or restrict liability for loss or damage caused by goods which are defective or work which has been badly performed.

unfair dismissal. If any rights have been infringed (under the Employment Protection Act 1975, amended by the Employment Act 1980), complaint is made to an industrial tribunal before whom the onus is on the employer to show that he has not infringed the employee's rights. A decision in favour of the employee may involve the employer in paying compensation; having to reinstate the dismissed employee in the same capacity as before; or to re-engage him/her in another capacity.

unincorporated associations. A body which has not been authorised by law to act as one individual – i.e. not made into a CORPORATION or LIMITED COMPANY – and not enjoying limited liability. Examples of unincorporated associations are partnerships, trade unions and social clubs.

union dues. Membership fees which trade unionists pay to their particular union. In some organisations the dues are deducted from pay and the total collected remitted to the union. In such cases the dues are classed as a *voluntary deduction* from a salary or wage.

unit cost (of production). The average cost of a unit of production; the total cost (i.e. the sum total of fixed and variable costs) divided by the number of units produced.

unit costing. A system of costing used where production is continuous and the unit of cost identical throughout, e.g. in coal mining where the unit of cost is a tonne of coal.

unit shop/unit trader. *See* SOLE TRADER.

unit trusts. Those where groups of small investors pool their resources to buy shares through a professionally managed company. Each unit is spread over a large number of investments, thereby reducing the risk of loss to the small investor. A unit trust is a legal trust and so an investor only holds units and does not become a shareholder.

United Kingdom Association of Suggestion Schemes (UKASS). Established with help from the Industrial Society. It has taken the place of the 'suggestion box' used by organisations to collect innovative ideas from employees, and will pool the suggestions for the benefit of industry and commerce as a whole.

United Nations Commission for Trade and Development (UNCTAD)/United Nations Food and Agriculture Organisation (FAO). All states of the European Community are members of these organisations, and also of other UN subsidiary bodies. At the general assemblies of these organisations they combine in their efforts to try to arrive at a common policy – on development aid, trade preferences for developing countries, special measures in favour of the least-developed countries, and similar issues.

United Nations Organisation. The UK became an original member of the UN and subscribes to the Charter which, as its constitution, sets out the rules. The chief of these are: all members are equal; international disputes must be settled by peaceful means; force will not be used in any way not allowed by the Charter; they will assist the UN in any action taken. The General Assembly which meets in New York every September resembles an international Parliament, and every member state is represented equally, having one vote each. The Security Council is primarily responsible for keeping international peace. An important achievement of the UN was the Universal Declaration of Human Rights, proclaimed in 1948.

unlimited liability. Some corporations choose not to have the advantages of LIMITED LIABILITY. Usually these concerns are very small and their liability in the event of failure would not be considerable. Sole traders and partnerships always have unlimited liability and in the event of failure are liable to the limits of the personal wealth of one or all owners of the business.

Unlisted Securities Market (USM). The Stock Exchange's market for medium-sized companies who do not qualify for, or do not wish, a full listing.

unlisted security (Stock Exchange). One which has not been admitted to the *Official List.* Usually the issuer will be an *unlisted company,* but not always. It is not uncommon for a company to apply for its ORDINARY SHARES to be listed but not its loan stocks, or vice versa.

unsecured loan stock (ULS). A type of DEBENTURE.

unsocial hours. Paid employment worked at a time which falls outside the normal working day and precludes participation in normal social activities.

Unsolicited Goods and Services Act 1971. Goods sent by a supplier to anyone who has not requested them are 'unsolicited' and under this Act it is illegal to demand money from those who receive such goods. If the recipient asks for the goods to be removed and no action is taken to do so, the goods become the property of the recipient. If no action is taken by the recipient and the goods are not collected by the sender within six months they automatically become the property of the recipient.

utility. The basic concept connected with demand is that before there is a demand for any kind of good or service it must possess utility for those who want to buy it; it must have a capacity to satisfy a desire or serve a purpose. As long as a commodity or service gives satisfaction in some form to those who demand it, it possesses utility in the economic sense. *Total utility* is the total satisfaction which is derived from the possession of a commodity though there might come a point where total utility has reached a maximum and a further supply would not be wanted. *Marginal utility* is the satisfaction of possessing one more unit of any commodity, or the satisfaction lost by giving up one unit. Choice is fundamental to economic life, but only when an item's marginal utility to the consumer exceeds the marginal utility of the income that must be given up to buy it, is that item actually bought.

utmost good faith *(uberrima fides).* A CONTRACT OF INSURANCE is voidable if any fact is withheld by either party which may affect the judgment of the other. At the time of completing the proposal form, it is expected that the person taking out the insurance, or assurance, will acquaint the insurer with all the true facts, and any risk the insurer accepts is based on what he believes to be the true facts. The would-be policy-holder also has a right to be provided by the insurer with complete information regarding the proposed contract.

V

valuation of assets. The valuation of assets shown on a BALANCE SHEET, which has regard to DEPRECIATION and outstanding debts, is necessarily an estimate only of the assets of the business as a going concern, but there must be no overstatements of value, and all precautions taken to present a true and honest statement.

valuation of stock account. It is unusual to value stock at cost price, but if there is a current fall in prices the value should be at the current market price. If the current price is rising there should be no marking-up of stock values; the rise may be temporary and it is always unwise to overstate profits and allow inflated values to appear on the BALANCE SHEET.

value added. The difference between the cost of raw materials, supplies and services bought from outside the organisation, and the amount received from customers when they are sold. The resulting figure represents wealth created and is distributed to employees, the government (taxes of all types), the providers of capital, and the organisation itself. Incentive schemes for employees based on the 'value added' concept offer employees a percentage share of such created wealth.

Value Added Tax (VAT). An indirect tax levied by the government on goods and services by way of business; it is a *commercial tax*. A standard rate of tax is payable on any goods and services which fall within its scope, which is collected by HM Customs and Excise. Zero-rated goods and services carry no VAT. Whenever a trader buys goods or services to which VAT applies, he receives from the supplier a tax invoice indicating the cost of the goods and the tax charged on them. When, in turn, the trader supplies taxable goods and services to his customers, he charges them tax at the same rate. At regular intervals, normally every quarter, the trader makes a tax return to the Customs and Excise, showing the tax charged to him (input tax) and the tax he has charged his customers (output tax) and will pay the difference. Tax point is the time when VAT becomes chargeable and is usually the date when goods or services are delivered or invoiced.

value analysis/value engineering. The critical examination of a product, its functions and component parts, with the object of producing a product to an equally high standard at the least total cost. The operation is carried out by an interdepartmental team of investigators.

value quotas. *See* QUOTA LICENCES.

variable costs. *See* COSTS.

variable pricing/price differential/price discrimination. The price of one commodity, produced by the same supplier, may vary. Two reasons for this are: the granting of cash, quantity or trade discounts; 'off-peak' or 'out of season' pricing – the cheap 'day returns' of British Rail which put an embargo on the use of rush-hour trains, and hotel prices which escalate during school holidays when hotels are most in demand. The object is to switch demand to periods when demand is lying idle.

variable proportions, law of. Also called the law of non-proportional returns, but more commonly known as the LAW OF DIMINISHING RETURNS.

variance report. *See* OPERATING STATEMENT.

variety chain store. The chain store is a multiple which sells a variety of goods; it is one of a large number of branch shops, each of which usually exhibits the same appearance, especially in the shop front and window design.

vending machines. A slot machine which can provide a large range of goods, including cigarettes, drinks, packaged meals, etc. They are useful out of shop hours or on premises away from a normal retail outlet.

venture capital. Capital provided by financial houses specialising in loans to unquoted companies. *See* INVESTORS IN INDUSTRY (3i).

verbatim. Word for word; e.g. *Hansard* is a full record (verbatim report) of each day's proceedings in both Houses of Parliament.

vertical integration. *See* MERGERS.

vicarious liability (law of tort). In general, a person is only liable for a TORT committed by himself (strict liability) but he may be *vicariously liable* for the faults of another if that person is his servant (employee) and if the tort is done while carrying out his duties.

videoconferencing. *See* ELECTRONIC OFFICE (conferences – Confravision)

viewdata. The name for a class of information services by which a specially adapted television set or a computer terminal is linked via the public telephone network to a host computer. PRESTEL is a public viewdata service run by British Telecom, but a number of large companies and institutions operate their own private viewdata systems, allowing information retrieval to staff and paying subscribers.

visible balance/visible trade (international trade). The excess of imports over exports, or exports over imports is called the BALANCE OF TRADE; this is the figure for 'visibles', i.e. trade in *goods*.

visual display unit (VDU) (computers). Similar to a television screen, this can display text or diagrams as output from a computer.

voice synthesizer (computers). A device for creating voice-like sounds from computer data.

volenti non fit injuria **(law of tort).** 'No wrong is done to one who consents.' An occupier may limit his liability by requiring a visitor to accept the risk of coming onto the premises by placing a warning notice – provided the visitor is reasonably safe.

volume quotas. *See* QUOTA LICENCES.

voluntary chains/groups. *See* RETAILER/WHOLESALER COOPERATIVES.

voluntary deductions from salaries and wages. *See* DEDUCTIONS FROM SALARIES AND WAGES.

voluntary liquidation/voluntary winding up (of businesses). In the case of a voluntary winding up either a member or a creditor petitions the court which makes a winding-up order. A liquidator is appointed who proceeds to wind up the affairs of the company by realising the assets and paying off the creditors. When this is done the company is dissolved and ceases to exist.

voucher. A documentary record of a business transaction; a written document acknowledging receipt of a sum of money and serving as proof of payment.

voyage charter. *See* CHARTER PARTY.

voyage policy. *See* HULL INSURANCE.

W

wage differentials. *See* DIFFERENTIALS.

wages. 1. A payment for services especially of a manual kind, usually according to contract and on an hourly, daily, weekly or piecework basis. 2. (economics). The share of the national product attributable to labour as a factor of production.

Wages Councils. The Wages Council Act 1979 brought about the establishment of Wages Councils in various occupations. Each Council comprises representatives from trade unions, employers and public bodies and its function is to regulate the pay (especially the minimum pay) and conditions of workers in the industry for which it was established. Workers in these industries (mostly the lower-paid service industries) are often the most vulnerable and isolated members of the economy.

waiver. The act of refraining from claiming, demanding, taking or enforcing.

wants. The *needs* of mankind are for food (and water), clothing and shelter. *Wants* are not needed for survival, but production is undertaken in order to supply people's wants. The goods and services produced are called 'utilities' – things which have the power to satisfy wants.

warehousing. The method used to store manufactured goods until they are required. It is an essential part of the production process – the commercial service which enables consumers to obtain their goods at the right time, at the right place, in the right quantity and the right condition. 'Condition' is particularly important – it is the warehouseman's obligation to keep the goods in saleable condition (e.g. frozen foods which might go bad, metal objects which might rust, etc.), and make seasonal goods like Christmas crackers and beach toys available at the right time. The traditional warehouse has been eliminated by the large supermarket chains who provide their own warehousing services, and this is an area where the wholesaler as a warehouseman has been affected. The CASH AND CARRY

WAREHOUSES and the RETAILER/WHOLESALER COOPERATIVES, both of which cater for the small retailer, have also affected traditional warehousing. Traditionally warehouses have been owned by wholesalers whose function must be performed by someone in the chain of production even if his traditional role is disappearing. It is impossible to consider warehousing without considering the position of the WHOLESALER whose role and function is discussed under its own title. *See* BONDED WAREHOUSE.

warrant (securities). A special kind of option, given by a company to holders of a particular security, giving them the right to subscribe for future issues, either of the same or some other security.

waybill. A list of passengers or goods being carried and the fares charged.

wealth. The wealth of a country is determined by its resources. A nation's wealth consists of its lands, minerals, forests, crops, railways, canals, factories, warehouses, dwelling-houses and the great mass of consumable goods lying in warehouses, shops, etc. Economic growth means an increase in the national income (or national wealth) in real terms – it means there are more goods and services about, and that the country is wealthier.

welfare. The welfare of the workforce, both physically and socially, is the responsibility of the personnel department of an organisation, as also is the implementation of all Acts regarding the health and safety of staff. *See also* EMPLOYMENT LEGISLATION.

'Which?'. The magazine of the CONSUMERS' ASSOCIATION.

white-collar worker. A worker in an office, or other non-manual worker.

White Paper. Before a government Bill is introduced, the government may issue to the press and public a 'Green Paper' explaining the proposals with a view to creating public discussion. This is followed by a 'White Paper' outlining the proposals more fully; after further consultation and discussion with interested bodies, the Bill is submitted to the Cabinet, put into proper legal wording by lawyers who specialise in such work; it is then introduced into Parliament.

whole-life policies. Provide for a sum to be payable on the death of the insured.

wholesale trade. Whatever commodity he may deal in, the wholesaler is a middleman, an intermediary in the chain of distribution, and the profit he makes must necessarily add to the cost of the goods to the final consumer. If he deals in raw materials the wholesaler may act as a link between the different branches of an industry, or he may be a source of supply to the retailer. The wholesaler has an important function in the chain of distribution and even if he is 'eliminated' – such as when a large retailing group buys direct from a manufacturer and delivers to its own outlets – the work he would have performed must still be done by somebody in the organisation. These functions include buying in bulk and breaking bulk; taking on the risk that demand for the goods may cease, the price drop, stock deteriorate or become out of date; the wholesaler is also responsible for the safeguarding of goods when in transit or in a warehouse. The traditional wholesaler buys from the manufacturer and sells to the retailer. *To the manufacturer,* his services enable the production lines to be cleared, and often the whole marketing function (advertising, packaging, branding, etc.) is performed by the wholesaler. His position in the chain gives him the opportunity to mediate between the manufacturer and retailer and also, through the retailer, to learn the views of the consumer. Very importantly, the 'time gap' between manufacturing and retailing is covered by the wholesaler. *To the retailer,* the wholesaler is a constant source of supply, allowing him to stock up to suit his own requirements. For the retailer, the wholesaler breaks bulk, gives credit, offers a choice of wares, and will transport the goods if required. *The consumer* is usually unaware of the services he receives from the wholesaler, but it is through him that a steady flow of goods is maintained in the shops and he is the one who, through information obtained from retailers, provides 'feedback' to the manufacturer of consumer preferences. An efficient wholesaling transport system is also effective in helping to keep down the price of goods. A modern wholesaling venture is the CASH AND CARRY WAREHOUSE. Large

MAIL ORDER firms which sell from catalogues are wholesalers operating from warehouses. *See* DISTRIBUTION.

Winchester disk (computers). Name of a compact, high-speed, high-capacity hard disk, which is completely sealed in its disk drive.

winding up (of companies). A company may cease to exist by winding up (liquidation). There are two principal ways in which a company may be wound up: one is by voluntary liquidation, the other is by a compulsory winding up order by the court. A liquidator is appointed who proceeds to wind up the affairs of the company by realising the assets and paying off the creditors. When this is done the company is dissolved and ceases to exist.

with particular average (WPA) (marine insurance). An 'against all risks' (aar) policy. It covers not only complete loss, but any particular loss or injury which may be suffered in marine transit.

Woolsack. Seat of the Lord High Chancellor in the House of Lords, where as a politician he is speaker of that House.

word processor. *See* ELECTRONIC OFFICE.

work experience. The Work Experience Act 1973 restricts work experience to young people in their final year of compulsory schooling (i.e. aged 15 – 16). Its main purpose is to give young people at school a chance to find out what it is like to be at work. All such work is unpaid.

work in progress. Uncompleted work (any material, components, product or contract) at any stage in the production process.

work legislation. *See* EMPLOYMENT LEGISLATION.

work measurement. The analysis and timing of a work task over a period of time in order to arrive at a correct time to do that job. Tasks are broken down into small elements and each element is watched and timed several times. The observer must decide how quickly or slowly the job is being carried out in relation to a standard – this is called 'rating'. The times for each element are added together and an allowance added to the total for fatigue, rest or contingencies. The result becomes the standard time for the job.

work study. The scientific study of work tasks to establish standards against which individual performance may be compared for planning and control purposes. There are two major components to work study: method study and work measurement, which are explained under their separate titles.

work-to-rule. Industrial action involving slow working and meticulous observance of rules which are made to become time wasting.

worker cooperatives. A cooperative is a group of workers working together in the production or distribution of goods or services. Worker cooperatives are completely owned and controlled by those who work in them. All members are concerned with decision-making.

worker directors (of companies). An employee of a LIMITED COMPANY who is appointed to the board of DIRECTORS.

worker participation. The inclusion of employees in the decision-making process of an organisation. An amendment in 1982 to the Companies Act 1967 requires companies of 250 employees or more to make an annual statement of the action they have taken to forward worker participation in their companies; this statement to appear in the Directors' Report.

working capital. *See* CAPITAL (TYPES OF).

working party. A committee of experts appointed to investigate and advise on a particular issue.

working population. This comprises every person in the 16 – 64 age group who are working or available for work (i.e. those registered as unemployed); all persons who are 65+ but still working are included in the figure. Excluded are housewives, those of private means and those who cannot work (the chronically sick and prisoners).

World Aid Section (British Overseas Trade Board). Finance for very large projects and programmes is arranged through international aid agencies, such as the World Bank; UK companies are eligible to tender for the resulting contracts. Advance information covering the full range of agencies is brought together by the BOTB and is available to UK firms.

World Bank. *See* INTERNATIONAL BANK FOR RECONSTRUCTION AND DEVELOPMENT.

worldscale. An international standard rate of charges for the chartering of bulk carriers.

XYZ

yield (securities). The annual return on money invested, based on the current price of the security, on the assumption that the next DIVIDEND paid will be the same as the last. *Flat yield* is the income on fixed-interest stock, ignoring any capital gain that may be made if the stock is due to be redeemed at Par at some future date. *Redemption yield* is the same, but allowing for the expected capital gain.

$$\text{Yield} = \frac{\text{Par value}}{\text{Market value}} \times \text{Rate of dividend percentage}$$

zero-rated (VAT). Zero-rated goods are those on which the purchaser pays no Value Added Tax.